The Future of Air Power
in the Aftermath of the Gulf War

Edited by

Richard H. Shultz, Jr.
Robert L. Pfaltzgraff, Jr.
International Security Studies Program
The Fletcher School of Law and Diplomacy
Tufts University

Air University Press
Maxwell Air Force Base, Alabama 36112-5532

July 1992

Library of Congress Cataloging-in-Publication Data

The Future of air power in the aftermath of the Gulf War/edited by
 Robert L. Pfaltzgraff, Jr., Richard H. Shultz, Jr.
    p. cm.
  Includes index.
    1. Air power—United States—Congresses. 2. United States. Air
Force—Congresses. 3. Persian Gulf War. 1991—Aerial operations,
American—Congresses. I. Pfaltzgraff, Robert L. II. Shultz, Richard H.,
1947-.
UG633.F86   1992   92-8181
358.4'03'0973—dc20   CIP
ISBN 1-58566-046-9

First Printing July 1992
Second Printing June 1995
Third Printing August 1997
Fourth Printing August 1998
Fifth Printing March 2001
Sixth Printing July 2002

Disclaimer

Opinions, conclusions, and recommendations expressed or implied within are solely those of the editors and do not necessarily represent the views of Air University, the United States Air Force, the Department of Defense, or any other US government agency. Cleared for public release: distribution unlimited.

Contents

Page

DISCLAIMER ii

FOREWORD vii

PREFACE ix

PART I

Strategic Factors Reshaping Strategies and Missions

Introduction 3

Air Power in the New Security Environment 9
   Secretary of the Air Force Donald B. Rice

Air Power in US Military Strategy 17
   Dr Edward N. Luttwak

The United States as an Aerospace Power
in the Emerging Security Environment 39
   Dr Robert L. Pfaltzgraff, Jr.

Employing Air Power in the Twenty-first Century 57
   Col John A. Warden III, USAF

The Role of the US Air Force in the
Employment of Air Power 83
   Maj Gen Charles D. Link, USAF

PART II

Air Power as an Element of US Power Projection

Page

Introduction 91

Air Power since World War II: Consistent with Doctrine? . . 95
Dr Williamson Murray

Aerospace Forces and Power Projection 115
Lt Gen Michael A. Nelson, USAF

The Relevance of High-Intensity Operations 127
Lt Gen Glenn A. Kent, USAF, Retired

Air Power in Low- and Midintensity Conflict 139
Gen Larry D. Welch, USAF, Retired

PART III

Air Power: Deterrence and Compellence

Introduction 167

Compellence and the Role of Air Power
as a Political Instrument 171
Dr Richard H. Shultz, Jr.

Reinforcing Allied Military Capabilities
in a Global-Alliance Strategy 193
Dr Jacquelyn K. Davis

PART IV

Designing Aerospace Force Structures

Page

Introduction 213

Force Structure for the Future 217
   Maj Gen Robert M. Alexander, USAF

The Air National Guard Today:
Looking to the Future 225
   Lt Gen John B. Conaway, National Guard Bureau

Space: A New Strategic Frontier 235
   Lt Gen Thomas S. Moorman, Jr., USAF

PART V

Factors Affecting Force Structure and Missions

Introduction 253

Congress and National Security 257
   Hon Bud Shuster

Balancing Budgetary and Force Constraints 263
   Brig Gen Lawrence P. Farrell, Jr., USAF

The Impact of Arms Control on the US Air Force 277
   Dr Edward L. Warner III

The Sky's the Limit: The Pentagon's Victory
over the Press, the Public, and the Peaceniks 295
   Ross Gelbspan

PART VI

Acquisition Priorities and Strategies: A View from Industry

                                                                           Page

Introduction 311

Research and Development Strategies 315
   Harold K. McCard

Advanced Technology Challenges
in the Defense Industry 329
   Dr John Blair

CONTRIBUTORS 347
INDEX 357

Foreword

Air University is proud to have joined the Air Staff and the International Security Studies Program of the Fletcher School of Law and Diplomacy at Tufts University in sponsoring the April 1991 conference on aerospace challenges and missions that produced this collection of essays. Written by a distinguished group of specialists from academia, the military, government, business, and the media, these essays examine American national security policy and Air Force issues from a variety of perspectives. Aside from their remarkable perceptiveness, the contributions of the authors are especially timely because they address the pivotal role of air power in the war with Iraq. The essays leave no doubt that the employment of both established and innovative methods of air combat in that crisis has important implications for the global-security environment of the future. In that sense, this book provides a foundation for evaluating the complex policy challenges that we face in the 1990s and into the next century.

CHARLES G. BOYD
Lieutenant General, USAF
Commander
Air University

Preface

The United States has recently emerged victorious from a war fought in the Persian Gulf against an opponent seasoned by eight long years of war with Iran and armed with heavy armored and mechanized divisions, as well as high-performance aircraft and ballistic missiles. The results of the engagement of US air and ground forces were unmatched in American military annals—the complete defeat of the enemy's forces, first through a devastating air campaign and then through a brilliant "Cannae-style" envelopment. In the aftermath of this victory, it is incumbent upon the US military services to undertake a sober reading of the diverse issues and implications that arose from the Gulf war and to bring these to bear in planning for the international security environment of the 1990s and beyond. This volume is an effort to do so with respect to the US Air Force. It is the product of a major conference on the role of air power and the Air Force in future American defense policy. The conference was the first major reassessment, in an open forum, of the role of air power following the Persian Gulf war.

When the International Security Studies Program (ISSP) of the Fletcher School of Law and Diplomacy, Tufts University, decided to hold a conference on "The United States Air Force: Aerospace Challenges and Missions in the 1990s," we of course had no idea that the dates of the conference would fall at the end of the largest engagement of American military power since the Vietnam War. The symposium was to be part of a series that the ISSP has designed to assess the future of American national security through the prism of each military service. The first conference had as its topic "US Defense Policy in an Era of Constrained Resources," and the 1990 program focused on challenges and missions for the US Army. The next two programs will assess future doctrines, missions, and force structures of the US Marine Corps and the US Navy in American defense policy.

This volume has as its goal a broad examination of the spectrum of issues and choices facing the Air Force in the 1990s and beyond.

Several of the contributors present diverse and thoughtful insights into the major lessons from the air campaign in Operation Desert Storm. The book is divided into six parts. Part I focuses on the emerging international security environment and the new strategic factors that are acting to reshape Air Force strategies and missions. Part II assesses the future role of air power as an element of US power projection. Part III examines two strategic principles—deterrence and compellence—and applies them to current and future air power roles and missions. Part IV highlights the need for and the ways to design a new aerospace force structure in this changing strategic environment. Part V identifies those domestic and arms control factors that will influence the force structure and missions of the Air Force in the years ahead. Part VI presents the defense industry's view of acquisition priorities and strategies for the future Air Force. Each section is preceded by a policy-focused introduction which highlights and integrates the key points and major recommendations of each of the contributors to the volume.

The book is intended for a broad spectrum of foreign- and defense-policy professionals, including civilian government officials; military officers in command and staff positions; members of Congress and their staff assistants; public-policy analysts and researchers at major think tanks; academics engaged in the study and teaching of international security; the media; and lay readers with a particular interest in national security issues.

Given the major role of the US Air Force in Operation Desert Storm and the decisive impact of air power on the outcome of the Gulf war, what formerly may have been a debatable question is now generally accepted—air power will be a formidable and essential tool in the future international security policy of the United States. The importance of this volume lies in its ability to cogently outline those new doctrinal, strategic, organizational, and structural challenges and missions facing the Air Force in this decade and beyond, and to provide thoughtful recommendations for addressing these and related policy issues.

The experience in the Gulf conflict comes at a time when the United States is faced with a rapidly evolving international environment. The policies and strategies tailored for the Soviet Union during the cold war era, in several respects, have become less compelling as the Soviet military threat to Western Europe has subsided, and as Soviet policy in the third world has abandoned its expansionist logic. As the Gulf conflict made apparent, the restraints placed upon third-world powers by the superpower rivalry have been erased, leaving few deterrent structures in the way of aggressors like Iraq's Saddam Hussein. The strategic environment, as Secretary of the Air Force Donald B. Rice has stated, "is not going to be free of conflict, and . . . there will be future challenges to American vital interests through military means."

The contributors to this book have concluded that the US Air Force, indeed all the US military services, must prepare for an international security arena of vastly different dimensions from that which they faced during the cold war. The likely complexion of the future international environment will feature, according to one writer in this book, an "increasing number of actors in possession of the means for conducting military operations at the higher end of the [conflict] spectrum." Such potential aggressors "will have available the means to launch strategic strikes that previously were possessed by the United States and the Soviet Union." The prospect of radical, unstable states possessing the ability to strike with ballistic missiles and other advanced weapons is daunting, yet the Air Force must accept the danger as inevitable and plan for these as well as a host of other challenges. Hopefully, this volume will contribute to the debate over how it can do so.

As mentioned above, this book reflects the proceedings of a conference held 3–4 April 1991 on the US Air Force in the 1990s. That event was the nineteenth in a series of annual conferences of the International Security Studies Program. In organizing the conference and this volume, we received the support of a number of organizations within the US Air Force. Of particular importance were the conference cosponsors: Air University and the Office of the Deputy Chief of Staff, Plans and Operations, Headquarters US Air Force. We would like to extend our deep gratitude to Lt Gen Charles G. Boyd, commander of Air University, and to Lt Gen Michael A.

Nelson, deputy chief of staff, Plans and Operations, Headquarters US Air Force, for all their support and advice. We would also like to express our appreciation for the support given by Secretary of the Air Force Donald B. Rice and Air Force Chief of Staff Gen Merrill A. McPeak.

We are most grateful to individuals within the US Air Force, without whose assistance this conference and volume would not have come about. In particular, Lt Col Frank Kistler, Brig Gen Jacques Klein, Maj Fred Ruggiero, Col Rod Payne, and Lt Col Ed Mann were indispensable in a number of ways. At Air University Press, Dr Elizabeth Bradley, director, and Dr Marvin Bassett, project editor, assisted in the publishing preparation of the conference papers.

We would also like to extend our gratitude to the support staff at the International Security Studies Program for their outstanding work with the conference and volume. Freda Kilgallen, ISSP administrator, did an outstanding job handling all conference arrangements and making sure the meeting ran on time and with no bottlenecks. Sam Blake, ISSP research and program associate, played an instrumental role in the editing and preparation of the manuscript for publication. Roberta Breen, staff assistant, likewise made an important contribution to the overall success of the program. Each year the ISSP has the good fortune of having the assistance of a US Air Force research associate. This year's officer, Lt Col Gary Gunther, like those who preceded him, actively contributed to the success of the conference and to other ISSP programmatic activities. We wish to thank both Colonel Gunther for his outstanding efforts and the US Air Force for having made his participation possible.

PART I

Strategic Factors Reshaping Strategies and Missions

Introduction

The recent events in the Persian Gulf have demonstrated that the post–cold war world is not going to be free of conflict and war, as several specialists suggested prior to Iraq's invasion of Kuwait. Unfortunately, there will be future challenges to American vital interests in various regions of the world through military means. The use of medium-range Scud-B missiles against Israel by the Iraqis, the large and (at one time) formidable ground forces of the Iraqi army, and the brutal occupation of Kuwait have likewise left the indelible impression that the international arena will become increasingly perilous as other states acquire similar—or more sophisticated—weaponry. The five writers in this section outline the dimensions of this future international security environment and suggest measures that can best prepare the United States—and the US Air Force in particular—to meet the challenges posed by aggressors in the years ahead.

Secretary of the Air Force Donald B. Rice points out in his paper that Operation Desert Storm "answered questions about America's relative military strength and the use of the military as an instrument of national power." Citing Lech Walesa, who proclaimed, "The world is awaiting your signal. It is watching you," Secretary Rice notes that the use of military force, with international sanction and a worldwide coalition, sent an unambiguous message to future aggressors that the US would respond to threats to its vital interests.

Although Secretary Rice sees little chance of the future security environment involving the US in a global war, he points to a Rand Corporation study which identified 35 conflicts of varying intensity that were raging at the time of Desert Storm. He foresees that most military operations will entail "quick action, few casualties, and the use of national and coalition strengths." The importance of air power will be paramount, as witnessed in the air campaign of Desert Storm.

Secretary Rice emphasizes the decisive part played by air power in the effort to break the back of the Iraqi military machine by destroying its strategic nodes; blinding its command, control, and communications; and shattering the morale of Baghdad's ground forces. That the air campaign was so crucial to success suggests to Secretary Rice that we must exploit revolutionary concepts of air power to give the US Air Force a decisive edge over any potential adversary. Such concepts and attributes would include the ability to see through clouds; to wage advanced electronic warfare to disrupt enemy command, control, communications, and intelligence; to quickly deploy forces; to field improved antiballistic missiles; and to develop enhanced bomb-damage assessment capabilities. Force-modernization programs should also be carried through to conclusion, including the B-2 stealth bomber, the F-22 advanced tactical fighter, and the C-17 airlifter.

In his paper, Dr Edward N. Luttwak observes that "the sharply diminished plausibility of Soviet aggression" around the world calls for a defense strategy that abandons the past reliance on "fixed garrisons based on heavy ground forces with air, naval, and strategic-nuclear complements" and ushers in an era that requires the US military to plan for "contingencies that could materialize as threats in unpredictable locations." Dr Luttwak sees the importance of "globally deployable air and naval forces, as well as of expeditionary ground forces" to meet future challenges similar to those presented by Iraq. In a brilliant analysis of the air campaign element of Operation Desert Storm, Dr Luttwak argues that, unlike the mixed performance of air power during the strategic bombing campaigns of World War II, the allied experience in Iraq was proof that air power can be strategically decisive.

A key lesson for the Air Force that Dr Luttwak draws from the air war against Iraq is that the US strategy of "Instant Thunder," as opposed to the gradual escalation of the war in Vietnam, allowed the US to seize control of the air battlefield overnight and to essentially blind and incapacitate Iraq's national command authorities and air defenses. This in turn permitted the Air Force to carry out a medium-altitude air campaign at its leisure, with extremely few losses, supreme accuracy, and little collateral damage.

Last, Dr Luttwak identifies the following funding priorities for future US military requirements: (1) sea lift and airlift, (2) Army and Marine Corps expeditionary forces, (3) carrier-centered naval forces, and (4) tactical air forces.

Dr Robert L. Pfaltzgraff, Jr., agrees with the assessment of Secretary Rice and Dr Luttwak that the United States will be faced with an "increas[ing] . . . number of actors in possession of the means for conducting military operations at the higher end of the conflict spectrum." He sees the future security arena involving adversaries who "will have available the means to launch strategic strikes that previously were possessed only by the United States and the Soviet Union."

In order to deal with these possible threats, Dr Pfaltzgraff argues, the US will need to have a military capability "that, in all of its elements, is highly mobile, flexible, firepower intensive, interoperable, and survivable under a broad range of combat conditions." The US military of the future will have to be capable of fighting on a wide range of terrains and will rely heavily on air power. The Air Force of the future will have to be strong in the areas of payload, range, speed, and penetrability. In addition, space assets will become increasingly critical to effective military action, as demonstrated by the successful use of space systems in the Gulf conflict.

Col John A. Warden III, the architect of the Instant Thunder bombing plan, also provides important insights into what future conflict will be like for the United States. Like Dr Luttwak, Colonel Warden emphasizes the revolutionary nature of the air campaign against Iraq and its implications for war in the near to midterm. In his words, with the total air superiority of the allied air forces over Iraq and the attendant ability of the coalition to work its will, "this victory provides the strategic model for American operations well into the twenty-first century."

According to Colonel Warden, "whether a world war takes place in the first quarter of the next century . . . will depend significantly on how we conduct our foreign affairs and how well we maintain the decisive military advantages we now enjoy." Like Dr Pfaltzgraff, he believes that—from the US perspective—our future enemies are "likely to be small to midsize powers with high-tech weapons capabilities." In responding to hostile actions by one of these powers,

> air power . . . has a unique ability to get to the combat area with massive power and to affect enemy operational and strategic centers of gravity. . . . Air operations . . . are very much likely to result in fewer casualties to either side.

Colonel Warden, like Dr Luttwak, emphasizes the potential of air power in the future, given the winning combination of precision, stealth, and intelligence in the war with Iraq. But he warns that while air power may dominate warfare, the realization of that very dominance will induce frantic efforts on the part of many countries "to develop defenses or to acquire a similar offensive capability." It is therefore incumbent on the Air Force and the other military services to continue to develop and field forces, for "if we refuse to accept the Gulf war as a milestone in history, then we risk losing the war of 2014—and that war may be for even higher stakes than the war of 1991."

In the final selection of Part I, Maj Gen Charles D. Link recognizes the constraints that complicate the use of military force by a democratic society. He asserts that the failure to successfully apply rational principles of conflict is most often "the result of our attempt to apply principles envisioned largely for implementation by authoritarian sovereigns to a government of checks and balances, which functions only on the basis of broad consensus."

General Link then considers the definition of air power and the degree to which the Air Force exercises a proprietary right over air power. He observes that while all three departments of the US military operate platforms in the aerospace medium, "only the Air Force looks at air power from the perspective of the department charged with fully exploiting the entire aerospace medium in the nation's security interests." As such, the Air Force has a preeminent interest in the application of jointness to ensure that air assets are used efficiently to prevent "parceling [or] subordination to subtheater objectives based in two-dimensional operations."

INTRODUCTION

In the author's estimation, air power is the most valuable commodity of combat because with air superiority "all is possible—without it, all is at risk." One of the critical values of air power is that it can compensate for the inadequacies in land power and sea power to a greater extent than is true of the reverse. But effective use of air assets depends on the broader vision of the joint commander in consultation with the joint force air-component commander, who must "bring an unsurpassed competence in the employment of air power across the spectrum of theater missions."

Air Power in the New Security Environment

Secretary of the Air Force
Donald B. Rice

Operation Desert Storm answered questions about America's relative military strength and the use of the military as an instrument of national power. It focused debates about the conduct of nations in the new order and about US leadership.

In 1989 Polish leader Lech Walesa told Americans, "The world is awaiting your signal. It is watching you."[1] Those were prophetic words. A year later, Saddam Hussein invaded Kuwait. Backed by the coalition, the United States responded. Military force was not the first choice for resolution. Diplomacy and economic sanctions were—and are—preferred tools for settling disputes in the new world order.

Witness President George Bush's frank talks with world leaders, his choice of trade embargoes before force, and his deference to the United Nations (UN) to convince Saddam he was playing with fire. In a recent newspaper column, George Will wrote of the American presidential legacy: to wield power well but also to set the example of available power not wielded, and to refuse unwholesome eminence.[2] That describes President Bush's conduct of Operation Desert Shield and Operation Desert Storm.

As war clouds darkened the desert, the president offered a vision to divergent people joined in a common purpose: peaceful resolution, if possible; resolve to act, if not. Remarkable alliances formed to liberate Kuwait. The Soviets voted with us in the UN and against their old ally Iraq. Syrian and Egyptian ground troops in Kuwait fought under Saudi command. And 10 air forces—some of which don't share the same alphabet, much less the same language—flew off the same daily air tasking order.

The aura of cooperation opens doors for better relations in the Middle East. Despite internal strife, from the debris of war has emerged a flicker of hope for lasting security through peaceful relations.

Security Environment

Geopolitics in other quarters also brings to mind a quote from an issue of *The Economist*: "The difficult takes time; the impossible can happen overnight."[3] After 40 years of a difficult cold war, almost overnight the superpower struggle relaxed. The defense of Western Europe drove US defense strategy and force structure. As the cold war thaws, new rules of the road apply.

Some people argue that in Eastern Europe Soviet control has been replaced with the "Sinatra Doctrine"—each country "doing it my way." More accurately, these countries are doing it *our* way—edging toward market economies, attacking infrastructure problems, cutting military outlays, and focusing on territorial defense. They are also groping for firmer ground than their "strategic limbo" after the demise of the Warsaw Pact.

NATO may change some features too, but its value remains—political, military, and economic. The outlines of an updated alliance strategy are already emerging. Across another ocean, Pacific nations ended the 1980s with the strongest economic growth record of any region in the world. With more competitors and more opportunities, nations staking a claim in world trade will have more interests to protect—interests that will conflict at times.

Though the chance of an Armaggedon-like battle is slim—from a statistical and historical standpoint—the number of conflicts in the years ahead could increase. Mike Rich of the Rand Corporation counted 35 conflicts being fought around the world during the height of Desert Storm.[4]

Only a fool would take us on again, but some fools are still out there—terrorists, drug warlords, guys like Saddam who would choke the world's economic lifeline or use weapons of mass destruction. If we have to engage again, the object will again be quick action, few casualties, and the use of national and coalition strengths. One of those strengths is the global reach and power of aerospace forces.

New Era in Warfare

Air power—of the Air Force, Navy, Army, and Marine Corps—has emerged as a dominant form of military might. The term *air campaign* is fixed in the lexicon, and warfare has entered a new era.

In June 1990 the Air Force published a strategic vision called *The Air Force and U.S. National Security: Global Reach—Global Power*, a white paper outlining air power's contributions to US national security. We just didn't expect such an early opportunity to dramatically demonstrate the ability to reach out and watch a volatile part of the world with the joint surveillance target attack radar system (JSTARS), the airborne warning and control system (AWACS), or the electronic reconnaissance capabilities of RC-135s, to name a few. Air power also had to reach out and help allies. When Israel needed Patriot missiles, airlifters delivered the first ones to Tel Aviv 11 hours after the order.

Air power also reaches out to block aggressors. Saddam checked his cards when he came up against the first F-15s and ground forces in the theater. Further, the integrated employment of air power can reach out to incapacitate. F-14s flew escort for Air Force attack aircraft, EF-111s jammed for the Navy and Marines, tankers increased the striking range of joint and allied forces, F-117s flew strategic bombing missions, and B-52s delivered close support for frontline troops. One commander orchestrated air assets for one integrated air war.

This new age also realized the concept of a strategic air campaign. Air power did exactly what air power visionaries said it could. With roughly 1 percent of the bombs dropped in 11 years in Vietnam, allied air assets shut down Iraq's gasoline production, electricity, transportation, communications, offensive-weapons production, and air defenses.

Coalition air forces concentrated power, taking low tolls in civilian life. Air power divided Iraq from its army in Kuwait. Iraq could not feed it, talk to it, reinforce it, or withdraw it. The army was strategically isolated. Iraq remained in this vise until it agreed to the UN Security Council's terms.

Strategic air power in previous wars suggested future potential. What is different now is the recognition by planners that technology caught up with theory. We can plan a strategic campaign and carry it out. We can go around and over the enemy, strike critical nodes precisely, and paralyze him with strategic and tactical assets. We see his every move and block it.

Potent testament to the effects of air power has come from battle-hardened Iraqi prisoners of war (POW). One senior officer said the air campaign shocked them in its length, massing of aircraft, organization, precision, and total control of the air.

Air power had an almost mystical effect on some Iraqi soldiers. They were in the middle of the desert in a country they didn't want to be in and had no bearings. They thought heroic words or deeds could win the war.

All of a sudden, someone knows where they are, and they can't fight back. One officer referred to the A-10 as "the silent gun because it flew so high and quiet that you assumed it was not going to do anything to you. Then suddenly equipment would begin exploding all around you and you realized it was him."

Some POWs said the most terrifying aircraft were B-52s, whose effects heightened psychological warfare. We would drop leaflets saying that B-52s would be by the next day and it would be a good idea to surrender. The Iraqis learned that these leaflets had what Henry Kissinger, former secretary of state, would call "the added advantage of being true."

Desertion rates skyrocketed, far surpassing the number of Iraqi troops killed in action and wounded. Air attacks also caused shortages of food and water. Many Iraqis chose to leave the battlefield rather than be killed by something they were powerless to defend against.

One officer, asked why his army collapsed, simply said, "The airplanes."

Holding the Edge

So where do we go from here? In the near term, we will refine systems—build planes stealthier and bombs more precise—to retain global reach and power. Downstream, we will need revolutionary capabilities such as

- the ability to see through clouds and guide bombs through;
- advanced electronic warfare to disrupt enemy command, control, communications, and intelligence;
- deployability advances for when, as Federal Express would say, "You absolutely, positively have to get there overnight";
- improved ability to destroy enemy missiles on the ground or intercept them while they are still over enemy territory; and
- high-confidence, effects-oriented, near-real time bomb damage assessment.

We won't fight the same war in 20 years. Other militaries are working now on the ability to defend against the tactics and weapons of Desert Storm. We need to forge ahead too.

There is one capability that no one can ever approach: our people. Their ingenuity solved desert combat challenges in real time. They figured out how to use imaging-infrared Maverick missiles on A-10s to identify tanks at night. The A-10 is a low-altitude daytime fighter designed around its gun. The crews turned it into a high-altitude nighttime tank-plinker.

Our people also discovered how to find Iraqi tanks buried in sand. In daylight, the camouflage was very good. At night, tank metal cooled at a pace slower than that of the sand and could be picked up on F-111 infrared scopes. So, F-111 crews became tank stalkers in addition to performing their normal deep-interdiction missions.

Our people were experts with precision bombs. Several times a two-ship formation of F-15Es with 16 bombs destroyed 16 tanks. The crews also used keen judgment under tough conditions about whether or not to drop.

The talents of our planners and warriors remind me of when Gen George Marshall was asked during World War II if he had a secret weapon. He said, "Yes—the best kids in the world."[5] They still are.

Aerospace Nation

The brainpower of the aerospace industry also deserves high credit. The development of stealth is an example. Its value is an overarching lesson of the air war. No other country is likely to catch up in this area—unless we give away our lead. No one else can manufacture stealth or defend against it. Holding the edge will take a healthy aerospace industry.

The US aerospace industry is a national asset. It is America's leading net exporter of manufactured goods. The aerospace trade surplus offsets the trade deficit and helps keep the nation competitive in defense, travel, and technology.

However, a downturn in defense has taken effect, and reductions lie ahead. The Defense Department's budget saw a real decline of 11.3 percent from FY 1990 to FY 1991. It will shrink an average of 3 percent a year in real terms for each of the next five years. At that point, the Air Force will have only about one-half the purchasing power in the procurement accounts that it had in fiscal year 1985.

Fiscal realities demand solid strategic planning for the defense research and development and procurement portfolio. These include investing in high-payoff technologies, using types of contracts commensurate with the risk involved, and paying close attention to industry trends. Aerospace stocks, bond ratings, and Wall Street issues are not just industry issues. They are national issues. This is an aerospace nation.

This is not to say that national defense should be determined by the analyst on Wall Street. Rather, it recognizes that sound defense requires a sound defense industry that is globally competitive and fiscally responsible. Our actions in the Defense Department affect that condition.

Priority Programs

The challenge ahead for both industry and the Air Force is to stay fit in lean times. Top-quality people come first, along with readiness, training, and equipment as priorities for the 1990s. In the investment accounts, we cannot afford to cut further the modernization programs for our three major systems. The B-2, F-22, and C-17 are essential for very different mission areas.

Every program has three phases: "It will never work"; "It will cost too much"; and "I thought it was a good idea all along." Most of the systems heralded as brilliant performers in the Gulf were stuck in the "it will cost too much" phase five, 10, or 20 years ago. We are still there with the B-2. The fact of the matter, however, is that in a world where flexibility, range, and payload are at a premium, the B-2 is right for the times.

With this next generation of stealth, we will buy about 10 times the ton miles of munitions per dollar with the B-2 as we get with the F-117. This is one measure of the value of a plane that combines stealthier operations than an F-117 with the payload range of a B-52 or B-1B. The B-2's mission is deterrence—of all conflicts. Wouldn't a future Saddam think twice about inciting a war if 75 B-2s were revving on the tarmac only hours away?

Across the board, our focus has to stay on qualitative improvements if we are to outrange, outrun, outgun, and outclass the next bad actor on the world stage.

Conclusion

Operation Desert Storm proved that the aerospace lead which America built over the last half century—and especially over the last decade—lets us approach crises on our terms. Whether it's smart bombs from an F-117, ship-launched Tomahawk cruise missiles, or space-based support, air power affords the speed, range, flexibility, and precision to do the job fast and get home.

Remaining a preeminent aerospace nation will help us prevail in future wars. Better yet, as a wise general said, it could afford a level of deterrence to bypass conflict altogether.[6]

Notes

1. Lech Walesa, "The World Is Awaiting," speech to the AFL-CIO, Washington, D.C., 14 November 1989.
2. George Will, "Person of the Millennium," *Washington Post*, 16 December 1990, K7.
3. "The Difficult Takes Time," *The Economist*, 6–12 January 1990, 16.
4. Michael D. Rich, vice president for national security research, the Rand Corporation, "National Security in the 1990s: The Future Geopolitical Environment," speech at the Town Hall of California, Los Angeles Council of Engineers and Scientists, Los Angeles, Calif., 19 February 1991.
5. Quoted by President Ronald Reagan, remarks at a rally for Sen James T. Broyhill, Raleigh, N.C., 8 October 1986.
6. "Bernard Schriever," in *Military Air Power: The CADRE Digest of Air Power Opinions and Thoughts*, compiled by Lt Col Charles M. Westenhoff (Maxwell AFB, Ala.: Air University Press, October 1990), 86.

Air Power in US Military Strategy

Dr Edward N. Luttwak

Once the cold war was militarized following the outbreak of the Korean War in 1950, US military strategy rapidly acquired the basic form it was to retain for decades, even as its nuclear content first waxed and then waned. Its key elements were (1) fixed ground/tactical-air garrisons in Western Europe and Northeast Asia that were never so weak as to be mere "trip wires" but never so strong as to be sufficient for a high-confidence, forward defense; (2) the upkeep of varying reinforcement capabilities for these garrisons; (3) superior (mostly vastly superior) naval strength to secure the sea-lanes across the Atlantic and Pacific, primarily against submarine interdiction; (4) the complement of strategic-nuclear capabilities, for which the deterrence of direct nuclear attack against the United States itself was always a lesser-included case of a more ambitious "extended deterrence"; and (5) the upkeep of varying expeditionary capabilities, including those narrowly specialized for so-called low-intensity conflict.

After decades of continuity, the retreat of the Soviet Union from central Europe and the sharply diminished plausibility of Soviet aggression in Northeast Asia have fundamentally altered the key determinants of US military strategy, mandating equally basic changes in defense policy which have only just started. Fixed garrisons based on heavy ground forces with air, naval, and strategic-nuclear complements were appropriate to cope with geographically fixed threats. They are not appropriate to cope with contingencies that could materialize as threats in unpredictable locations.

To be sure, Soviet strategic-nuclear capabilities remain as formidable as ever; beyond that, there are still residual Soviet "theater" capabilities in various directions, in addition to a variety of new dangers (as opposed to willful threats). Some of those dangers are associated with the possibility of a reversion to a centralizing dictatorship, while others are associated with the opposite tendency towards disintegration on national lines. Yet even before 2 August 1990, it was perfectly clear that in a post–cold war context, the *salient* dangers to US interests as commonly defined were likely to arise within the North African–West Asian "zone of conflict" centered on the Levant and the Persian Gulf, and not because of Soviet initiatives.

It follows that the relative importance of globally deployable air and naval forces, as well as of expeditionary ground forces, must necessarily increase, obviously at the expense of the heavy ground forces and short-range tactical air power associated with the former garrison element in US strategy. It remains only for US defense policy to acknowledge the change and reallocate resources accordingly, notably from heavy ground forces to other capabilities and from shorter-range to longer-range air power.

What was not at all clear until now, however, was whether the forces that were globally deployable could in fact cope with the sometimes very heavily armed opponents likely to be encountered in the North African–West Asian regions. That light ground forces could do little offensively against large armored/mechanized forces of even minimal competence (and not much defensively in open, trafficable terrain) was understood and accepted. That US naval forces could secure the sea lines of communications and blockade opponents was also taken for granted (though the relevance of blockade as an instrument of war obviously depends on the nature of the opponent). What was strongly debated, however, was the crucial question of how much could be expected from air power—a debate that became downright furious after the August 1990 decision to deploy US forces to confront Iraq.*

---

*The remarks that follow often reflect insights gained from others, notably Col John Warden and Lt Col Frank Kistler, both of the USAF Air Staff as of this writing.

Air Power in the 1991 Gulf War

After years of bombing, much of Berlin was in ruins by January 1945, but Joseph Goebbels could still broadcast nationwide; Hitler could still freely send out orders and receive reports from all fronts by radio and teleprinter; the German army could still supply and move its forces by rail; the Luftwaffe could still sometimes challenge Allied bombers with its new jets; and Berlin's population at large still had electricity, telephone service, water, and adequate supplies of all basic necessities. After less than 48 hours of bombing in January 1991, Baghdad was still largely intact—as it remained throughout the war (Cable News Network showed some of the 50-odd destroyed buildings again and again)—but Saddam Hussein could no longer broadcast on television or nationwide AM radio; all major government, military, and party headquarters were wrecked; both civil and military telecommunications were totally silenced; Iraqi air defenses were largely incapacitated; and in Baghdad the population at large was deprived of electricity, telephone service, and piped water. During the next few weeks, the Iraqi army was cut off from food, fuel, and ammunition resupply by the destruction of rail and road bridges; more and more Iraqi tanks, artillery pieces, aircraft in and out of shelters, and naval vessels were destroyed by direct hits from guided weapons; and any forces that moved out of their dug-in positions were quickly detected and attacked, so that the Iraqi army in and around Kuwait was almost entirely immobilized. The six years of bombing during the Second World War killed many Germans and ruined many German towns and cities without defeating Nazi Germany. A few weeks of bombing hardly damaged Iraqi towns and cities but totally paralyzed Iraq's military power, so that the final ground offensive of Operation Desert Storm was not offensive at all but an almost unopposed advance. Heavily protected American M1 tanks got through unscathed, but so did lightly armored troop carriers, the jeeps of the French foreign legion, and even the rented cars of adventurous journalists. Air power had finally done it.

It is obvious that the bombing of Iraq was *qualitatively* different from that seen in all previous wars. It was certainly not the sheer tonnage of bombs that did it. Contrary to the impression left by the triumphalist briefings with their daily "total sortie" counts of 2,000 and more—which conflated transport, refuelling, defensive patrol, reconnaissance, and escort flights with the minority of actual strike sorties (appendix A)—the total bomb tonnage dropped in Desert Storm (under 80,000 tons) was by no means huge: in March 1945 alone, the American and British air forces dropped 134,000 tons of bombs on Germany. Actually, the qualitative difference was even greater, for it was the 17,109 precision weapons (especially the 9,297 laser-guided bombs) employed by US forces and the few more delivered by the allied air forces that made all the difference, rather than the plain "iron" bombs that accounted for some 90 percent of the tonnage dropped on Iraq and Kuwait (appendix B). The latter were not much more effective than the bombs of previous wars.

The outcome of the air campaign against Iraq was more unexpected than it should have been. Seventy years of overpromising by air power advocates had left a deep residue of distrust in Washington's military culture. Because air power was thought to have failed in Indochina in some very general sense and because it was not deemed to have been "decisive" in either the Korean War or the Second World War, many people believed that its role against Iraq would also be "indecisive"—with some of them expecting outright failure, as that term was variously defined. These negative expectations overlooked the profound implications of both the permanently *situational* character of air power and of its novel capabilities. In fairness, the air power advocates of the past also slighted the supremely situational character of air power in making claims for it independently of the context.

In regard to *conflict intensity*, the attack of targets from the air has always been much more effective in high-intensity conflicts, when the destruction of high-value/high-contrast targets seriously weakens the enemy, rather than in low-intensity conflicts, when there are only low-value, low-contrast targets in most cases. In regard to the *geographic setting*, the attack of targets from the air has always been much more efficient in the arid Middle East with its (often) clear skies than in temperate zones with their frequent mists, fogs, and clouds, or in tropical zones with their recurrent blinding rains and abundant natural cover.

When one reviews the debate that began in August 1990, it is remarkable to note how widespread was the tendency to apply negative assessments of the value of the air power straightforwardly drawn from the (mostly) low-intensity and decidedly tropical setting of Indochina to the high-intensity/arid-zone setting of the projected war with Iraq. What made the transposition so remarkable was that in the Middle East, air power has *always* been much more successful than elsewhere. As early as 1916, the German air squadron that supported the Ottomans had a decisive effect, and then in turn British Field Marshal Edmund H. H. Allenby's airmen were decisive (along with the cavalry!) in the Palestine campaign. Later, air power was clearly decisive in both the North African campaigns from 1941 to 1943 and the Arab-Israeli wars from 1956 onwards. The parallel failure to recognize the full implications of the new capabilities of the US Air Force—a failure shared even by many advocates of air power—is far more understandable because a number of rather subtle considerations were involved whose interaction remains far from obvious, even in the wake of the Iraq air war.

Now is the time to recall that in the 1920s when the first theoreticians of air power issued their promises of what bombardment could achieve, they implicitly—*and legitimately*—assumed a high degree of precision in finding, identifying, and attacking targets. Giulio Douhet navigated to his targets from 1915 onwards by following the course of known roads, railway lines, and rivers. Such visual terrain following was of course very much weather-limited, but when practicable at all, it virtually guaranteed that one target location would not easily be mistaken for another. No doubt, it never occurred to Douhet that in subsequent decades more elaborate means of navigation would be used, which could provide no such assurance of bombing the right target. Likewise, Douhet dropped his bombs at speeds of less than 100 miles per hour and at very low altitudes—a perilous means of delivery even in those days, but also inherently very accurate. No doubt, it never occurred to Douhet that in subsequent decades fighters would chase bombers to much higher speeds and higher altitudes that would preclude the precision that he took for granted. Finally, Douhet could see well enough if he had hit the target, if the bomb had exploded, and if there were any immediate signs that damage had actually been inflicted—a far cry from the hopeful presumptions of most of those airmen who bombed after him in decades to come.

One may, therefore, say that from 17 January 1991, the F-15Es, F-111s, and F-117s that were accurately navigated over their intended targets to drop laser-guided glide bombs within three feet of the aim points, with the concurrent filming of the attack sequence, finally recovered the lost qualities of air power that Douhet, Gen William ("Billy") Mitchell, Air Marshal Hugh Montague Trenchard, and the other theorists of the 1920s had taken for granted. That is why the promise of "victory through air power" was finally redeemed in the Iraq air war, after a 70-year detour through competitively increasing speeds, tentative acquisition, and often gross imprecision in delivery.

It would obviously be grossly premature to attempt any sort of overall assessment of the Iraq/Kuwait air war and of its complex implications for US military strategy as a whole. Nevertheless, some preliminary observations are in order.

The Political, Strategic, and Geographic Contexts

First, the international context was decisive, not merely in a broad diplomatic sense but also specifically in regard to the air war. Because Iraq was diplomatically isolated before it was attacked, the bombardment was unchallenged by any third-party intervention. Otherwise, the very success of the bombing could have evoked adversarial reactions by those countries newly motivated by that success to diminish the scope of the American victory. In the past, we might have witnessed a Soviet airlift of the latest and best air defense equipment, possibly complete with crews. Regardless of the technical effectiveness of such help, the airlift itself could have inhibited the air attack.

Second, one must not overlook the *situational* limits of air power in celebrating its signal achievement in Iraq. The value of bombardment depends on the strategic value of the targets it can actually destroy. The less conventional a war, the fewer the stable and easily identifiable targets of high value. Against elusive guerillas who present no stable targets of any value at all, bombardment remains of little use, even if it is perfectly accurate. In lesser degree, the geographic setting is also significant. In spite of the extreme accuracy of the latest blind navigation techniques, even in the Iraq air war, bad weather with dense clouds and low ceilings was sufficient to drastically restrict air operations for days at a time. Against moving targets that had to be spotted with the naked eye to be attacked at all—most famously the mobile Scud launchers—the effect of bad weather was very direct. At a time when the felt urgency of striking at Scud launchers was at its height, on D+13 (30 January) only three sorties were flown to look for Scuds. On D+14 only one sortie could be flown, rising to a mere nine on D+15, and none at all on D+16. Even against targets of known location, bad weather seriously impeded the air attack—partly because the most accurate precision bombs must still be guided down visually and partly because the effect of prior sorties could not be photographed to establish if further attack was warranted.

As it happens, the reduced pace of air operations caused by bad weather that was most unusual for the region merely delayed and did not change the outcome, because the Iraqis were unable or unwilling to take advantage of the respite to carry out ground attacks of their own. Against a more aggressive enemy, however, the consequences could have been severe. Obviously, this factor must be taken into account in applying any lessons of the war to other possible wars that might unfold in less favorable geographic settings, against more active opponents.

Strategy in Prewar Planning

As regards the use of air power in war, all of the strategy lies in the selection and prioritization of the targets. Much more than the mere technicalities of targeting is involved. Even in a most uneven encounter, the planners of a bombing campaign must contend with scarcity—they cannot attack all possible targets immediately and concurrently. Some targets, notably those associated with defense suppression, automatically warrant the highest priority. Others, notably urban areas as such, may easily be dismissed as near useless or even counterproductive. It is between these extremes that planners must select what to bomb and in what sequence, according to their best estimate of the especial vulnerabilities of the enemy and especially of the enemy's strategy. The latter in turn can be deduced (not determined) only from a serious, multidisciplinary analysis of (1) the country, (2) its political leadership and current goals in the conflict (subject to constant reassessment, as below), (3) the peculiar strengths and weaknesses of its armed forces, and (4) the presumed military modus operandi down to the tactical level. The aim is to construct an "anatomical chart" that identifies the key nodes of the enemy *as an operating system*. From that total array of more significant potential targets, planners can then derive a priority list on the basis of standard urgency and physical vulnerability criteria to formulate the initial bombing plan.

In that regard, it is now necessary to rediscover and revive the lost art of vulnerability analysis. Now that bombs can be guided down the air shafts of aircraft bunkers and onto a specific segment of a large bridge, the expertise of structural engineers and a host of other such specialists has become correspondingly important in planning an air campaign. A pontoon bridge that loses one of its middle segments is soon repaired, but if cut from its moorings to float downstream, it will have to be entirely replaced. Likewise, different types of buildings in Baghdad called for radically different forms of attack (critics of modern architecture will be reinforced in their beliefs by the extreme vulnerability of the most modern high-rise buildings). This sort of engineering-in-reverse was highly developed by the end of the

Second World War, but it became a lost art with the advent of nuclear weapons, when strategic bombing was equated with wholesale destruction.

Much of the success of the air campaign against Iraq was in fact due to the quality of the original "Instant Thunder" Air Force plan that was broadly accepted by Gen Norman Schwarzkopf and Gen Colin Powell on 10 and 11 August 1990. The plan's very name alluded to the rejection of Vietnam-era gradualism. Instead of attacking peripheral targets, mostly of modest importance—as in President Lyndon Johnson's "Rolling Thunder" bombing campaign of 1965–68—Instant Thunder called for the concentrated precision bombing of the most important sites in Baghdad from the very start of the war.

In broad outline, the plan amounted to a self-sufficient air offensive in three phases. The first and shortest was intended to win air superiority over the whole of Iraq and Kuwait by the systematic attack of the main Iraqi radar and air defense command centers, the runways of the civil and military airfields where Iraqi military aircraft were already dispersed, and some of the major antiaircraft missile batteries. In addition to these typical "defense suppression" targets, the first phase also included the most urgent strategic targets. Notable among these were the major military and regime headquarters with their communications, mostly in Baghdad, and the fixed launchers and known storage sites of Iraqi Scud missiles and biological and chemical weapons. The latter were targeted to diminish the then much-feared threat of chemical-missile attacks against Israeli and Saudi cities, as well as US ports of entry.

The second phase was to focus the air attack against Iraq's entire logistic infrastructure, starting with ammunition dumps, oil refineries, petroleum-product tank farms, and the major depots for weapons of all kinds. Success in attacking those "military support" targets would henceforth limit Iraqi military units to the fuel and ammunition they already held in their forward areas—enough for only 72 hours or so of intense operations. The larger effort of this second phase, however, was to be the bombing of weapon assembly lines, factories, and repair workshops, as well as the laboratories and plants where nuclear, biological, and chemical weapons were being developed or actually produced. In addition, Iraq's civil infrastructure was also to be incapacitated by precision attacks on electrical power plants, radio and television stations, telephone exchanges, water-treatment plants, and so forth.

The third phase, starting on the second week of the air offensive, was to focus on Iraq's main strength—its ground forces. It called for air strikes against the rail and road bridges between Baghdad and Kuwait, the area bombing of Republican Guard and other selected Iraqi ground forces, and precision attacks against naval vessels and Iraqi aircraft in and out of their shelters, among other such high-value targets. As far as detailed targeting was concerned, Instant Thunder was prepared with the help of whatever experts could be found, but something resembling a "vulnerability encyclopaedia" would have served the planners much better.

In any event, by the time the war began, there were more US and allied aircraft in hand than had originally been anticipated, so the three phases were greatly compressed. Still, Instant Thunder was to remain the essence of the war plan that was actually carried out.

Strategy in the Conduct of War

As soon as the bombing actually starts, the enemy's operating system will begin to change as he seeks to circumvent the effects of the bombing he has already absorbed and of the subsequent bombing that he anticipates. Hence, precisely to the degree that the anatomical chart *was* accurate and the bombing *is* effective, the results of the prewar analysis are undone. This creates the possibility that if the initial bombing plan is followed mechanically and without change, the bombing will diminish in effectiveness. Against that, the feedback from combat results and bomb damage assessment also begins, and so does the more general observation of the enemy's actual modus operandi, which may diverge in ways large or small from prewar presumptions.

There is no alternative other than continuously reappraising the anatomical chart and reformulating target priority lists with changes large or small, so as to ensure that the destruction of the chosen targets continues to serve the overall strategic purpose at hand.

Institutional Factors

Because the effectiveness of the air attack thus depends on the continuous reassessment of the anatomical chart, it follows that any delay between the bombing and the flow of damage assessment feedback caused by institutional arrangements exacts a proportionate penalty. If the feedback is also deformed by the imposition of irrelevant criteria that do not correspond to the purposes of the air attack (e.g., by requiring destruction when shutdown is sufficient), the penalty is yet greater. There are indications that the greatest weakness revealed by the Iraq air war was precisely in the feedback process as a whole—from the collection of evidence to the dissemination of analyzed results. Actually, the institutional requirements for the optimal use of offensive air power are much more demanding. In bare outline, they are summarized in appendix C.

Three Operational Lessons

The advent of systematic defense suppression as well as stealth in the Iraq air war did more than minimize aircraft losses. They also allowed the *reconquest of the middle altitudes*, which are most suitable for a deliberate process of target acquisition, accurate attack, and the observation of immediate damage effects. The very low-altitude/high-speed penetration and bombing tactics developed over the years—especially by the Royal Air Force (RAF)—to circumvent Soviet missile air defenses were, of course, quite unsuited to the conditions of the Iraq war, where surface-to-air missile defenses were weak while antiaircraft artillery was abundant. But in all circumstances, those tactics turn the aircraft into a blind and unresponsive missile which cannot usefully employ the most reliable and most economical of current precision weapons—laser-guided glide bombs. Flashing over their targets, the RAF Tornados scattered their area munitions to good or ill effect and exited again without collecting any damage feedback data. Likewise, very high-altitude flight is incompatible with the effective use of economical precision weapons, allowing only area bombing in most cases.

A second discovery of the Iraq air war was that "all bombing nowadays is [should be] precision bombing," in the words of Col John Warden, the architect of Instant Thunder. Assuming that both the prewar planning and the ongoing war planning do allow the bombing of key systemic nodes and not merely enemy structures and forces en masse, nonprecision bombing remains valid only against a narrow range of targets in a narrow range of circumstances. In other words, *general-purpose unguided bombs have become specialized weapons*, while the various precision weapons have become the standard weapons of air bombardment. It was the generalization of bombing with three-feet median inaccuracies (versus the 30 feet of past best efforts and the 3,000 feet of most World War II "strategic" bombing) that resulted in the transformation of air power manifest in the Iraq air war.

A third discovery of the Iraq air war was that insofar as stealth diminishes vulnerability to detection and interception, it is wonderfully economical. Certainly, in expeditionary scenarios the superior economy of stealth persists, even if each aircraft is much more costly than a nonstealth counterpart. The reason is simple enough: under current standard operating procedures, nonstealth bombing aircraft are now escorted by fighters flying top cover, by dedicated aircraft armed with antiradiation missiles, and by active jamming aircraft, as well as tankers for all of these aircraft. Hence, only a fraction of the aircraft that go into action carry any ordnance. During the Iraq air war, the use of as many as eight or 10 aircraft to deliver a total of four or six bombs was rather common. Inevitably, the economy of air power is degraded as the allocation of aircraft for self-protection rather than the positive strategic purpose increases.

It is obvious that striving to avoid any combat losses whatsoever can *overshoot the culminating point of strategic utility*. Of course, the degree to which combat losses should in fact be minimized at the expense of such self-imposed "virtual attrition" depends on the specifics of the situation. Losses tolerable in a great life-and-death struggle of the nation would not have been acceptable in an expeditionary setting such as the Iraq air war.

In any case, stealth can eliminate this type of virtual attrition altogether. Insofar as X targets can be attacked by Y stealth aircraft or by three times Y nonstealth aircraft, the life-cycle cost of stealth and nonstealth aircraft should be compared accordingly to the very great advantage of the former.

Technical Lesson

The importance of feedback in maintaining the validity of target selection stage by stage increases correspondingly the value of bombing modes that allow at least partial immediate feedback (identifying the attacked target, hitting the same, witnessing the primary explosion, and viewing the primary and secondary effects). Likewise, the value of bombing modes that reduce such feedback to target acquisition (e.g., most air-to-surface missiles)—even more, of modes that deny feedback altogether (e.g., air-launched cruise missiles, sea-launched cruise missiles)—is correspondingly degraded. In addition, the sea-launched cruise missiles employed in the Iraq war had much larger median inaccuracies than the best of the air-launched weapons—and the difference was quite often decisive.

Conclusion: The Role of Air Power in US Strategy

In the aftermath of Desert Storm, many commentators chose to insist that the role of all four services was (equally?) essential in achieving victory. Insofar as Desert Shield is accepted as a valid precedent, it follows that the US would again require several months and very elaborate preexisting basing facilities to deploy sufficient force to fight a medium power such as Iraq. Hence, US strategy should now take advantage of the diminishing costs of the US garrison forces in NATO countries in order to keep up as much as possible or even increase funding for (1) airlift and sea lift, (2) Army and Marine Corps expeditionary forces, (3) carrier-centered naval forces, and (4) tactical air forces.

But there is another reading of the evidence, based on the actual operational content of Desert Storm rather than the preparations made under Desert Shield. The latter assembled a "balanced" five-service array of forces (including the Coast Guard), but the former was in fact an air war that might have ended with Iraq's surrender in a few more weeks, but which was concluded by a ground advance that turned out to be almost administrative in character. It is evident that the air power used in Desert Storm was already mostly in place, while the Desert Shield deployment was still months away from completion.

On that basis, the alternative to a general-purpose increase in airlift/sea lift would be to assign a higher priority to *globally applicable air capabilities.* The latter would consist of an evolving combination of present-day tactical aircraft with rapidly deployable base-infrastructure modules, and future aircraft with much longer combat ranges (i.e., B-2s with suitable nonnuclear ordnance, operable from a small number of well-equipped bases from which they could reach all points of interest). Because of the situational character of air power, the exact budget priority to be assigned to globally applicable air capabilities depends on the estimated nature and geographic locations of potential conflict situations. At present, for example, a very high priority would seem to be justified by the centrality of the North African–West Asian "zone of conflict" in virtually all forecasts.

Appendix A

Sorties Flown in Operation Desert Storm
17 January–27 February 1991
(Numbers approximate and rounded off)

Type of Mission	Allies	USAF	Other US	Total Coalition
AI[a]	4,600	24,000	11,900	40,500
OCA[b]	1,400	4,500	600	6,500
CAS[c]	0	1,500	1,500	3,000
Total strike sorties[d]	6,000	30,000	14,000	50,000
Aerial refuelling	1,500	10,000	1,500	13,000
DCA[e]	4,100	3,200	2,700	10,000
SEAD[f]	0	2,800	1,200	4,000
Tactical airlift	4,300	14,000	0	18,300
Other[g]	1,100	6,000	7,900	15,000
Total nonstrike sorties	11,000	36,000	13,300	60,300
Approximate grand total of all Desert Storm sorties				110,300

Sources: Department of the Air Force, *Air Force Performance in Desert Storm* (Washington, D.C.: Government Printing Office, April 1991), and author's collation of published data.

[a]Air interdiction—in this case a conflation of both strategic (against Iraqi installations) and operational (against Iraqi air, ground, and naval forces) bombing, including battlefield interdiction (against Iraqi forces behind the front).

[b]Offensive counterair (i.e., attacks against Iraqi air force bases and related facilities).

[c]Close air support (i.e., attacks against Iraqi ground forces at the front).

[d]*Strike* as here defined includes all aircraft that penetrated hostile airspace in the course of ground-attack missions, *with or without* ground-attack ordnance of their own.

[e]Defensive counterair (i.e., air defense patrols and intercepts).

[f] Suppression of enemy air defenses (i.e., attacks against Iraqi antiaircraft missiles, guns, and related radar and other facilities).

[g] Airborne early warning, airborne electronic surveillance, electronic warfare, and other.

Appendix B

Aerial Ordnance Used in Operation Desert Storm
17 January–27 February 1991

Part I
US Forces (Air Force, Navy, and Marine Corps)

Air-to-ground missiles
AGM-65 Maverick variants
    -65B (TV guidance)   1,703
    -65D (imaging infrared)   3,536
    -65G (imaging infrared)   187
    -65E (laser)   41   (used by Marine Corps aircraft)
AGM-84E/supersonic low altitude
  missile (SLAM/Harpoon)   7   (500 lb, used by Navy aircraft)
AGM-62 (Walleye)   131   (2,000 lb, used by Navy aircraft)

Total air-to-ground missiles   5,605
Total estimated warhead weight   1,416   tons

Guided bombs
GBU-10 (2,000 lb)   2,263
GBU-15* (2,000 lb)   71
GBU-24 (2,000 lb)   284   (used by F-117s and F-15Es)
GBU-10/I-2,000   403
GBU-24/I-2,000   877
GBU-12 (500 lb)   4,542   (used by F-111Fs against tanks)
GBU-16 (1,000 lb)   208
GBU-27 (2,000 lb)   718   (used by F-117s against hard targets)
GBU-28 (4,000 lb)   2

Total guided bombs   9,368
Total estimated weight   5,852   tons

---

*Electro-optical, all others laser-homing.

THE FUTURE OF AIR POWER

Radiation-homing missiles (for SEAD, see appendix A)
AGM-45 (Shrike) 31
AGM-88 (high-speed antiradiation
 missile—HARM) 1,804

Total antiradiation missiles 1,835
Total estimated warhead weight 133 tons

Total number of all air-launched guided weapons 16,808
Total estimated warhead/bomb weight
 of all air-launched guided weapons 7,401 tons

Tomahawk sea-launched cruise missiles
RGM-109C 264 (1,000-lb warhead)
RGM-109D 27 (bomblets)
RGM-109B 10

Total number launched 301
Total warhead weight, at 1,000 lb each 142 tons

Unguided bombs
Mk 82 (500 lb) 64,698
Mk 83 (1,000 lb) 10,125
Mk 84 (2,000 lb) 11,179
Mk 117 (750 lb) 34,808
UK (1,000 lb) 288
Mk 20 (500 lb) 27,735 (Rockeye, multiple)
CBU-78 (1,000 lb) 215 (cluster type)
CBU-89 (710 lb) 1,107 (cluster type)
CBU-52/58/71 (800 lb) 17,029 (cluster type)
CBU-87 (950 lb) 10,815 (cluster type)

Total Mk 20 and cluster types 56,901
Total number of unguided bombs 177,999
Total weight of unguided bombs 64,996 tons

Number of bombs delivered in bulk
 by B-52s 72,000+
Weight of bombs delivered in bulk
 by B-52s 25,700 tons

Summary totals
Total aerial tonnage delivered by US forces 72,539 tons
Weight of guided weapons of all types 7,543 tons (10.4%)

Total number of aerial weapons used
    by US forces   195,108
Total number of guided weapons   17,109 (8.8%)

Part II

Estimate of Aerial Tonnage Delivered by Non-US Forces

In the absence of other data, the calculation that follows generously assumes that the average non-US "strike" sortie tonnage was the same as the US average minus that of the B-52s.

Total air-ground ordnance delivered by US aircraft, excluding Tomahawk cruise missiles (142 tons)	72,397 tons
Less 25,700 tons delivered by B-52s	46,697 tons
Number of US "strike" plus SEAD sorties, minus 1,624 B-52 sorties	46,376
Ordnance delivered per (non B-52) "strike"/SEAD sortie	1.007 tons
Total number of non-US "strike" sorties	6,000
Estimated aerial ordnance delivered by non-US forces	6,042 tons

Estimated Grand Total of Aerial Ordnance Delivered in Desert Storm

US (including cruise missiles)		72,539 tons
Estimated non-US		6,042 tons
	Grand Total	78,581 tons

Sources: Department of the Air Force, *Air Force Performance in Desert Storm* (Washington, D.C.: Government Printing Office, April 1991), and author's collation of published data.

Appendix C

Organizing for Success: Five Preconditions

Precondition 1. Recognition of the priority of target selection requires more or less the inversion of ordinary air force hierarchies. If the organization is commanded by sortie maximizers, effective bombing is unlikely. Targeting generals must outrank administrative generals, training generals, and flight generals. If targeting is treated as an afterthought, left to institutionally marginal figures, bombing is unlikely to succeed. Target selection must be carried out concurrently at all levels, but *starting* with the strategic. It is useless to be technically, tactically, and operationally successful in bombing the wrong targets, and it may even be counterproductive.

Precondition 2. Bombing without a backflow of data on the bombing's immediate and broader results may be a purposeless scattering of ordnance or, at best, blind "theory bombing" (e.g., the groundless World War II British hypothesis that "dehousing" equals progress towards victory). The essential complement of effective bombing is the systematic collection, analysis, and dissemination of data on both its immediate and cumulative effects, specifically to determine whether

- the targets attacked have in fact been damaged;
- subsequent targets can continue to be damaged, given that damage will evoke a defensive reaction; and
- the damage achieved is actually *and* cumulatively damaging the enemy's war effort.

In practice, effective bombing thus depends on the effectiveness of the information backflows, namely

- the technical and tactical backflows to assess the damage achieved, which inherently also determines if extant enemy defenses are being overcome;
- the operational-level backflows to identify adversary reactions currently under way because of prior bombing and to provide guidelines for preparations designed to counter them in turn; and
- the strategic backflows to determine if the bombing—howsoever effective at the technical, tactical, and operational levels—is actually achieving the strategic objective.

Precondition 3. The dynamic assessment (over time) of the workings of the backflow loops is necessary in order to guard against "theory" feedbacking, which is only one notch above theory bombing. That is an especial danger because

- Strategically important results will often be cumulative, easily inducing the belief that the bombing is successful because progress is being made in a process (e.g., urban areas *are* being destroyed). But the progress might be illusory if the nexus between the process and victory is itself illusory.
- Success in a process that is related to victory will cause the enemy to try to evade, if not outmaneuver, that process (e.g., bombing of ball-bearing production induces the importation of ball bearings, retroactively falsifying a theory perfectly valid ex ante). In other words, backflow loops correct blind bombing, while dynamic assessment of the backflow loops corrects for "drift" caused by delusive accumulation or enemy reactions to cumulative effects in fact being achieved.
- While enemy reactions at the technical (e.g., electronic countermeasures) and tactical (e.g., new fighter tactics) or operational (e.g., day/night redeployment) levels are in general easily identified because of their direct impact on combat operations, enemy reactions at the strategic level can be very elusive. These include the avoidance of bombing effects by dispersal and their circumvention by

substitution. One complication is that substitution can be masked by the upkeep of facilities no longer valued. For example, the Allies continued to bomb heavily the large, fixed V-1 launch sites in the Pas de Calais when the Germans had long since switched to light, mobile launchers (the bombing of fixed Scud launchers during the Iraq air war is an exact analogy; there is no evidence that any Scud was launched from any of them).

- Modality changes (e.g., when supplies for heavy forces are interdicted, the enemy may still attack with light forces under certain conditions, as the Chinese did in the Korean War after Operation Strangle).
- Reconstitution (the enemy that can build weapon factories can reconstitute his production capacity after these factories are damaged—not the case for Iraq in the Gulf war).

Precondition 4. Air Force responsiveness is necessary (i.e., an institutional willingness to accept plan changes and to bomb usefully rather than maximally). Air forces naturally fall into a "sortie production" rhythm. Hence, they tend to resist plan changes that interfere with sortie generation (as most will).

Precondition 5. Military-wide responsiveness is also necessary. If bombing is dynamically effective, will other services allow it to continue till victory?

The United States as an Aerospace Power in the Emerging Security Environment

Dr Robert L. Pfaltzgraff, Jr.

For more than two generations, the United States has relied largely on strategic air power in its various forms as the basis for deterrence and for the actual conduct of military operations in the event of deterrence failure. In the bipolar setting of the several decades since World War II, the requirements for strategic deterrence have been met with spectacular success. That this has been the case represents a tribute to the strategic concepts and force structures that have guided the United States as a superpower with goals encompassing both the deterrence of attack against its own national territory and the extension of security guarantees to allies. The ability of the United States to deter strategic warfare in consonance with the principal tenet of deterrence logic resided in the capacity both to inflict unacceptable levels of devastation on its adversary the Soviet Union and to minimize the ability of the Soviet Union to execute a crippling strike against the United States. Such an achievement on the part of a strategic nuclear force structure, however formidable its requirements and however questionable its prospects at the time, was the outcome of policies consistently pursued by successive administrations since the dawn of the nuclear age.

The security environment for which American air power at the strategic level was largely configured was essentially bipolar in structure, although the actual contingencies in which such capabilities came to be used were conflicts at intensity levels lower than, and outside, the immediate superpower confrontation. In this international system of superpower deterrence at the strategic level, the air assets of the United States were utilized in a broad range of other situations in which deterrence clearly had broken down. To a large extent, the condition of strategic deterrence between the United States and the

Soviet Union contributed to a situation in which lesser powers, including Soviet proxy states, were prepared to use maximum military force available to them to achieve political objectives. At the same time, the United States—for a host of reasons, including the perceived threat of escalation involving the Soviet Union—was unwilling to employ the ultimate weapons at its disposal in the various regional or local conflicts in which it became militarily engaged. Beneath the stability of strategic deterrence in the bipolar structure of the generations after World War II, there were numerous conflicts of varying intensity levels to which American military power in all but its strategic nuclear dimension was committed.

In this sense, the international security environment has long displayed numerous features of military power diffusion. The wars in Korea and Vietnam were fought with the high-intensity capabilities that were available at the time—excluding, of course, nuclear weapons. The large number of wars that have shaped the international security landscape of the past 40 years provides vivid evidence of the increasing availability of a broad spectrum of military capabilities to actors in regions characterized by major conflict potential. To a large extent, the dominant features of the emerging security environment bear considerable similarity to a familiar past. On a continuing basis, the United States has found it necessary to project military power into distant conflict zones in support of vital interests. Such a need, as demonstrated by Operation Desert Storm, remains a likely prospect in the 1990s.

What can be projected for the future, however, is the acceleration of the diffusion of technologies that will increase the number of actors in possession of the means for conducting military operations at the higher end of the conflict spectrum. This includes the proliferation of missiles; advanced aircraft and maritime platforms; and nuclear, biological, chemical, and conventional warheads. It has been widely assumed that the world of the early twenty-first century will contain as many as 15–20 states in possession of all or some of such capabilities. To the extent that the weapons inventories of an increasing number of actors contain these types of systems, the capacity to wage war at a level previously associated exclusively with the superpowers will be more widely diffused. A large number of states will have available the means to launch strategic strikes that previously were possessed only by the United States and the Soviet Union.

The unfolding of such a strategic multipolarity is likely to be a gradual process. Initially, crude delivery systems such as those possessed by Iraq will be replaced or supplemented by capabilities that have greater accuracy and extended range. Ultimately, technologies will give to increasing numbers of actors the ability to target any point on the earth's surface from any other site. To the extent that range and accuracy no longer pose inhibiting factors, the concept of bipolar strategic deterrence with which we have been critically concerned for the past two generations will be transformed in its requirements. As we move toward military multipolarity with large numbers of actors in possession of increasingly sophisticated capabilities, the requirements for deterrence will have to be reconsidered. Indeed, the most important issue for the United States as an aerospace power will be framed by deterrence needs—together, of course, with appropriate force structures under conditions of deterrence failure if American vital interests are at stake.

The security environment for which we must plan deterrence and war-fighting requirements will have as a defining characteristic an increasing number of actors capable of acquiring or producing a range of advanced military capabilities for the conduct of operations at the higher end of the conflict spectrum. Such states will emerge in most, if not all, of the regions of the world. To the extent that the process of such military power diffusion proceeds at an uneven pace, the potential for destabilization—as we have seen in the Middle East—will be substantial. It should not automatically be assumed that the United States will choose to intervene in the fashion of Desert Storm. Nevertheless, the role that the United States has chosen to play—especially in the second half of this century, as well as in the two world wars—has been that of a balancing power. American policy has been designed to preserve (as in the case of NATO) or to restore (as in the war in the Persian Gulf) a regional equilibrium that was deemed in some broader strategic sense to be of vital importance to the United States. In a world of larger numbers of actors in possession of high-intensity capabilities, the international security environment is likely to feature periodic challenges in what has been termed a regionalization of conflict. Additional threats to equilibrium, as in the recent history of the Middle East, will arise. To the extent that the United States and other actors committed to some form of world order will seek to preserve or restore the independence of states within such regions, they will need to develop appropriate concepts of deterrence based on collaborative frameworks and joint force structures for the conduct of military operations and peacekeeping.

The diffusion of military power holds numerous important implications for deterrence, which in turn will shape the role to be played by the United States as an aerospace nation. First and foremost, the greater availability of capabilities of increasingly high intensity places a premium on the ability to deter the outbreak of conflict in regions in which the United States has vital interests. The requirements for multipolar deterrence, more complex and onerous than in the simpler bipolar era, have yet to be fully understood. At a minimum, they will confer on the United States the need to have available time-urgent capabilities. Our ability to deter a would-be aggressor will be determined by the extent to which we are perceived to be able to inflict unacceptable levels of devastation, as in the traditional meaning of deterrence. What such a requirement will mean for ballistic missile capabilities forms an important question that, as military multipolarity unfolds, will have to be addressed.

Equally important will be the extent to which the United States will have the means, if deterrence fails, to prevail with air power against actors with substantial air assets and ground forces. The security environment in which US military power would be deployed will be characterized by adversaries at least some of which will be more fully capable than the United States of deploying substantial ground forces. Operation Desert Storm occurred at a time when deployable US and allied ground forces were numerous; those numbers will diminish greatly as we move toward the end of the decade. The NATO-Europe force structure, still intact in 1991, will not be available as a strategic reserve for high-intensity ground operations. At all levels of our military structure, to be sure, greater emphasis will be placed on the qualitative factors of strategic planning and technology. The obvious need to operate with smaller forces enhances the importance of deterring the outbreak of war and, once conflict begins, utilizing air assets to achieve decisive and quick results.

In the emerging security environment, the spectrum of potential threats is likely to be broadened. While present possessors of lower-intensity capabilities will be strengthened as a result of technology diffusion, new actors at the lower end of the spectrum can be expected to emerge. The United States will face threats ranging from terrorism practiced by state and nonstate actors to potential warfare at the nuclear level. Technology will confer upon groups at all levels the means to make them formidable enemies in armed conflict. This proliferation of capabilities is taking place in a security environment containing numerous flash points. They encompass disputes over resources, including oil and water, as well as deeply rooted differences based on ethnicity, nationalism, ideology, and religion. The extent to which such conflicts will engage American forces remains to be seen. In the absence of a clearly defined Soviet threat, the United States may be less likely to intervene than when such states were menaced directly by the Soviet Union or by a Soviet client state. Yet the reverse proposition, as we saw in Operation Desert Storm, is also evident, namely that the sharp reduction in the military threat facing NATO in Europe—together with the ability of the Bush administration to achieve major power agreement, including the Soviet Union, in the United Nations Security Council—enhanced the willingness of the United States to take decisive military action against Iraq's aggression.

The extent to which such conditions will prevail in the emerging security environment cannot be fully determined in advance. However, it is likely that the requirements for a collective imprimatur in the form of an international coalition that shares the burden of deploying, using, and paying for authorized military operations will be shaped by the recent Gulf experience. There will be an obvious preference for operations patterned on Desert Storm, based on reinforcing levels of international and domestic consensus. Nevertheless, the United Nations will remain an uncertain reed on which to base such action, for the interests of the United States and its allies may diverge sharply from those of a large number of other members of the international organization. It may even be necessary to envisage—as in the case of the 1983 Grenada and 1989 Panama interventions, as well as the air strike in 1986 against Libya— unilateral US action on a time-urgent basis. Desert Storm unfolded over a period of several months, during which time it was possible masterfully to create a broad international coalition of support while deploying the capabilities required for the conduct of high-intensity military operations. Therefore, an immediate lesson of the experience of the United States over the past decade—in post-Vietnam military power projection—becomes apparent. In preparing for a spectrum of conflict contingencies, we will find it necessary to consider our responses in both multilateral and unilateral contexts. The greater the level of effort that will be required over a lengthening time span, as in Operation Desert Storm, the more extensive and obvious will be the need to sustain an international coalition. The more restricted the operation, both in its time frame and the level of military resources needed, the more plausible it will be that the United States will be prepared to act unilaterally. It is amply evident that, in both categories, air power will form a decisively important element of military operations.

Although ground forces will remain vitally important elements of the campaign, as in Grenada, Panama, and the Gulf war, wars on land cannot be won without air superiority. By the same token, the ability to destroy an enemy's military infrastructure, including his advanced weapons-production facilities and military assets, will be increasingly important in the emerging world of greater military multipolarity. The projection of military power into regions of major importance will depend increasingly on our capacity, at the beginning of war, to neutralize or destroy the military assets of a would-be regional hegemonist such as Saddam Hussein. More likely, however, are contingencies in which the task facing the United States will be that of launching limited strikes against specific, discrete targets that will not necessarily involve a coalition effort in support of interests deemed vital to the United States. In short, the United States, while seeking always to act in concert with allies and coalition partners, will find it necessary to be prepared for contingencies in which vital interests can be safeguarded only by unilateral action.

In such a global-security setting, it is possible to categorize the requirements for American power projection with obvious implications for the United States as an aerospace nation. First, the highest priority will continue to be attached to the deterrence of war at all levels—especially nuclear war. Second, it will be essential that the United States be prepared to intervene in situations, of which Desert Storm is illustrative, in which major conventional forces are employed by one or both sides to the dispute. Finally, we will find it necessary in the emerging security environment to be able to respond in the form of retaliatory raids—as in Libya in 1986—against specified targets if, for example, US interests are attacked by terrorist groups. For each of these categories of contingencies, air power will form an indispensable element of American capabilities. In light of the characteristic features of each, the requirement will be apparent for a military force structure that, in all of its elements, is highly mobile, flexible, firepower intensive, interoperable, and survivable under a broad range of combat conditions.

Deterrence will remain a central concern of military planners as we move into a world of additional nuclear powers, as well as possessors of biological and/or chemical weapons. Simply as a result of the entry of new actors, the possibility—if not probability—of deterrence failure will grow. In addition to the US-Soviet strategic nuclear balance, it will be necessary to base deterrence planning on the emergence, within an anticipated time frame, of increasing numbers of other powers having capabilities of varying levels of sophistication. Under such circumstances, the offense-defense deterrence mix will increase in importance. The ability of larger numbers of actors to strike distant targets will have major consequences for both the retaliatory and defensive components of deterrence. A would-be aggressor may be deterred by a combination of countervailing means, including the virtual certainty that he could be struck in retaliation as well as the knowledge that his attacking force could not reach the intended target as a result of defensive measures. The implications of nuclear, biological, chemical, or even conventional warheads deployed on delivery vehicles of greater range and accuracy will be destabilizing, for such capabilities will become available to actors whose value systems, goals, and interests are certain to be widely divergent with respect to each other and to the United States. It is useful, in retrospect, in thinking about such a future to ponder the problems that would have been created for the United States—and for its coalition partners outside the Middle East—if Saddam Hussein had possessed a demonstrable capability to strike targets in Western Europe or North America. The psychological dimensions of such a capability would have been enormous for populations in such target countries. The ability on the part of the United States to deploy Patriot air defense systems in Israel, Turkey, and Saudi Arabia—as well as their performance as area defense systems despite their original mission as a point defense—provided in itself a major contribution to the cohesiveness and success of the coalition against Saddam Hussein.

Although the precise configuration of an offense-defense posture for the United States as an aerospace power in the emerging multipolar security environment demands extensive analysis, it is apparent that a combination of active and passive measures—together with counterair and theater missile defense—will be required. On the one hand, we will face an air defense environment—a logical outgrowth of technology diffusion—that is itself more hostile as a result of the deployment of new-generation air defense systems by adversaries. Therefore, the requirements for stealth technologies, together with other means designed to assure that our retaliatory assets reach intended targets, will intensify. At the same time, on the other hand, we will confront the need to provide a defense against enemy strikes aimed at military targets and civilian populations. It is apparent that the requirements for such defenses differ substantially from a capability configured specifically to deter a Soviet attack. Therefore, the issue is how best to protect vital power-projection assets—especially forward-deployed forces, including air, ground, and naval units—as well as civilian targets against the increasingly lethal, accurate, and extended-range capabilities that will be more widely available as we move into the next century.

In its essence, deterrence will encompass the necessary means to prevent nuclear war, as well as combat biological, chemical, and conventional warheads under conditions of multipolarity. The conceptual needs of offense/defense will place a premium on technologies that provide for highly sophisticated reconnaissance and surveillance systems, including the greater use of space. To an extent that is unprecedented, the architectural requirements for such capabilities will make necessary the integration of space and terrestrial elements of strategy and forces. Such a synergism was apparent in the utilization of space-based sensors in the targeting of the Patriot air defense system. Deployment of space-based missile defense in itself provides abundant evidence of the increasing requirement to command the heights of space, just as control of the skies immediately above and around the battlefield is the sine qua non of military victory. In a geostrategic sense, there is an obvious indivisibility of the aerospace mission that is already apparent by the utilization of the exosphere and endoatmospheric environment in both the offensive and defensive components of deterrence. This condition can only grow in importance in the emerging security environment.

Ideally, our national security strategy should have as a continuing objective to provide for deterrence at all levels in a multipolar security environment. From their advent, we have thought of nuclear weapons as deterrents, not only against the use of such systems in the hands of an adversary, but also as a basis for the deterrence of all armed conflict between their possessors. Thus, the United States and the Soviet Union have gone to the brink, but not beyond, in their strategic military interaction. Instead, nuclear weapons have provided the defining parameters of a relationship that has been shaped by other forms of conflict across a range of other capabilities. Whether armed conflict between the United States and the Soviet Union would have been avoided in the absence of nuclear deterrence will never be known. Similarly, we cannot at this point in time be certain that a more multipolar world, including additional possessors of nuclear weapons, will be more stable. Indeed, there are portents that point in the opposite direction as a result of likely differences in the composition of the risk-gain calculus in a culturally diverse world. In the logic of multipolarity, we face the prospect of larger numbers of conflicts if only as a result of a greater diversity of actors having profoundly important political differences and in possession of more lethal advanced military capabilities. As the frequency of conflict grows, it is not necessarily the case that its intensity will diminish, especially as the lethality of diffused capabilities is magnified. In such an environment, the objective of our deterrence concept will be to minimize the frequency and intensity of armed conflict.

In achieving such a goal, we face uncertain prospects, given the uneven pace at which regional actors will acquire advanced technologies that will be available for employment—as in the case of Iraq—against less advanced neighbors. Such gaps at the regional level will enhance the prospects for high-intensity warfare unless such combat can be deterred by countervailing power that is rapidly and credibly available to a threatened region and state. The configuration of deterrence assets for such contingencies will impose major requirements on air power as an element of regional equilibrium. In the eventuality that wars break out at the regional level, the task confronting the United States in cases where vital interests are at stake will be to terminate such armed conflicts before large-scale ground forces need to be deployed. In the eventuality, as in Operation Desert Storm, that major land forces are moved into position, air power will have the role of destroying the political, military, and psychological will of the enemy. Taken together, the possession of the means to operate effectively under such circumstances may serve to reinforce deterrence at all levels. The common denominator and linking feature at each level is provided by air power.

The third set of contingencies, likely to be most frequent, will be the projection of power in clearly discrete operations designed to inflict limited damage on an enemy such as a state that sponsors terrorist activity or threatens a neighbor with capabilities which, if identified and destroyed, will effectively disarm the aggressor. However successful we may be in deterring the outbreak of conflict or its escalation at the higher-intensity level, the frequency of conflict at the lower end of the spectrum can be expected to increase under conditions of multipolarity. The numbers of actors will rise dramatically in a world that contains numerous groups, large and small, seeking by whatever means is available to alter the balance of forces to their political, military, or economic advantage. The extent to which small groups—terrorist organizations—acquire such high-intensity capabilities as nuclear weapons remains to be seen. In some cases, nonstate actors will operate on their own. Only if they can be targeted will deterrence based on retaliation be a potentially effective instrument of policy for the United States. Nonstate actors, lacking clearly delineated territorial boundaries, present unique problems with respect to retaliation. Deterrence has operated within a security environment in which the opposing parties held at risk assets deemed vitally important by each other, including territory and population that could be easily targeted. Such targets are not as readily identifiable in the case of nonstate actors that do not occupy a clearly defined territory or whose population may be scattered or interspersed with that of other units within, for example, existing states. Nevertheless, the accuracy levels of air power, again so clearly demonstrated in Operation Desert Storm, will confer on the United States an unprecedented ability—once targets such as headquarters and terrorist personnel are identified—to strike decisively and discretely against them.

Somewhat easier will be the task confronting the United States in the case of state-sponsored terrorist activity, for which the retaliatory strike against Libya in 1986 forms a model. In low-intensity operations, air power will be utilized in a time frame that will be based on greater or lesser urgency requirements. In some cases, the need will be apparent for preemption, as in situations in which a state is poised to attack a neighboring state (e.g., Iraq against Kuwait). More likely, however, the United States—as in the recent Gulf war—will find itself in a reactive mode. Whatever the contingency, it will be essential to enhance our ability to acquire, transmit, and analyze intelligence as part of a deterrence and war-fighting strategy. The accelerating pace of change, both at the strategic and tactical levels, will place an even higher priority on our ability to monitor and forecast the actions of our opponents and to transmit directives and orders to all levels of command.

The emerging security environment will be characterized by a multiplicity of threats whose dimensions are far more diverse than anything the United States has faced in its previous history. The territory of the United States will become vulnerable to attack from a larger number of weapons possessors and from points anywhere on the globe. Beyond a continuing Soviet strategic threat, the United States will eventually find it necessary to take into its security calculations the ability of a larger number of actors to inflict strikes of varying levels of destructive potential on its national territory. Such a situation will coincide with an intensification of economic links and other relationships between the United States and the external world. The frontiers of the United States, together with those of other states, will continue to be made permeable to an unprecedented extent as a result of advanced technologies providing for instantaneous transmission of information and communication of ideas—as well as the transfer of goods and services—in addition to military capabilities.

Among the implications of such factors that will reduce the significance of formal territorial boundaries, especially in technologically advanced and politically pluralistic societies, will be a greater blurring of the historic distinction between foreign policy and domestic politics. Hence, a discussion of the emerging security environment that does not encompass the nexus between such factors, within and outside the national unit, would be less than complete. In practical terms, we face a situation in which diverse external forces shape domestic constituencies that, in turn, play a decisively important role in determining the national security policy options—including force structures—available to governments. For the United States, the conduct of military operations in such a security setting is constrained by numerous public considerations. They include a relatively low level of tolerance for protracted military action resulting in high casualty levels, depending of course on the extent to which vital national interests are perceived to be at stake. In retrospect, Operation Desert Storm took place in a context in which US military casualties could be drastically limited by high-tech weaponry, combined with an effective strategy leading to the rapid and decisive military defeat of Iraqi forces. Such a combination of factors and circumstances accords fully with the late-twentieth-century American strategic culture that is easily projected into the years leading into the next century. This assessment leads immediately to the self-evident proposition that no strategy designed to defend American vital interests in the emerging security environment will be possible without air power as an indispensable ingredient. Massive deployments of ground forces will be undertaken only under exceptional circumstances. Although we must be prepared for contingencies in which such capabilities—as in the Gulf war—will be sent into battle, it will be essential that they achieve their political-military goals quickly with minimal casualties so that they can be expeditiously withdrawn. In keeping with American values placing high emphasis on technology to save American lives, the military force of the future—designed to fight on a wide range of terrains—will be based heavily on air power.

Domestic constraints in host countries—and in the United States itself—on the types, levels, and stationing of forces will affect US military deployments abroad. The constriction in overseas basing structure that has already been evident for many years will continue to reduce the ability of the United States to deploy military forces in forward positions. Those few facilities that will remain as we move toward the end of this decade will be restricted in the uses to which they can be put. Such conditions have already existed for many years. The United States has been unable, for example, to rely on bases in Europe in certain Middle East operations—excluding, of course, Operation Desert Storm. By the end of this decade, we will have terminated a large number of existing basing arrangements, even though in the aftermath of the Gulf war the United States may be encouraged to develop in some form a greater forward presence based on maritime and air power, as well as the positioning of equipment in or near the Persian Gulf. Nevertheless, the overall trend points clearly to the need to reconsider future requirements for the lift of military units and their equipment in timely fashion to zones of conflict. To the extent that the deterrence of war or its escalation will depend on our ability to engage in the preemptive prepositioning of such forces (air and ground), mobility based on speed of transport becomes a crucially important consideration. Because of the rapidity with which destabilizing elements are likely to pose threats to vital US interests— as in Iraq's invasion of Kuwait and the imminent danger that Saddam Hussein posed to Saudi Arabia—the need for extensive lift capacity will assume greater importance, both as a deterrent and as an actual war-fighting capability.

If the future international security environment features more powerful regional states, as described earlier, together with a sharp reduction in American forward-basing arrangements, it follows that range and payload—as well as speed and penetrativity—become increasingly important characteristics of the force structure to be acquired by the United States. Because our force structure is likely to contain fewer numbers, both in equipment and personnel, those reduced units—if they are aircraft—will need to have the ability to fly longer distances unrefueled and to carry larger amounts of ordnance and equipment required for their respective missions. Because of the high value of emerging-generation manned capabilities, greater emphasis necessarily will be placed on unmanned systems able to deliver warheads with more precision on priority targets. The speed characteristics of aircraft will continue to assume greater importance in the increasingly lethal air environment of regional conflict in the years leading into the next century. Even more important will be the development of a range of stealth technologies designed to foil enemy defenses and thereby to enhance penetrativity and minimize losses.

In the emerging security environment, space as a strategic frontier will grow dramatically in importance. Assets for surveillance and intelligence—as well as command, control, and communications—will be even more vital to the United States as a result of dynamic political changes having important implications for US interests, including the need to forecast impending developments and to take appropriate steps either in anticipation of, or in response to, such events. As a vital dimension of the emerging security environment, space will become an arena available to larger numbers of actors as we move into the next century. The military multipolarity which increasingly will characterize the emerging security environment will be extended to space. As additional states acquire ballistic missile systems, they will seek to take advantage of associated technologies that provide access to intelligence and surveillance, as well as command, control, and communications. For the United States, the ability to control space as a part of the seamless web of the emerging security environment will be no less important than command of the airspace over the battlefield and the surrounding seas. Historically, the geostrategic importance of the terrestrial environment has been shaped decisively by the ability conferred by technology to move military and other capabilities from one point to another on or above the earth's surface or over, on, or under its oceans. Those states best able to master the technologies of the day that provide for mobility on the seas (Great Britain as a dominant sea power) or on land (the aspirations of Germany earlier in this century) have become major powers in their time.

American military power has been measured by its ability to control the vital theaters in which combat operations have been undertaken. Space has become such an arena. In the first instance, space has already provided an indispensable adjunct to the conduct of terrestrially based military operations, as well as to the monitoring of arms control agreements. The need for surveillance, reconnaissance, communications, and targeting capabilities deployed in space will increase in the emerging security environment. The ability to launch air strikes on designated targets, as well as the requirements for early warning against missile attack and the tracking and interception of incoming warheads, points up the importance of space. Meteorological information for accurate weather forecasting, navigation satellites, geosynchronous communications satellites, and satellite early-warning systems are illustrative of the crucially important role played by space. In the decades ahead, space will emerge as an arena for control beyond our respective interests on earth. The establishment of space stations and other facilities, including commercial activities such as access to new sources of energy and manufacturing in space, will enhance the intrinsic importance of space far beyond its value as simply an adjunct to terrestrial activity. For the United States as an aerospace power, the task will be to develop adequate launch capacity to provide greater access to space. This will be a priority need if the United States is to exploit the opportunities available in space as a strategic arena. At the same time, the need to be able to defend assets deployed in space will grow in importance as additional powers develop their own technologies for entry into this arena. Although presumably the United States will strive to preserve its lead, the inevitable process of technology diffusion that is transforming the emerging security environment on earth will have its counterpart in space. Therefore, the United States cannot assume that its present position in space will remain secure in the absence of an aerospace strategy designed both to exploit present technological advantages and to offset potential threats from hostile sources.

In sum, the era that lies ahead will contain numerous challenges to US interests in a world that will continue to be transformed by emerging technologies that drastically reduce distances, penetrate national frontiers, and make available a vast array of increasingly sophisticated military capabilities. To a large extent, aerospace—in its fullest dimension—will form the cutting edge of the ongoing revolution in technology. This will impose on the United States the need to pursue actively and aggressively research and development programs to exploit scientific advances in the form of technologies that will be the key to future capabilities. As the structure of deterrence is transformed to a more multipolar configuration with threats more numerous yet less clearly defined, the need for flexible, mobile, highly accurate forces will intensify. In such a global-security environment, the challenge for the United States as an aerospace power will be clear: to assure technological superiority as a basis for the maintenance of air power capable of dominating outer space and the airspace closer to earth. Conceivably and ideally, such an objective will be pursued with the support of allies and other friendly states capable of contributing to the effort—both in political-military and financial terms. However it is done, the key lies in the ability of the United States to protect and project power with air assets as the indispensable element, as we define and move toward whatever "new world order" lies beyond the present decade in a rapidly changing global-security environment.

Employing Air Power in the Twenty-first Century

Col John A. Warden III, USAF

In the winter of 1991, American air power overwhelmed Iraq, paralyzing it strategically and operationally. Air power incapacitated the country's leadership, made communication nearly impossible, took away its electricity and gasoline production, inhibited significant movement, and wreaked destruction on every part of its military machine. The cost in American blood for complete domination of a country of 16 million people and its million-man military was astoundingly low. This significant victory satisfied the legitimate demands of the American people that their wars use technology to keep human losses—on both sides—to an absolute minimum. This victory provides the strategic model for American operations well into the twenty-first century.

The Grand Strategic Context—A New Challenge

The world today is changing at a great rate—one comparable in magnitude and scope to the pace of changes which followed the defeat of Napoléon in 1815 and the defeat of Germany and Japan in 1945. These changes have significant implications for national strategy, military strategy, and force structure.

For almost 40 years, the United States based the majority of its national strategy and military thinking on the fact that the Soviet Union presented a significant and imminent threat. Now, however, the Soviet Union is suffering from a number of internal economic and political problems which are leading that country to focus the majority of its energy internally, hoping to rescue itself from chaos. This Soviet introspection, combined with the unification of Germany and the probable acceleration of the disarmament movements within

Europe, means that the chances of the US meeting the Soviets in a short-warning battle are small. Likewise, as the Soviets turn increasingly to internal matters, the chance of our confronting them elsewhere in the world as a necessary part of our containment strategy is much reduced.

German unification has changed the map of Europe and has also made the fear of a battle across the inter-German border a thing of the past. Should a conventional conflict materialize within Europe in the next decade, it most certainly has to start someplace other than where both sides spent four decades preparing for it.

What effect will the enormous changes afoot in the world have for US grand strategy? Of great significance, the US can no longer depend on containment as a unifying concept. In the past, the US could make a reasonable assumption either that almost any disturbance anyplace in the world was inspired by the Soviets or that if such a disturbance went the wrong way, the Soviets would stand to benefit from it. Containment strategy was relatively straightforward because it was seen as a zero-sum game: either the Soviets won or we won. Now, however, as the Soviets begin to withdraw from international political and military competition, we no longer can assume that any disturbances are Soviet inspired or that the Soviets would benefit from or even have any interest in the outcome of a particular conflict. In short, there is no longer any automatic guide to who is friend or foe. The old dictum of British foreign policy that Great Britain had neither permanent friends nor enemies, only permanent interests, may again be relevant and useful.

In this developing world, we cannot predict who our enemies are going to be, but on the basis of an exclusion analysis, we can conclude that they are likely to be small to midsize powers with high-tech weapons capabilities. Midsize powers are not necessarily insignificant. For example, many of the countries around the world with which we might clash have almost as large a military—or in some cases a larger military—as a midsize power such as Germany has today. Furthermore, many of them have as many tanks as the

Germans had at the start of World War II. Iraq, for example, had twice as many.

A small chance exists of a violent clash of interests with a large power, but it seems rather unlikely in at least the next two to three decades. There is also some prospect that the Soviets could reverse themselves in a way that could lead to war; however, that also seems very unlikely. Twenty years from now, a state not currently a great power may become great and plunge the world into war. Whether a world war takes place in the first quarter of the next century, however, will depend significantly on how we conduct our foreign affairs and on how well we maintain the decisive military advantages we now enjoy.

The US will find a replacement for containment; what it will be is unclear. It may be something like the role that Great Britain played prior to World War I when it acted as a balancer between striving coalitions and states in other parts of the world. Or it may be like the role the US played until World War I—not isolationist by any means, but very selective in its global intervention.

This leads to a discussion about the kinds of wars the United States might fight since, unfortunately, the historical record suggests that we will be in some kind of armed conflict periodically for the foreseeable future. In fact, if we look back through our history, it is difficult to find a period of more than 10 or 20 years when we were not fighting. Possibly, our dramatic victory in the Gulf war may reduce the likelihood of further conflicts, but prudence demands that we assume the worst and be prepared for war.

Of all the wars that might develop, the least likely is a global conventional war centered around a mature, prepared theater like the one that grew for 40 years over the inter-German border. The notion that no conflict is likely to center around a mature theater has some very significant implications.

The most likely wars will be those to stop offensive behavior on the part of a country that is working its own agenda, that is trying to steal something from us or from some other country, or that is doing something entirely unacceptable to us. We would enter such wars not to prove that the US is the world's policeman, but to stop interference with very legitimate American interests. The wars we conduct to stop this offensive behavior by other states will be characterized by sharp, decisive action on our part and will be designed to reach a conclusion as quickly as possible—with few or no US casualties and with the least number of enemy casualties consistent with political and military objectives.

The next most likely war is a "cutting-out" operation like Urgent Fury (Grenada) or Just Cause (Panama), whose primary goal is to separate a tyrant or a small group of tyrants from an otherwise friendly and innocent population. Such an operation can best be accomplished by ground power because only this type of power can go directly to an offender like Manuel Noriega without extensively damaging the surrounding population and infrastructure, which could make the realization of political objectives impossible. Also occurring, but on a much smaller scale, will be covert and quasi-combat operations against terrorists or drug traffickers.

Another change of enormous importance has also taken place. With the exception of North Korea, nowhere in the world can an enemy force us into nonnuclear war at the time and place of his choosing. Nor is there any place where truly vital interests can be threatened in the short term. We have the option of choosing when, where, and how we will respond. That is, America will decide whether it goes to war. Optional wars, however, are far more difficult from a policy standpoint than no-choice wars. The president of the United States must assess the seriousness of the threat, the possibility of a diplomatic solution, and the backing of the electorate if military operations seem best. In turn, the need to acquire the backing of the electorate means that for almost all cases, the president must be able to offer a military solution that entails few American casualties. In addition, any operations that we undertake are almost certain to be offensive, for we will be responding to an enemy action that has already taken place—a situation which calls for offensive action to redress the problem. Very simply, our national security world has turned upside down. We have moved from a defensive posture where our principal enemy had absolute control over war and peace to an offensive posture where we decide if, when, where, and how we will fight.

We will also be doing things that are not combat operations per se but in the coming world may have significance approaching that of such operations. We do not have a good name for the concept, but it may be termed the rapid movement of national influence. This means using the great mobility of the US to break a blockade such as the one against Berlin in 1948, to provide materiel to a friend in need—such as Israel in 1973—or to provide disaster relief to Armenia following an earthquake in 1988.

How does air power fit into all this? Very briefly, we would suggest that it provides indispensable support for the cutting-out operations like Panama and Grenada in the form of airlift, electronic detection, and very accurate and precise attacks to complement ground operations. In the movement of national influence, air power is the nation's capability for quick response. When we think about real power projection, about protecting our interests against small to midsize power threats, air power becomes dominant, and our primary defense problem becomes one of responding with sharp, decisive actions. Air power becomes important because it has a unique ability to get to the combat area with massive power and to affect enemy operational and strategic centers of gravity.

All components can attack centers of gravity, but only air power can frequently circumvent enemy forces and attack strategic centers of gravity directly. Other components, on the other hand, need to fight their way in—normally with large casualties. Air operations—especially with modern weapons and accuracy as used in the Gulf war—are very much likely to result in fewer casualties to either side. Air power then becomes quintessentially an American form of war; it uses our advantages of mobility and high technology to overwhelm the enemy without spilling too much blood, especially American blood. This last point cannot be overemphasized: excluding any imminent threat to our survival, no American government is likely to undertake military operations that promise more than the handful of casualties we suffered in the Gulf.

To understand the role of air power, we must think about our war objectives. Most wars are fought to convince the enemy leadership to do what one wants it to do—that is, concede something political. That something may be a province, a trade route, or an ideology. The enemy leadership agrees that it needs to make these political concessions when it suffers the threat or the actuality of intolerable pressure against both its operational and strategic centers of gravity.

Centers of Gravity

Thinking about war and actually conducting war require that we have a good understanding of what war is, what we intend to gain from it, and what the links are between the instruments of war and the ends desired. Too frequently, our vision of war concentrates almost exclusively on its most obvious manifestation—the clash of the contestants' fielded military forces. Indeed, Clausewitz identified the battle as the essence of war.[1] Perhaps, however, Clausewitz identified battle as the essence of war because from his vantage point in time and place, battle dominated the process of war. Indeed, his native Prussia was known as an army with a country; thus, the only way to defeat Prussia was to defeat its army. Furthermore, in reaction to the stylized magazine wars of the preceding century, Clausewitz tended to focus his attention on the actual clash of men and to see that clash as the dominant form of war. Clausewitz may have been right for his time and place and accompanying technology, but it is not clear today that the actual clash of men on the front is the only way or the best way to wage war. To the contrary, we suggest that it may be the most costly and least productive approach in perhaps the majority of cases. To understand why this may be so, one must examine the objectives of waging war at the strategic and operational levels and then look at descriptive models of modern-day combatants.

Objectives

States employ air, sea, and ground forces to conduct military operations that will lead to attainment of their political objectives. The political and military objectives of the opposing sides, as well as domestic and cultural constraints, establish the nature of the conflict. The political objective of a war can range from demanding unconditional surrender to asking the opponent to grant favorable terms for an armistice. The military objective that will produce the desired behavior on the part of the enemy will be related to the political objective and will in turn heavily influence the campaign plan designed to attain it. Basically, a state realizes its political objectives when the enemy command structure (i.e., the enemy leader or leaders) is forced by direct or indirect action to make concessions. Control of the enemy command structure, civil and military, must be the ultimate aim of all military operations. At the strategic and operational levels, inducing the enemy to make the desired concessions requires identification and attack of those parts of the enemy state and military structure which are most essential to his ability and desire to wage war. What concessions might the enemy be asked to make?

An enemy can concede his right to existence, or he can concede his desire to destroy his opponent. In between these extremes, he can concede a province, a trade right, or his intention to conduct a military offensive. It is important to note that most wars have dealt with concessions far removed from conceding a right to exist. Indeed, wars carried to this extreme have been so rare that we still refer to them as "Carthaginian solutions." Since most wars end with concessions short of utter destruction, the defeated parties are left relatively intact. Even in the extreme cases of Japan and Germany in World War II, the defeated states made their final concessions long before the total destruction of their fielded military forces. Most recently, Iraq offered to concede its right to Kuwait while its army occupied all of the contested area.[2] This is a key point because it implies a relatively high degree of rationality on the part of most states and military forces. That is, states and military forces make concessions based on some kind of a cost-benefit calculus. The Japanese, for example, surrendered—made a concession—based on the assessment that continuing the war would be very costly and would not produce much benefit.

Although all states and military forces assess costs and benefits differently, they have similar concentrations of strengths. These strengths are centers of gravity, but they are also vulnerabilities in the same way that Samson's hair was at once his strength and his weakness. When a state's centers of gravity are put under sufficient pressure, either the state will make appropriate concessions to relieve the pressure (the anticipated costs of not doing so are too high for likely gains) or it will make concessions because the pressure has become so intense that it is no longer physically capable of continuing its prior course.

The concept of centers of gravity is simple to grasp but difficult to realize because of the likelihood that more than one center will exist at any time. Further, each center will have an effect of some kind on the others. It is also important to note that centers of gravity may in some cases be only indirectly related to the enemy's ability to conduct actual military operations. As an example, a strategic center of gravity for most states beyond the agrarian stage is the power generation system. Without electric power, production of civil and military goods, distribution of food and other essentials, civil and military communication, and life in general become difficult to impossible. Unless the stakes in the war are very high, most states will make desired concessions when their power generation system is put under sufficient pressure or actually destroyed. Note that destruction of the power system may have little short-term effect at the front—if there is a front.

Every state and military organization will have a unique set of centers of gravity—or vulnerabilities. Nevertheless, it is possible to create a general model as a starting place for analysis. The next few paragraphs discuss the model in terms of rings. That is, because some centers of gravity are more important than others, they can be laid out in the form of five concentric circles. The most important element—the enemy command—is in the center circle; essential production is second; the transportation network is third; the population is fourth; and the fielded military forces—the shield and spear—are fifth.

The most critical ring is the enemy command structure because it is the only element of the enemy—whether a civilian at the seat of government or a general directing a fleet—that can make concessions. In fact, wars through history have been fought to change (or change the mind of) the command structure—to overthrow the prince literally or figuratively or to induce the command structure to make concessions. Capturing or killing the state's leader has frequently been decisive. In modern times, however, it has become more difficult—but not impossible—to capture or kill the command element. At the same time, command communications have been more important than ever, and these are vulnerable to attack. When command communications suffer extreme damage, as they did in Iraq, the leadership has great difficulty in directing war efforts. In the case of an unpopular regime, the lack of communications not only inhibits the bolstering of national morale but also facilitates rebellion on the part of dissident elements.

When the command element cannot be threatened directly, the task becomes one of applying enough indirect pressure that the command element rationally concludes that concessions are appropriate, realizes that further action is impossible, or becomes physically unable to continue combat. Normally, reaching these conclusions is a function of the degree of damage imposed on the surrounding rings. Excluding a rational response by the enemy command element, it is possible to render the enemy impotent by destroying one or more of the outer strategic rings or centers of gravity.

The next most critical ring contains key production, which entails more than just war-related industry. Indeed, war-related industry may not be very important qua war industry in many cases. The growth in the size of cities around the world and the necessity for electricity and petroleum products to keep a city functioning have made these two commodities essential for most states. If a state's essential industries (or, if it has no industry of its own, its access to external sources) are destroyed, life itself becomes difficult, and the state becomes incapable of employing modern weapons and must make concessions. The latter could be as little as forswearing offensive operations outside its own borders or as much as offering total surrender. Depending on the size of the state and the importance it attaches to its objectives, even minor damage to essential industries may lead the command element to make concessions. The concessions may come because (1) damage to essential production makes fighting difficult or impossible or (2) damage to essential production has internal political or economic repercussions which are too costly to bear. The number of key production targets in even a large state is reasonably small, and all of the targets in key industries such as power production and petroleum refining are fragile.[3]

The third most critical ring contains the enemy state's transportation system, which moves goods and communications—civil and military—around the state's entire area of operations. The system includes rail lines, airlines, highways, bridges, airfields, ports, and a number of other similar systems. For both military and civil purposes, it is necessary to move goods, services, and information from one point to another. If this movement becomes impossible, the state ceases to function. Compared to key industrial systems, transportation facilities are more numerous and more redundant; thus, one may have to expend more effort to effectively damage the transportation system.

The fourth most critical ring holds the population and its food sources. Moral objections aside, it is difficult to attack the population directly because targets are too numerous and in many cases—especially in a police state—the population may be willing to suffer grievously before it will turn on its own government. Indirect attack on the population, such as North Vietnam used against the United States, may be effective, especially if the target country has a relatively low interest in the outcome of the war.

The last ring holds the fielded military forces of the state. Although one tends to think of military forces as the most vital element in war, in fact they are a means to an end. That is, their only function is to protect their own inner rings or to threaten those of an enemy. One can certainly persuade a state to make concessions by reducing its fielded military forces. Indeed, if all of its fielded forces are destroyed, it may have to make the ultimate concession simply because the command element knows that its inner rings have become defenseless and open to destruction. This view of fielded forces is not a classical one, in large part because the majority of the classical writing and thinking on warfare has been done by Continental soldiers whose only choice was to contend with enemy armies. Modern technology, however, makes possible new and politically powerful options that in fact can put fielded forces into the category of means and not ends.

In most cases, all the rings exist in the order presented, but reaching more than one or two of the outer ones with military means may not be possible. For example, by the end of 1943 the Germans were incapable of making serious attacks on anything but the fourth and fifth rings (population and fielded forces) of their primary enemies because they did not have a useful long-range attack capability. The Japanese could attack only the fifth ring (fielded forces) of their primary enemies. Conversely, the Allies could attack every German and Japanese ring of vulnerability. The Iraqis had an even more difficult problem: they could not reach any of their principal foe's strategic rings unless the United States chose to put its fielded forces in harm's way. For states, like Iraq, that cannot employ military weapons against their enemy's strategic centers, the only recourse is to attack indirectly, through psychological or unconventional warfare.

It is imperative to remember that all actions are aimed against the mind of the enemy command. Thus, one does not conduct an attack against industry or infrastructure because of the effect it might or might not have on fielded forces. Rather, one undertakes such an attack for its direct effect on national leaders and commanders who must assess the cost of rebuilding, the effect on the state's economic position in the postwar period, the internal political effect on their own survival, and the cost versus the potential gain from continuing the war. The essence of war is to apply pressure against the enemy's innermost strategic ring—its command structure. Military forces are a means to an end. Dealing with enemy military forces is pointless if they can be bypassed—by strategy or technology, either in the defense or offense.

Before continuing, we must ask ourselves if there are any states that do not have all five rings or centers of gravity. The further back we go in history, the more we find that the second, third, and fourth rings decreased in importance or disappeared entirely. As an example, when William the Conqueror developed his campaign plan for the conquest of England, he could not have identified key production, critical transportation, or the population as centers of gravity. King Harold II and his army constituted the only real centers of gravity—neither the state nor the army depended on key production; little or no transportation system was needed to serve the meager needs of the state or army; and the people had little to say about Harold's policies (and perhaps didn't care). William's only choice, therefore, was to clash with Harold and his army. Today, it is difficult to imagine a similar situation; we have all—even in the third world—become too dependent on elaborate production and transportation systems for both our daily subsistence and our ability to fight. The one exception may occur when an entire people rises up to conduct a defensive battle against an invader. If the people are sufficiently motivated, they may be able to fight for an extended period by using the resources naturally available to them. This may be possible for the defense but not for the offense.

To this point, we have discussed centers of gravity that we tend to identify as "strategic." Operational-level commanders may be told that their objective is to attack strategic centers of gravity. On the other hand, the commanders may be forced to deal with the enemy's fielded military forces if they cannot reach strategic centers without first removing enemy defenses or if their political masters will not permit them to attack strategic centers. In such instances, they must still concentrate on the centers of gravity.

Centers of gravity exist not only at the strategic level, but also at the operational level and, indeed, are very similar. At the operational level, the goal is still to induce the enemy operational-level commanders to make concessions—such as retreating, surrendering, or giving up an offense. Like the state command structure, however, the operational commanders have rings of vulnerability—or centers of gravity—surrounding them. In fact, each major element of their command will also have similar centers of gravity.

The focus of war operations must be on the enemy leadership. When the leaders, whether in the nation's capital or in the field, believe they are defeated or bested, the nation or forces they lead are beaten—at least until a new leadership is installed. To affect the enemy leadership, we must understand what the enemy looks like conceptually. If we accept the idea that the enemy leader is surrounded by centers of gravity, we can think more clearly about how to affect him. By thinking in these larger strategic and operational-level terms, we simplify our tasks enormously. We may not have to find and destroy 30,000 tanks if we can destroy their few hundred associated fuel or ammunition distribution points. We may not have to destroy the few hundred fuel distribution points if we can immobilize an entire society by destroying dozens of electrical generation systems. And we may not need to destroy dozens of electrical generation systems if we can capture, kill, or isolate the enemy leader. Our task is to look and work as close to the center of the enemy's operational and strategic rings as possible. When we have identified where the real centers of gravity lie, we must then decide how best to strike those centers. If we go through this process honestly and rigorously, we can be confident that we have crafted a good campaign which will lead to realization of the political aims of the war with the least cost in blood and treasure—to both sides.

The Air Campaign against Iraq

Gen Norman Schwarzkopf attacked every one of Iraq's strategic rings with the exception of population, going to great lengths to avoid hurting Iraqi civilians and succeeding admirably in that effort. A short recap of the effects of attacking the strategic rings of Iraq is useful in understanding the implications for the future.

The coalition attacked the command ring—the Saddam Hussein regime—by striking at its command centers, its communications, and its many internal control mechanisms. The major source of Iraqi communications—the telephone system—went out in the first minutes of the war. Likewise, the national television system was an early casualty, which meant that the regime lost one of the most effective modern public communications media. The Iraqi communications system was very good and very hard—probably built to survive a nuclear war. However, from prisoner reports we know that within about three weeks the regime was unable to communicate effectively with most parts of the country, including the army deployed in Kuwait.

Internal control mechanisms were too pervasive to destroy quickly, but the first-day attacks did considerable damage to headquarters buildings (and presumably to files, computers, and communications). According to current newspaper reports, serious dissident plotting began immediately after the war started. One can presume that impairment of the internal control mechanisms facilitated this plotting and permitted large-scale action to take place in Kurdish areas relatively soon after the war's end. In addition to direct attacks on the regime, the coalition attacked it indirectly by destroying the very expensive nuclear, chemical, and biological warfare facilities that Saddam thought would make him the dominant power in the region.

Coalition air attacks did not bring down the regime, but they certainly set the stage for the widespread rebellion that may eventually succeed politically, even though it failed militarily. The air attacks did, however, make the regime helpless to affect the outcome of the war. Because its facilities, personnel, and communications were so disrupted, it was hard-pressed to understand what was happening, had nearly insurmountable problems in planning, and was able to communicate only the most rudimentary instructions to agencies within Baghdad or in other parts of the theater. Despite the obvious success of direct attacks against the command ring, they were not sufficient unto themselves. Attacks on the other rings were necessary in order to impose the strategic paralysis requisite to victory.

Air attacks against key production—the second ring—were enormously successful. The lights went out in Baghdad minutes after the war started and have yet to regain their former intensity. As the lights went out, military and secret police communications and computers crashed. Subsequent attacks on other parts of Iraq's power production system led the Iraqis to cut off the whole national grid. The collapse of the electric system created insurmountable difficulties for almost every activity in Iraq that supported the war effort. Equipment ranging from radar screens to electric typewriters was largely dependent on long-haul power. Only a small portion of the loss could be made up by using standby generators. It was never the goal of the coalition to destroy Iraqi generation capability; instead, the goal was to do only enough damage consistent with military capabilities that Iraq would not be able to provide wartime work-arounds or to recover with its own resources. Iraq's postwar dependence on massive outside technical assistance meant that the strategic campaign would provide the coalition with long-term leverage to help enforce the eventual peace agreement.

The next element of the second ring to come under attack was Iraq's oil refining capability. Here, the goal of the coalition was to shut off the production of refined products such as gasoline, diesel fuel, and jet fuel that would support the war effort and provide strategic and operational mobility for Iraq. As with the attacks on electric generating plants, the plan was to limit damage as much as possible to key parts of the refining operation so that rebuilding would be quick when the coalition had realized its political objectives.

Oil refining and power production are essential to almost every state in the world today. Undertaking and sustaining strategic offensives—and defensives—without them is not feasible. As mentioned previously, however, each country will normally have unique features to its five rings. In the case of Iraq's second ring, it was important for the coalition to attack Iraqi nuclear, biological, chemical, and specialty weapons production because their destruction at once served long-term political objectives in the region and imposed psychological stress on the regime. Success in this area was nearly complete: nuclear and biological research production and storage appear to be so damaged that Iraq would have to start from the beginning to restore nuclear and biological research and production.[4] In the much larger chemical production area, the coalition destroyed at least three-quarters of production and storage. In the specialty weapons category, the coalition set back for years Iraq's production of Scuds, guidance units, liquid propellants, rocket motors, long-bore artillery, and similar items.

In summary of the second-ring attacks, the coalition imposed temporary strategic paralysis on Iraq and emasculated its offensive weapons production. Without significant outside technical and monetary assistance, Iraq cannot return to the prewar conditions that allowed it to attack its neighbors. Assistance with repair of electric and oil facilities can take place quickly—and is very desirable as soon as the Iraqi government adheres to coalition terms. Conversely, it appears unlikely that any country or firm will find either the political or financial incentives to rebuild Iraq's special weapons production facilities, at least for the remainder of this century. The coalition thus realized enormous political objectives with relatively little effort and, due to the precision weapons generally employed against these targets, did so with very little collateral damage and very few Iraqi civilian casualties.

Attacks on the third ring—the transportation system—were relatively simple in the case of Iraq—as they are against most states at a strategic and operational level. The most significant military and civilian transportation systems in Iraq either originate or terminate in the southern part of the country. Connecting the upper part of the state with the lower was a railroad—which moved the majority of prewar tonnage between Baghdad and Basra—and a number of highways passing over a series of bridges across the Tigris and Euphrates rivers. The coalition brought rail traffic to a halt in the first week of the war by destroying the key Euphrates rail bridge with a single bomb. Attacks on highway bridges in the next two weeks reduced supplies to the army in Kuwait to below the subsistence level. Of special note is the rapidity with which the coalition destroyed nearly 50 bridges in a four-week period.

In past wars, destroying a bridge was an enormously expensive proposition because only direct hits were effective and bombing accuracy before the advent of guided bombs meant that several hundred bombs (meaning hundreds of sorties) had to be dropped in order to have even a hope of destroying a single bridge. In other words, before the days of guided bombs, destruction of 50 bridges would have consumed 10,000 or more sorties; in the Gulf war, 50 bridges fell to a few hundred sorties. Likewise, in past wars, it would have taken many months to knock out 50 bridges. As the time spent in bombing bridges stretched out, the time available for the enemy to rebuild or to work around the damage increased. In the case of Iraq, the destruction of bridges was so overwhelming that repair and significant work-around were not feasible. Although it is hard to generalize about such matters, it is unlikely that any state or army is prepared to redress the loss of 50 key bridges in a four-week period. Those who doubt this statement should remember how long it took to restore the damaged Oakland Bay bridge after the 1989 earthquake and should consider the effect if the 50 most important bridges in the US—including all of the ones across the Mississippi—fell within four weeks. Such attacks on the transportation ring were so successful that Iraq was unable to provide any significant reinforcement, resupply, or succor to a 40-division army barely 200 miles from its capital.

The coalition announced from the beginning that its quarrel was with the Hussein regime, not with the people of Iraq—the fourth ring. To that end, coalition forces went to extraordinary lengths to avoid hurting civilians. F-117 pilots attacking targets in Baghdad did not drop unless they were positive of their target and all their systems were functioning properly. Planners chose targets and attack vehicles to avoid collateral damage. Although it is difficult to measure the success of this effort, the Iraqi government was claiming only 40 people killed in Baghdad as late as the second week in the war. Thereafter, Baghdad began to realize the potential propaganda value of claiming civilian casualties, so subsequent figures are suspect. Prewar estimates suggested that 400 to 2,000 civilians might die as a result of bombs destined for military targets going astray or otherwise affecting innocent civilians; as of now, there is no evidence to suggest that estimate to be in error.

Although the coalition very properly chose to avoid direct attacks on the population, it could have availed itself of an intense strategic psychological campaign to induce the population to withdraw support from the regime. This is a difficult area for a variety of reasons, but one that requires increased attention.

From a strategic standpoint, the coalition identified Iraqi offensive and defensive air forces and the Republican Guard as important in the strategic campaign against the fifth ring—fielded forces. Although the coalition faced a formidable air defense system, it was able to destroy it in the first hours of the war by brilliant use of revolutionary stealth technology. The F-117s made simultaneous attacks on nearly all the major air defense nodes—the Iraqi air force headquarters and the air defense operations center in Baghdad, most of the country's sector operations centers and their accompanying intercept operations centers, and even some forward radars. As a result of these attacks, combined with the first-ring attack on communications and the second-ring attack on electricity, the Iraqi high command found itself instantly blind, deaf, and dumb. The result: no possibility of coordinated air opposition to the subsequent attack of nonstealth coalition aircraft. Virtually every element of the shooting side of the Iraqi air defense system—fighters, missiles, and antiaircraft artillery (AAA)—was forced to operate autonomously; against the concentrated attacks of the coalition, piecemeal, autonomous opposition was futile.

The destruction of the Iraqi air force's conventional aircraft took more time, but because the air defense system was gone, the coalition faced a manageable problem. It solved this problem by doing something that many people thought aircraft shelters had made impossible—it attacked and destroyed the Iraqi air force on the ground. Even those Iraqi shelters believed to be proof against anything but a direct nuclear hit proved vulnerable to special penetrating bombs guided precisely to their targets by F-111Fs, F-117s, A-6s, and F-15Es. The shelters built on the European model proved vulnerable to normal ordnance. When its hardened shelters failed so dramatically, the Iraqi air force sent some of its aircraft to Iran and dispersed others to open areas. By the second week, the coalition had air supremacy and was able to roam freely—above the AAA fire—to accomplish the rest of its mission over Iraq. The loss of air superiority put Iraq completely under the power of the coalition; what would be destroyed and what would survive was up to the coalition, and Iraq could do nothing. It lay as defenseless as if occupied by a million men. For practical purposes, it had in fact become a state occupied—from the air.

Although the coalition destroyed the conventional part of the Iraqi defensive and offensive forces quickly, it found destruction of the Scud missiles to be much more difficult. The Iraqis clearly had a sound and competent system for hiding mobile Scud launchers and for firing with little or no warning. The coalition was unable to stop Scud firing but did reduce it to manageable proportions by working out a clever system to dispatch aircraft very quickly to locations from which Scuds had just been fired. Subsequent attrition to Scud crews and launchers cut firings by about 80 percent from the level of the first few days of the war.

The last element in the fifth ring was the Republican Guard. Although coalition attacks began the first day on Guard headquarters and units in the field, they were never heavy or sustained enough to destroy the deployed Guard.

The results of the attacks on Iraq's five strategic rings were impressive. Well before the start of coalition ground operations, Iraq was in a state of strategic paralysis from which it could not recover without massive outside assistance. Only two or three countries in the world might be able to restore themselves to prewar levels after a comparable strategic attack; thus, Iraq's predicament was not unique. The effects of a successful strategic attack continue to be felt long after the last bomb falls—which gives the attacker long-term ability to exercise control over his enemy. The coalition imposed strategic paralysis on Iraq with just over 10,000 sorties and just over 20,000 tons of bombs.[5] Compare this 20,000 tons with the over 8 million tons dropped on Vietnam in seven years and the 200,000 tons dropped on Germany's 69 oil refineries over a 12-month period. By the end of the strategic campaign, Iraq had lost the capability to maintain its forces in Kuwait, to conduct offensive operations anywhere, to restore a prewar strategic position and standard of living for its people, to defend itself against coalition attacks, to communicate effectively internally or externally, to move significant military units internally, and to prevent multiple uprisings in long-quiescent areas.

In the Gulf war, the coalition wanted Iraq to withdraw from Kuwait—and to lose the military hardware employed in the invasion and occupation. To ensure realization of this goal, the coalition decided to accompany the strategic attacks with direct air attacks against the Iraqi army in Kuwait. The results were again impressive. In some 38 days of air operations, coalition forces destroyed in excess of 60 percent of Iraq's deployed tanks, armored personnel carriers, artillery, and trucks. The Iraqis lost much equipment, whether it was on the move or dispersed and buried in the desert. The number of Iraqi soldiers killed or wounded by air operations is unknown, but prisoner interrogations have made clear that desertions inspired by the air operations brought personnel strengths in most units to well below 50 percent.

As mentioned above, the coalition had established air superiority over Iraqi aircraft through the strategic campaign. As coalition air forces began to operate over Kuwait, they made a concerted effort to knock out enemy radar-controlled weapons. This accomplished, the coalition owned the skies over Kuwait; further, by operating above 10,000 feet, it was also nearly immune to Iraqi AAA and infrared-guided surface-to-air missiles. The Iraqi army was unable to protect itself and could only hope that Hussein would order it to withdraw before suffering total destruction from coalition air attacks. The army was completely defenseless, a point mentioned repeatedly in prisoner interrogations as having had a devastating effect on morale.

Saddam Hussein faced a vexing problem. His strength was in his very capable army, which was judged to be one of the best defensive armies in the world. For an army to prevail on defense, however, someone must attack it. The coalition to this point had refused to engage on the ground, preferring to use its aircraft, which the Iraqi army was powerless to stop. Saddam's strategy was heavily dependent on significant ground warfare that would impose enough casualties on the coalition to break its political will. He was desperate for the ground war to begin, but General Schwarzkopf steadfastly refused to accommodate him. In a calculated attempt to ignite the ground war, Saddam launched an offensive at Khafji, Saudi Arabia.

The Iraqi plan appears to have been as follows: On the first night, take over the lightly defended town of Khafji; on the second night, strike south with a corps to provoke a coalition counteroffensive and then withdraw to pull the coalition counteroffensive into well-prepared Iraqi defenses in Kuwait. The expected result: high coalition casualties. The story of the first night of Khafji is well known; not so well known is the second night, when the Iraqis assembled at least two divisions (armored and mechanized) just inside the Kuwait border north of Khafji. Unfortunately for Iraq, the coalition discovered the assembly and dispatched aircraft to attack it. After several hours, the Iraqis had suffered such heavy casualties that they began a withdrawal; in the process, they lost the majority of their divisions. In a single night, air power destroyed a corps-sized force and stopped a major offensive before it ever crossed into enemy territory.

When the coalition ground campaign began on 23 February 1991, the Iraqi army was devoid of communications and supplies, had no way to move, had no idea what was happening, and had no desire to fight. Thus, the air campaign had imposed not only strategic paralysis on the whole state of Iraq but had imposed operational paralysis on the army in Kuwait. This disaster befell Iraq during the worst weather of the year, which was also the worst weather observed in the last 14 years over Baghdad and Kuwait.

Momentous Events of the Air War

With fewer than 1 percent of the bombs dropped on Vietnam, the coalition air campaign imposed strategic and operational paralysis on Iraq. Air power defeated ground power and held the line on the second night of the battle at Khafji. The coalition air offensive proved to be unstoppable. Precision weapons in conjunction with stealth made it possible to achieve maneuver, mass, and concentration on an entirely unprecedented scale. The coalition conducted the first true "inside to outside" war, beginning with the most important central ring in Baghdad and working its way to the outermost ring of fielded forces. Such a war was in marked contrast to wars of the past that by necessity started with the outermost ring and then worked their way painfully to the innermost ring of the capital. Air superiority allowed the coalition to do everything it chose to do on and over its territory and on and over Iraqi territory; conversely, the Iraqis could do nothing. When Iraq lost strategic air superiority—as it did in the first week of the war—its only hope was to sue for peace as quickly as possible. A new kind of war had its birth in Mesopotamia.

Implications of the Gulf War

Coalition air operations are the first example in history of a pure strategic and operational air campaign designed to be the primary instrument in achieving the political and military objectives of war.

The Gulf conflict was also the first example of "hyperwar"—one that capitalizes on high technology, unprecedented accuracy, operational and strategic surprise through stealth, and the ability to bring all of an enemy's key operational and strategic nodes under near-simultaneous attack. Hyperwar is very difficult to defend against or to absorb, which means that the offense again has clearly assumed the dominant position in warfare. Thus, the premium for striking first is higher than ever.

Let us recap the revolutionary developments of the Gulf war. The two with the greatest impact are stealth and precision. Stealth brings tactical and operational surprise back to air warfare; with precision, one needs only a few sorties to destroy targets that would have required many hundreds of sorties in World War II and even in Vietnam. In the first minutes of the war, without giving any useful warning to Iraq, F-117s struck sector operations centers, intercept operations centers, key command centers, and key communications nodes. At the same time, nonstealthy but hard-to-detect Tomahawk cruise missiles took out electricity. The effects were near catastrophic.

Not only did the F-117s arrive in Iraq undetected, they attacked very hard targets with precision bombs so reliable that planners had a high expectation that a single sortie would achieve its objective. Prior to precision, a simultaneous attack of this kind would have been impossible, because hundreds of sorties would have been required to produce the same level of damage to each of the targets against which one or two F-117s were pitted. Many thousands of sorties would have been needed to accomplish what 100 or so precision sorties accomplished in the first hours of the strategic air campaign—and no air force in the world has the capability to put thousands of sorties across an entire country in a few hours.

To precision one must add penetration. Our bombs penetrated all of Iraq's hardened aircraft shelters with ease. Iraq was certainly shocked, for it thought the best of its shelters were invulnerable to anything but nuclear attack.

THE FUTURE OF AIR POWER

Stealth has reinstated surprise to air war; precision has lowered the number of sorties required by orders of magnitude; and penetration has made almost all targets vulnerable. The day of the aircraft shelter is over, and the day of the air offense has returned. In many ways, we are almost back in the days before radar, when enemy aircraft were parked in the open.

Our ability to find even an enemy deployed in the field has increased significantly with forward looking infrared radar (FLIR) for night and with sensors such as the joint surveillance target attack radar system (JSTARS) aircraft. Our ability to find the enemy 24 hours a day and strike even his deployed armies with precision means that an army which has lost air superiority is an army in mortal peril. Each of its elements is exposed to destruction. The tank is easy to find, easy to attack, and dependent on a huge and vulnerable supply support structure. The Gulf war represented but the first installment: in its air attacks against the Iraqi field army, the coalition destroyed over 50 percent of the tanks, trucks, armored personnel carriers, and artillery pieces; forced over half its personnel to flee; sundered its tactical communications; immobilized it; and broke its will to fight. Conditions will vary, but it seems reasonable to presume that the same thing can be done against other armies in other places.

Some people are wary of drawing too many lessons from a single war or battle, although many vital lessons have flowed from isolated events in the past. The following are examples of lessons that should have been obvious at the time but were subsequently ignored, with great loss of life: the effect of the long bow on French heavy cavalry at Agincourt; the difficulty of attacking the trenches around Richmond; the carnage wrought by the machine gun in the Russo-Japanese War; the value of the tank as demonstrated at Cambrai; and the effectiveness of aircraft against ships as shown by the sinking of the *Ostfriesland* in tests after World War I. In today's world—or more properly in tomorrow's world—where information flows so rapidly and technology changes so fast, we do not have the luxury of waiting for 10 replications of an event before we decide that real lessons exist.

Such is the case in the Gulf war, wherein a revolution took place that we ignore at our peril. With certainty, other countries understand that something very different happened, and they will move quickly to develop defenses or to acquire a similar offensive capability. Fortunately for us, duplication of the technology, organization, theory, and training that brought us one of the great military victories of history is so expensive and requires such an extraordinarily broad scientific, military, and industrial base that it may take two decades for another country or countries to develop equal offensive capabilities or to construct appropriate defenses. We must use this respite to make more than marginal improvements in our capabilities.

Twenty years from now, we ought to be prepared with theory, technology, and training that permit us to wage another revolutionarily different war. What the next revolution will look like is up to us. It may include high-altitude, hypersonic aircraft that operate directly from the United States. It may include stealthy aircraft that operate from high altitudes of 80,000 feet or even higher (obviating the defenses that will be developed against our first generation of relatively low altitude stealth aircraft). It may include precision weapons designators that are immune to bad weather. And it may include whole new classes of nonlethal weapons. If we fail to develop a new revolutionary capability, if we bask in our great victory, if we refuse to accept the Gulf war as a milestone in history, then we risk losing the war of 2014—and that war may be for even higher stakes than the war of 1991.

Conclusion

The world has just witnessed a new kind of warfare—hyperwar. It has seen air power become dominant. It has seen unequivocally how defenseless a state becomes when it loses control of the air over its territories and forces. It has seen the awesome power of the air offensive—and the near impossibility of defending against it. It has seen a demonstration of the validity of strategic attack theory. It has seen a war waged primarily against things but one that produced remarkably few casualties, especially considering the outcome. For the next two decades—and perhaps for much longer—an American commander, whether the president in Washington or a general in the field, will turn first to air power, just as did President George Bush and Gen Norman Schwarzkopf. We have moved from the age of the horse and the sail through the age of the battleship and the tank to the age of the airplane. Like its illustrious ancestors, the airplane will have its day in the sun, and then it too shall be replaced. *Sic transit gloria mundi.*

Notes

1. Carl von Clausewitz, *On War*, ed. and trans. Michael Howard and Peter Paret (Princeton, N.J.: Princeton University Press, 1976), 95.

2. Iraq announced its willingness to begin withdrawal negotiations in mid-February 1991, just after the coalition attack on Iraq's Al Firdos command center. At that time, Iraqi losses in Kuwait were probably in the vicinity of 15 to 20 percent of major equipment, but Saddam Hussein was beginning to realize that his country, army, and cause were doomed.

3. Superficially, Allied attacks on German industry in World War II would seem to contradict the idea that essential industry is fragile. In that conflict, however, bombing accuracy was not good; more than half of all bombs missed their targets by well over 1,000 yards. When accuracies are improved so that more than half of all bombs fall within a few feet of their target, as did the majority of those aimed at petroleum and electric targets in Iraq, it becomes clear that what took thousands of sorties and many tons of bombs can now be accomplished with orders of magnitude less effort.

4. Iraq could easily have hidden small quantities of already-manufactured nuclear or biological weapons parts—and could assemble those parts in relative secrecy. Capability to do new production or research, however, appears virtually nil.

5. These figures are approximations and include only the bombs dropped on Iraq proper.

The Role of the US Air Force in the Employment of Air Power

Maj Gen Charles D. Link, USAF

The essays collected in this book reflect the extent to which the debate over air power—supported by a wide range of diverse and strongly held opinion—remains active and intense. These remarks attempt to rationalize or make more understandable this range of opinion.

Although the interest level among the participants in the debate over air power is uniformly high, the level of comprehension may not be. Many people are simply not prepared to think about air power at the level of abstraction that is routine for such authorities as Gen Larry D. Welch and Gen Glenn A. Kent. These men have spent a lifetime thinking about air power. When the rest of us attempt to apply our relatively elemental understanding of air power in more complex discussions, we are sometimes frustrated by discontinuities which result quite naturally from our not having thoroughly understood the underlying theses which support the assumptions of the higher-level arguments.

A case in point is Clausewitz, who ministers to the military's professional need for coherent, rational analysis of what are basically irrational acts. We officers work hard to apply the reason and logic of Clausewitz to the military affairs of the United States. As critics often note, we sometimes fail. But this failure is not always a function of military incompetence; more often, it is the result of our attempt to apply principles envisioned largely for implementation by authoritarian sovereigns to a government of checks and balances, which functions only on the basis of broad consensus. In that regard, a book such as this one serves the vital purpose of helping to inform the public debate in ways that increase the likelihood of wise public choices. Some of that responsibility for informing the public debate certainly falls to the military itself. Air University, for example, emphasizes that responsibility as part of the process of professional military education.

In that regard, another case in point is the definition of air power. The underlying question is, Does the United States Air Force have proprietary rights to air power? Of course, the answer is no, but a simple answer is deceiving. A brief review of the basis of organizing for the common defense of the United States would be helpful here.

Why are there three departments and four services? I submit that this division is simply a function of task organization. Americans inherited an understanding of the need for specialization in the two mediums of warfare which prevailed in the time our nation was founded. Land warfare and sea warfare were both characterized by, and limited to, two dimensions of maneuver on the earth's surface. The invention of the airplane and its subsequent military use required the development and cultivation of a new competence, a new expertise in the employment of air power, and a new force characterized by three-dimensional maneuverability. When we add speed and range to three-dimensional maneuver, we find that we have altered in a fundamental way the time-honored understanding of the principles of mass and maneuver. Before air power, mass and maneuver were competing principles. The outcome of battles frequently hinged on the careful selection and timing of one, always at the expense of the other. The full development of modern air power permits today's commander to employ the principles of mass and maneuver simultaneously and complementarily—a circumstance unique to air power.

The three departments, then, are charged with the exploitation of their associated mediums of warfare—land, sea, and air. The Department of the Navy has further specialized within the sea medium to address the requirements of amphibious warfare—hence, the Marine Corps.

The services associated with each of the departments operate platforms in the aerospace medium, and rightly so. The Air Force has no designs on these platforms, but it must be clearly understood that—except in the case of the Air Force—these platforms are envisioned, acquired, and then dedicated to the specific support of the operations of the associated land, sea, or amphibious mediums. Only the Air Force looks at air power from the perspective of the department charged with fully exploiting the entire aerospace medium in the nation's security interests.

In his essay for this book, Dr Edward N. Luttwak reminds us that the dreams of early air power prophets were not in error but merely postponed. Roughly 60 years ago, Giulio Douhet had the audacity to argue that instead of using air power to protect the army so it could do its job, one should use the army to allow the massing of air power to win the war. Given the events of the recent war with Iraq, that should sound quite familiar.

How does all this relate to the concept of jointness? First, jointness in the operational context is not a useful measure of military effectiveness. One could pile up the corpses of all the troops who have been killed by jointness in all wars and not be troubled by their presence. Enemy dead generally exhibit the effect of shock, blast, heat, or fragmentation of weapons first envisioned by specialists in one or another of the mediums of warfare. Jointness in the operational context is a measure of efficiency rather than effectiveness. Admittedly, efficiency is an appropriate pursuit of those of us who are concerned with military effectiveness, but it is not a substitute for effectiveness. Further, jointness is not a substitute for high levels of competence in a particular medium of warfare but rests on an appropriate degree of integration of these highly developed specialized competencies.

Is it not ironic that Air Force officers in the post Goldwater-Nichols time frame find themselves taking great care to address the successful air campaign of the Desert Shield/Desert Storm operations in such self-abnegating terms? We are specifically encouraged by those who wish us well to be circumspect and unassuming about the relative importance of the contribution of the United States Air Force to the "joint" air campaign. It is indeed ironic because, of all the services, the Air Force has the greatest stake in jointness, as well as an established record of serious commitment to jointness.

Jointness is important to the Air Force because of the versatility of air power. Everybody wants some. The Air Force depends on the judgement of the joint commander—the theater commander—illuminated by the broader responsibilities inherent to high command, to make sound decisions with regard to the allocation of theater air power assets. Without the joint commander's broad insight, air power assets are peculiarly vulnerable to parceling—to effective subordination to subtheater objectives based in two-dimensional operations. In such instances, air power can become little more than very expensive artillery.

The fact of the matter is that air power is *the* valuable commodity of combat. For example, air superiority may not be sufficient, in and of itself, to meet the theater commander's objectives—but it is necessary. With it, all is possible—without it, all is at risk. The extraordinary battlefield value of air power flows from its inherent and prevailing versatility. It is fundamentally important to understand the simple fact that air power can compensate for inadequacies in land power and sea power in much greater measure than either or both of these can compensate for inadequacies in air power.

This capability must be brought first to the joint commander and then—only as a matter of the commander's judgement—to the support of missions of the other components of the assigned forces. Granted, the joint force air component commander may not be an Air Force officer. When this is the case, the commander brings an air power perspective which has been largely developed within a two-dimensional construct of ground-maneuver support, amphibious warfare, or fleet defense. On the other hand, if we in the Air Force do our jobs right, an Air Force officer serving as the joint force air component commander will bring an unsurpassed competence in the employment of air power across the spectrum of theater missions—from the strategic to the tactical, from airlift to bombardment, and from space to the surface of the planet.

I am proud to be an Air Force officer. I am especially proud to be part of the service whose superior competence in organizing, training, and equipping her forces contributed so substantially to the success of Desert Shield and Desert Storm.

PART II

Air Power as an Element of US Power Projection

Introduction

The Gulf war has taught American political and military leaders, not to mention the general public, that the United States will require a credible and potent power projection capability to respond to threats to its national security interests around the globe. As the authors in this section affirm, the US has to concentrate on the important lessons of the Gulf war, yet avoid any sense of complacency over its spectacular success. Within this context, they look to the possibilities of future conflict that may face the US in the next decade and beyond.

Dr Williamson Murray provides a historical summary of the uses and misuses of US air power since World War II. He looks back to the early days of the US Air Force and identifies deficiencies in doctrine and force structure that had a deleterious impact on American air power performance in two conflicts: "The air war in both Korea and Vietnam raised fundamental issues conflicting with USAF perceptions of how war should look. Adaptation was slow and hesitant; the US lost one of those wars and tied the other." The misreading of a lesson from World War II—that strategic bombing was highly effective—and the belief that nuclear bombardment was the only likely form of air war against the Soviet Union "hindered the preparation and utilization of air power in conflicts in which the United States has engaged."

According to Dr Murray, the emphasis on nuclear war with the Soviet Union overshadowed the crucial doctrinal lessons of World War II that were directly applicable to air power employment in conflicts like Korea and Vietnam. When war broke out in Korea, the Air Force—which had almost abandoned its Tactical Air Command—had to relearn many of the lessons of World War II. The Air Force experienced similar problems in the Vietnam War. There, it struggled to carry out an effective tactical air campaign against insurgent and highly evasive conventional forces by using "fighter-bombers [that] were designed and [whose] air crews [were] trained for high-speed delivery of tactical nuclear weapons." Murray observes that the Air Force's exchange ratio between 1965 and 1968 with the North Vietnamese MiG-21s was an "incredibly low" 1:2.29, whereas in Korea it had been between 1:7 and 1:10.

Lt Gen Michael A. Nelson emphasizes the importance of power projection capabilities by reviewing some of the lessons learned in the Gulf conflict and by examining some of the systems and capabilities the United States is pursuing for the future. He points out that the great nations of history have possessed power projection capacity superior to that of their adversaries. Such was the case with Rome and Great Britain. A central element in developing this power projection capability has been superior technology, which allowed those states to intervene in conflicts over great distances.

Today, the important power projection variables are speed and lift capacity, as witnessed in the Gulf war. As General Nelson notes, the US Air Force deployed the 1st Tactical Fighter Wing, airborne warning and control system (AWACS) aircraft, and tankers within 34 hours after receiving the order from President George Bush. The buildup of forces was immense, and the Air Force—through airlifters of the Military Airlift Command and tankers of the Strategic Air Command—was able to haul 46 percent of all combat forces stationed in the continental United States to the Persian Gulf.

For General Nelson, the lessons learned in the Gulf operation were severalfold. Of critical importance was the provision for a single air commander who had total operational control over the air campaign. Additionally, key technological advantages were exploited, including precision guided munitions and stealth, excellent intelligence-collection capabilities, superior communications, and the effective use of space assets for a variety of purposes. The top-notch performance of the US Air Force and ground forces demonstrated that dollars allotted in the 1980s for training, readiness, and spare parts were well spent.

General Nelson offers a caveat for Americans who have developed an overly sanguine picture of future conflict from the experience in the Gulf. He asserts that "16 January 1991 was the right time, Southwest Asia was the right place, and Saddam Hussein was the right opponent." It would be folly to assume that the next conflict will provide such favorable circumstances.

Gen Glenn A. Kent agrees with General Nelson and the other contributors to this volume that the new international security environment "mandates the objectives of quickly projecting sea power, air power, and ground power to the far reaches of the globe and of being able—once forces are deployed—to sustain high-intensity operations as required." He proposes that the US follow four critical stages in the next war:

- Project effective firepower early on (within a few hours).
- Project massive firepower soon thereafter (hours to days).
- Deploy very capable ground forces (days to weeks).
- Sustain high-intensity combat operations as long as required.

General Kent sketches a notional conflict that breaks out on 2 August 1998 and involves an invading Iraqi army bent on conquering not only Kuwait but also Saudi Arabia. The Iraqis, as Kent's scenario proceeds, "did not stop to park in the sand at the border," but proceeded into Saudi Arabia. The US commits forces immediately with three operational objectives: "(1) disrupt the enemy command and control, (2) slow or halt the invading armies, and (3) maintain the viability of the ports and airfields." In the scenario, once the US achieves air superiority, it concentrates on utilizing its massively enhanced airlift capacity to ferry troops and armor into the theater of operations. The United States is able to prevail because the planning and acquisition process had added "truly superior forces" to the US Air Force over the previous eight years.

In his paper, Gen Larry D. Welch reviews the challenges of low-intensity conflict (LIC) to American air power. He points out that the emphasis on LIC grew out of revolutionary strategy prosecuted by the Soviet Union and the Warsaw Pact, a threat no longer extant. Although the LIC challenge was a real one, he asserts that in the last 30 years, low-intensity conflict solutions have never been particularly effective. Most of the problems addressed as LIC have either been too big—forcing military escalation—or beyond military solution (e.g., essentially internal political or economic problems).

General Welch sees the era of low-intensity warfare as a thing of the past, while the most pressing challenges to the US military will be a conflict of midintensity "in areas where the issues are intense and intractable—the Middle East and South Asia." The United States will intervene in a manner "to commit overwhelming forces at any level of conflict to control the level of violence and to resolve the issue quickly." General Welch believes that air power is well suited to this "preferred 'American way of war': short, decisive, as bloodless as possible for US ground forces."

Air Power since World War II
Consistent with Doctrine?

Dr Williamson Murray

Early in 1991 we saw an awesome display of military technology and force employment. Quite literally, 40 days of pounding by allied air forces removed whatever inclination the Iraqi army might have had to stand its ground and fight in Kuwait. Nevertheless, before we abandon ourselves to reveries that military power is no longer needed or—even more dangerously—to the belief that everything worked so well that we can escape serious analysis of our efforts, we should take a long, hard look at what we are about and what we believe the purpose of air power to be.[1] This essay aims to suggest certain historical and doctrinal problems that have substantially hindered the understanding of the nature of war by airmen since 1945 and that have consequently hindered the preparation and utilization of air power in conflicts in which the United States has engaged.

Our victory over Iraq, at an almost unbelievably low cost, represents a relatively small success in comparison to the changes that shook Eastern Europe in the fall of 1989. Those events, which ended Soviet hegemony, were the culmination of 40-plus years of deterrence that locked the Soviet Union and its massive military machine within the confines of a self-imposed iron curtain. To make deterrence work, America's military institutions prepared with single-minded determination for Armageddon with their Soviet counterparts. Much of that effort involved the design and preparation of nuclear forces to fight and, if necessary, to win a nuclear war—if such a conflict could conceivably be considered winnable. From B-29s through B-52s to the B-1 and perhaps the B-2 of tomorrow, the US Air Force poured the national treasure as well as its intellectual lifeblood into preparing for a war that only madmen could have wished to unleash. Similarly, the preparation of missile forces placed an emphasis on a nuclear war that never happened. That such a war never occurred should *not* mislead us as to the immense contribution that those forces made to stability and peace in the world. Without that credible nuclear threat, there is no doubt that the Soviet Union would have embarked on extraordinarily dangerous ventures with its preponderant conventional forces.

Unfortunately, preparations for a nuclear war had other consequences for how the USAF prepared for war in other arenas and against other potential opponents. The overwhelming concern with the Soviet Union created a mind-set—a paradigm if you will—that has largely guided how American airmen have thought—and still do think, for the most part—about war.[2] Through the late 1960s, the emphasis within the Air Force remained firmly concentrated on Strategic Air Command (SAC); indeed, beyond the strategic mission, the other missions of the Air Force seemed puny. In the post-Vietnam era, other voices beyond SAC's came to dominate the Air Force, but those argued in terms of a conventional conflict over central Europe, a conflict in which we would win air superiority over the battlefield and then with the help of the Army's AirLand Battle sufficiently batter Warsaw Pact forces to end the conflict before it went nuclear. In the background, SAC continued to serve as a warning to the Soviets about the consequences of escalation or the possibility of American response should Soviet arms prove too successful in the conventional arena.

Both of these approaches had important consequences in how the USAF thought about and prepared for war in this period. Firstly, the emphasis on nuclear war with the Soviet Union resulted in a failure to come to grips with many of the crucial doctrinal lessons of World War II that were directly applicable to air power employment in the postwar world. Secondly, the stress on nuclear war resulted in an engineering, technological bias. As a result, the USAF's doctrinal conceptions across the spectrum were dominated by quantitative rather than psychological or historical factors. These two facets of the reaction to the nuclear world represent major themes throughout the remainder of this essay, but let us expand on them before we move to an analysis of the historical evidence.

The conduct of World War II raised substantial questions about the claims of airmen and air theorists in the 1920s and 1930s that air power, at least in a conventional sense, would be *the* decisive weapon of the next war.[3] The prolonged, five-year campaign of British and American air power against Germany, along with the land and sea campaigns, suggested a more complex picture. The analysis of the strategic bombing campaign was left to historians and academicians with strong biases against air power. Most of their words argued that the air campaign, at least in its strategic application, had proven to be a waste of resources.[4] The newly created Air Force did support a history of its efforts in World War II, but neither its postwar planning nor its doctrine was influenced greatly by historical "lessons learned."[5] In fact, general trends in USAF thinking after the war rejected the lessons of World War II in favor of the belief that nuclear weapons had now allowed air power to achieve a level of effectiveness claimed by its prophets before the war. Even as sophisticated an Air Force officer as Gen Lauris Norstad claimed that the advent of nuclear weapons would result in tactical air power having little role in future warfare.[6]

Consequently, airmen again looked to their weapons to provide a uniquely new form of warfare in which the traditional attributes of military power were no longer relevant.[7] The nature of a possible nuclear war remained largely opaque, however, because of the exponential increase of destructive firepower that nuclear weapons represented. Consequently, much of the military effort in regard to nuclear war resulted in an emphasis on targeting. By the early 1960s, the result was the single integrated operational plan (SIOP), an approach to potential nuclear war emphasizing quantitative factors to the exclusion of virtually everything else. There was, of course, considerable interest in the civilian academic community on strategic issues involved in nuclear war, but that interest centered on deterrence to a general exclusion of war. Moreover, there is little indication that the writings and arguments of civilian theorists had much influence on the targeting philosophy of military officers charged with designing plans for nuclear war.[8] Interestingly, few academic thinkers on nuclear strategy exhibited much interest in historical analogues.[9]

On the technological and engineering side, the nature of both aircraft and the systems upon which the Air Force depends served to reinforce a quantitative emphasis. This led to some serious misestimates on enemy capabilities in the Korean War, but its most dangerous impact came during the Vietnam War. In that conflict, the creation of numerical criteria by which the Air Force measured success—admittedly driven by Secretary of Defense Robert S. McNamara's bizarre lack of understanding of either military institutions or the nature of war—in some cases was counterproductive to the actual conduct of operations, particularly in a war so heavily dependent on political factors.

Since the subject of this essay is doctrine, it will be useful to say a few words on the creation and importance of doctrine to military organizations, as well as USAF attitudes over this period.[10] The current Air Force Manual (AFM) 1-1, *Basic Aerospace Doctrine of the United States Air Force*, defines doctrine as stating "the most fundamental and enduring beliefs which describe and guide the proper use of aerospace forces in military action."[11] Unfortunately, over the period since 1945, the Air Force has been generally cavalier in its approach to its basic doctrine, certainly in comparison to the Army and the Marine Corps.[12] Its clearest manual was written in 1943. As recently as 1979, it produced a doctrinal manual that a number of Air Force officers derisively but quite correctly described as "a comic-book version."[13] Nevertheless, whatever the failing of doctrinal manuals to articulate a coherent and consistent philosophy of war or of air power, the Air Force did evolve a general consensus and doctrine expressed in its actions and preparations for war. And those preparations—as this essay initially suggested—reflected the shifting paradigm of war against the Soviet Union: initially one of massive nuclear war but then shifting to a graduated response, beginning with conventional war in Western Europe and escalating up the ladder. Unfortunately, that paradigm did little to prepare the Air

Force, in a doctrinal sense, for the wars that it would have to fight—first in Korea and then in Southeast Asia.

When World War II ended, the Army Air Forces had amassed considerable experience in the employment of air power from strategic bombing to tactical missions that significantly enhanced employment of ground and naval forces. Yet, so strong was the pull of nuclear weapons, along with the inclination to return to comforting theories of prewar air power prophets, that almost immediately the new service's leadership shunned the tactical missions that had played so significant a role in World War II. Even before Hiroshima, Gen Frederic H. Smith, Jr., deputy chief of the Air Staff, argued against creation of a tactical air force in the postwar period; such a state of affairs was "'fallacious in principle and dangerous in implication'."[14]

In the acrimonious debates after 1945, Air Force senior leaders argued strenuously against the creation of a tactical air command. In October 1947 Gen Carl Spaatz suggested that "strategic and tactical aircraft" were essentially "interchangeable" and that as a consequence there was no requirement to create a separate command structure that would use up scarce resources.[15] Admittedly, much of the problem—up to the outbreak of the Korean War in June 1950—lay in severe shortages of resources in the retrenchment following World War II. Given the perceptions and long-range reality of the Soviet threat, the heavy emphasis on SAC's requirements was natural and wise. Nevertheless, the evidence suggests that more than just financial difficulties underlay the efforts to downgrade tactical air power and air defense.

In 1948 Tactical Air Command (TAC), having been on a starvation diet for the previous three years, found itself relegated to becoming an operational headquarters under Continental Air Command. It survived only because the Air Force needed a functional means to coordinate with the Army and Navy.[16] TAC's innovative and brilliant first leader, Gen Elwood Quesada, soon found himself shuffled off to meaningless assignments and eventually into retirement to run the Federal Aviation Administration. Even within TAC, shortly after World War II, little sense of the importance of tactical air power to

US defense capabilities remained. Gen William Momyer, then a colonel and an assistant chief of staff at Headquarters TAC, argued that TAC would be committed in hostilities only if "the atomic offensive failed and the war degenerated into a conventional air-surface action." That would not occur, according to his estimate, until at least two years after hostilities began. Moreover, Momyer saw no role for TAC's fighter assets in supporting SAC; only Air Defense Command might possibly use TAC's fighters in war.[17] In early 1950 Gen Hoyt S. Vandenberg went so far as to argue, in direct contradiction of historical lessons of World War II, that air superiority was not a prerequisite to conducting a strategic bombing campaign.[18]

The Korean War, however, suggested the weaknesses in Air Force doctrine. That conflict remained limited; the American government did not countenance the employment of nuclear weapons; and in most respects air power found itself employed in a broad spectrum of missions that mostly reflected the needs of the joint arena. Gen Omar Bradley set the mood of much of the American military towards the war when he remarked that the conflict was "'the wrong war, at the wrong place, at the wrong time, and with the wrong enemy'"; that comment certainly summed up the attitude of much of the USAF leadership.[19] It was not a war for which the USAF had prepared. On the level of national strategic policy, the US had real strategic reasons for wanting to protect the southern portions of the Korean Peninsula from Kim Il Sung's grasp; certainly in terms of protecting American interests in Japan, the war made sense. Moreover, the limits that were imposed prevented an expansion of the war into a far more dangerous conflict against China and perhaps even the Soviet Union—an escalation that might have resulted in the use of nuclear weapons.

The Korean War turned into an air war for which American air power was generally unprepared. Across the board, from aircraft to training to doctrine to employment concepts, the USAF had to relearn many of the lessons of World War II. As American ground forces found themselves hastily committed to stemming the onrush of North Korean forces towards Pusan, USAF aircraft from Japan attempted to interdict the flow of supplies and to provide support for hard-pressed, ill-trained ground troops. Meanwhile, B-29s rushed from continental US bases to attack North Korea. But the lack of prewar training and clear doctrinal conceptions seriously hindered early air efforts:

> The results . . . were often disastrous. American pilots attacked a column of thirty ROK [Republic of Korea] trucks, killing two hundred South Korean troops. An American officer working with an ROK unit said he was attacked by "friendly" aircraft five times in one day. . . . Four Australian planes blew up an ammunition train heading *north* to supply ROK units. Nine boxcars of vital ammunition were destroyed.[20]

Nevertheless, air operations—if they could not halt the enemy—did underline the importance of air power. American aircraft quickly disposed of the Yaks and Stormoviks that the North Koreans possessed and thus gained general air superiority over the peninsula. This then allowed B-29s to hammer North Korean industrial and transportation sites. The sustained air offensive, however, did not prove decisive; it made the counterattack of US ground forces easier and, along with the Inchon landings, contributed to the collapse of Communist forces around Pusan. However, the limited extent of North Korean industrial capacity provided a restricted set of targets for strategic bombing.

The war radically changed with the intervention of Chinese armed forces in the late fall of 1950. The savage battering absorbed by United Nations forces drove them south of the 38th parallel and for a time appeared to threaten the entire allied position in Korea. Again, air power played a crucial role in stabilizing the front, but by itself it could not defeat the enemy.

The resulting stalemate led to a battle for air superiority over North Korea and to one of the more acrimonious interservice squabbles in American military history. Flying from bases in Manchuria, the Chinese—with help from the Soviets—flew MiG-15s into the area south of the Yalu River that soon gained the nickname MiG Alley. The appearance of MiGs came as a nasty surprise to the USAF, which believed it enjoyed general technological superiority over the potential Soviet enemy; nevertheless, superior training and experience—rather than technology—provided significant advantages in air-to-air combat. However, the MiGs accomplished one goal that the Luftwaffe had failed to achieve in World War II: they ended daylight B-29 strikes against North Korean targets. On 23 October 1951 over 150 MiG-15s attacked B-29s that were bombing the North Korean city of Namsi. Despite the efforts of escorting fighters to protect the bombers, the Chinese shot down three B-29s and seriously damaged five others; thereafter, the B-29s came only at night.[21] Admittedly, the sanctuary provided by bases in Manchuria prevented the Americans from getting at the direct sources of enemy air power; given the importance of political considerations, the Americans had no other choice.

How air power could best contribute to the other war—the one along the 38th parallel—remained the great contentious issue. The new commander of Far East Air Forces, Gen Otto P. Weyland, argued in a letter to Vandenberg in June 1951 that Korea offered the Air Force a golden opportunity to show that air power could win a conventional war through its own efforts. The USAF should "fully exploit the first real opportunity to prove the efficacy of air power in more than a supporting role."[22]

Weyland's interest in "proving" this efficacy resulted in the great interdiction effort to isolate the battlefield and cause the collapse of the Chinese logistics. Some of the more optimistic officers on Weyland's staff argued that the campaign could force the Communists to retreat to within 100 miles of the Yalu.[23] The code name for the operation, Strangle, was singularly inappropriate, since a similar interdiction effort in Italy in 1944 with the same code name had failed to achieve its objectives. Strangle's results were mixed. On one hand, the interdiction operations probably prevented the Chinese from amassing the supply dumps necessary to launch another great land offensive. Significant portions of Chinese and North Korean manpower had to be diverted to repairing the damaged transportation system and to insuring the flow of supplies. Nevertheless, the logistical system continued to function, and the Chinese and their North Korean allies kept up a punishing and nasty war along the 38th parallel.

The largest arguments came over the way air power should provide close air support to American and allied forces along the front line. It is not worth rehashing the tired arguments about differing USAF and Marine Corps approaches to close air support.[24] The significant point here was that the Air Force system proved less responsive than that of the Marines and, in the final analysis, American lives were lost as a result. The real fault most probably lay not in the Air Force system, but in an apparently unfortunate unwillingness on the part of some USAF leaders to make their system as responsive as possible to the needs of the ground troops.

In the end, the Korean War appeared to be a completely unsatisfactory war from the American perspective. By 1953 it was thoroughly unpopular with the American people. American military forces suffered three grinding years of attrition, while the battlefront remained largely where it had started. Yet in retrospect, the war was more of a success than generally recognized. American forces stabilized the strategic balance in East Asia; the war galvanized the US into a serious military buildup to meet the Soviet threat; and that buildup allowed us to create military forces sufficient to serve as both conventional and nuclear deterrents.

In terms of doctrinal lessons, the war confirmed the lessons of World War II. Air superiority was a prerequisite to the employment of air power; air power could significantly reduce enemy military power through attrition; and close air support could save lives on the battlefield. Unfortunately, the period after the 1953 armistice reflected a flight within the USAF from the doctrinal lessons of the war. The paradigm of massive nuclear war with the Soviet Union provided the sole guiding light in the intervening years for the development of forces.

The post-1953 period was, of course, the time of the great buildup of SAC to meet the Soviet threat. That effort reflected pre–World War II theories of air power. As one Air Force general argued, "'A well organized air attack once launched cannot be stopped. . . . I think you have to stop it before it is launched and you can do so by offensive means only'."[25]

The single-minded focus on the Soviets and on preparations to fight an all-out nuclear conflict had serious consequences for other missions and force employments of air power. Fighter tactics became dominated by the Air Defense Command approach of launching platforms which, under radar control, could fire nuclear missiles at incoming bombers. Air-to-air combat—the dogfight—disappeared from the lexicon of those who flew fighters.[26]

On the other hand, TAC, saved from extinction as a result of Korea, turned itself into a mini SAC. The appearance of smaller nuclear weapons, allowing delivery by fighters or medium bombers, allowed TAC to carve out a niche on the lower end of the nuclear-employment spectrum.[27] Weyland, now commander of TAC, argued that nuclear capabilities were critical to tactical air power: "'With nuclear weapons these forces can be compact and yet be so effective as to provide the decisive balance of power'." Moreover, Weyland predicated the new approach on a belief that never again should the US "'restrict our selection of weapons or target area as we did in Korea'."[28]

The result of such a focus was a narrowing of capabilities and preparation to one form of war. Pacific Air Forces' training manual for F-100 pilots stated in 1961 that "nuclear training will in every instance take precedence over non-nuclear familiarization and qualification. . . . Non-MSF [mission support facility] units will restrict convention familiarization to accomplishment of only one event per aircrew per year."[29] As the foremost historian of Air Force doctrine has suggested, "The emphasis [was] in making war fit a weapon—nuclear air power—rather than [in] making the weapon fit the war. It was a weapons strategy wherein the weapons determined the strategy rather than the strategy determining the weapons."[30]

The Vietnam War, like Korea, however, turned out to be very different than USAF expectations. Admittedly, the commitment of American military forces to battle in 1965, both in the air and on the ground, took place within a misshapened political and strategic framework.[31] Nevertheless, even within the severe constraints within which that war was fought, the operational and tactical performance of American military institutions left much to be desired.

Two recent studies in military history—one on the British army in World War I and the second on the US Army in Vietnam[32]—underline the nature of the problem. Both studies suggest that military institutions take a particular framework or conception of what they believe the next war will look like into a conflict and then, disregarding the fact that the "real" war in which they are engaged is entirely different, rigidly apply their conceptions to the conduct of operations. In the former case, the result was the first day on the Somme River, 1 July 1916; in the latter case, the result was a firepower strategy that had little relevance to the political and strategic problems raised by an insurging war.

In many similar ways the performance of the USAF in the two separate air wars in North and South Vietnam reflected the inapplicability of tactics and doctrine, largely developed in response to the Soviet threat. Given the worldwide strategic situation confronting the US, such a state of affairs is understandable. What was less satisfactory was the inability to adapt to the "real" war. Admittedly, the overall framework within which the air campaigns against North Vietnam were executed was disastrous. Social science theories of gradual escalation as well as the heavy-handed and generally ignorant leadership of President Lyndon B. Johnson, Secretary McNamara, and their advisors proved to be a handicap that no skillful military leadership could have overcome.[33]

Political constraints aside, there is some doubt as to whether air power, alone and unconstrained, could have redressed the substantive political weaknesses of the South Vietnamese regime. Of course, that issue is impossible to answer; more important is the question of why no senior leader resigned in the face of constraints that were so inimicable to doctrinal conceptions. For example, in 1966 Johnson allowed the Joint Chiefs of Staff to strike only 22 of the targets that it proposed in support of Operation Rolling Thunder.[34]

Unfortunately, the conduct of operations hardly suggests a clear doctrinal or conceptual framework for handling the war that the

United States confronted in 1965. Equipment was largely inappropriate; heavy, high-speed fighters—either in or coming into the USAF inventory—had been designed for missions with little relevance to the requirements of the theater. Air Defense Command's fighters (the F-101B and F-102) were either inappropriate in an air-to-air environment or, if they could compete in the air-to-air environment, had inappropriate weapons. TAC fighter-bombers such as the F-101A, F-100, and F-105 were designed and their crews trained for high-speed delivery of tactical nuclear weapons, where pinpoint accuracy was not an essential element to weapon delivery. Under McNamara's pressuring, the USAF was in the process of buying the F-4, designed by the Navy as a high-altitude fighter, but the version bought by the Air Force had no internal gun.[35] Obviously, little work had yet been done on developing precision guided munitions, so fighter-bombers were reduced to dropping ordnance that reflected little improvement over World War II's weaponry.

It was in the air superiority realm that the USAF showed the most glaring weaknesses in doctrine and prewar preparations. Air-to-air combat had almost entirely disappeared from the capabilities of its fighter pilots. From 1965 to 1968 the exchange ratio in air-to-air engagement between US fighters (Navy as well as Air Force) and North Vietnamese MiG-21s was an incredibly low 1:2.29; the Korean ratios had varied between 1:7 and 1:10. At least the Navy, shocked by this low level, substantially upgraded air-to-air training in fighter tactics with its "Top Gun" school between 1968 and 1972. The USAF, however, failed to recognize that a problem existed and did little to alter its training approach. The Navy upped its ratio to 1:12 in its favor in the 1971 air war, while the Air Force rate during that time remained at the same low level as in 1965–68.[36] Depressingly, the lack of electronic countermeasures gear—which forced Air Force and Navy pilots to troll for surface-to-air missiles in 1966—only exacerbated loss rates and made a difficult and lethal environment even more dangerous and hazardous.[37]

The organization of the air war provided the most glaring sin against a coherent doctrinal approach to the war. The claims of airmen (including Navy aviators) that one airman should be in charge of the air campaign[38] dissolved in the face of interservice bickering that finally divided the air war against North Vietnam into two separate theaters. The level of cooperation between those two campaigns was often minimal, particularly when headquarters got into the act.[39] But even within the framework of the Air Force's own efforts, the organizational structure hardly bore any semblance to that tired but still crucial principle of unity of command. As one commentator has noted,

> The absence of a single air commander produced chaos. The 2d Air Division in Saigon, the Air Force headquarters with direct control over fighter wings participating in the campaign, received guidance not only from PACOM [Pacific Command] and PACAF, but also from [Thirteenth] Air Force in the Philippines.... To simplify the multilayer Air Force command arrangement, PACAF changed the 2d Air Division to the [Seventh] Air Force in early 1966. The confusion then increased, however. Instead of providing the [Seventh] Air Force with complete control over the 2d Air Division assets, PACAF gave the [Seventh] Air Force "operational" direction over the fighter wings, while the [Thirteenth] Air Force retained "administrative" control.[40]

SAC retained both command and operational control of its strikes into the south (and eventually the north in the Linebacker II operation of 1972). The nature of the organizational and doctrinal nightmare is clear.[41]

Finally, we should not forget the problems associated with adaptation to war in the "real" world. When the US committed large-scale forces to South Vietnam in 1965, the USAF had developed significant capabilities on the low end of the spectrum. That capability—furthered by creation of C-47, C-119, and eventually C-130 gunships—received significant enhancement from 1965 to 1972.

Nevertheless, there was a loss of perspective in much of the air war in the south as more and more conventional air power arrived in the theater. Much the same process occurred in the Air Force as was occurring in the Army: with more and more regular forces arriving to fight a political and social war within a framework of about one-year tours, the emphasis shifted to a high-intensity firepower war. In some respects, particularly from the perspective of ground troops, overwhelming firepower from the air was a matter of life and death.[42] But there were areas in the war where overwhelming firepower inflicted as much political damage on ourselves as it did physical damage on the enemy.

Moreover, the inability to arrive at a coherent definition of what we were attempting to accomplish on the strategic level resulted, on the operational and tactical levels, in meaningless statistical measures of merit that on occasion impaired our capacity to fight the war or even to damage the enemy. In one of many cases, the 487th Tactical Fighter Squadron (in TAC's 8th Fighter Wing at Udorn Royal Thai AFB, Thailand)—a squadron which carried the burden of much of the night air war over the Ho Chi Minh trail—found itself ordered to dispense with its flare racks and bomb only by radio control. The result was an increase in bomb tonnages dropped and a rapid drop in strike effectiveness, but the former was the measure of effectiveness used by Seventh Air Force.[43] Even more distressing, the initial strikes into North Vietnam during Linebacker I in 1972 largely ignored the combat experiences of 1968 against the high-threat environment that the North Vietnamese had emplaced with the help of the Chinese and the Soviets.[44] Heavy initial losses eventually brought a return to more realistic tactics, but the question of why we had to learn the lesson of 1968 over again is important. Moreover, SAC's B-52 strikes of Linebacker II—crucial to the North Vietnamese agreement to the Paris Peace Accords—suffered heavy losses as a result of both the predictability of their mission profiles and a general unwillingness to learn at the hands of others.[45]

We have seen great events in the first half of 1991. Air power may well have lived up to the potential that its early prophets Gen Giulio Douhet, Air Marshal Hugh Montague Trenchard, and Gen William ("Billy") Mitchell claimed. Nevertheless, we should not lose sight of the advantages that we enjoyed. Our opponent prepared, equipped, and trained for this war in a fashion almost exactly similar to the Soviet paradigm against which we have devoted as much of our efforts over the past 40 years. In this case a third-world society assumed the armor and guise of Achilles. We, on the other hand, possessed a resolute political leadership. In some respects we had learned many of the substantive lessons of Vietnam, although at the beginning of August 1990 Tactical Air Command proved incapable of conceiving of any air role for its forces other than serving as the Army commander's long-range artillery. Much of the credit for the actual success of effort is due to obscure battles fought in the Pentagon in 1985 and 1986 for a joint air-component commander,[46] and to a major research paper written at approximately the same time by an Air Force officer.[47] But in this case, the paradigm that we created to fight the Soviet Union gave us every advantage against Iraq. If you will, we had prepared a sledgehammer for use against a 100-pound rock and then used it against a three-pound sponge.

But the paradigm is gone; the Soviet Union—if it continues to exist at all—will diminish as a threat as its internal problems and its withdrawal from Eastern Europe continue. We may succeed in the creation of a new world order among the industrial states, but no matter how successful our Pax Americana, we will—from the point of view of military history—confront a war within the next three decades. The war, as with Korea and Vietnam, may well look nothing like our previous conflicts. How long and how well we have thought about war, about doctrine, and about the strengths and weaknesses of air power in the widest sense will determine how well we adapt to the "real" wars that we will face in the future. We may get much of that future war wrong in the period before it begins; the crucial issue, however, is how quickly and how skillfully we adapt. If we use our recent success as a stepping-off point for improving our conceptions and our performance, then we will do well. If we think that we have already learned everything that we need to know, then we will confront disaster.

The air war in both Korea and Vietnam raised fundamental issues conflicting with USAF conceptions of how war should look. Adaptation was slow and hesitant; the US lost one of those wars and tied the other. Admittedly, in the case of Vietnam, even had we done better militarily in addressing the conflict within a coherent doctrinal framework, the political realities as well as our political leadership had made the war unwinnable from the start. Nevertheless, air power requires, as does all military power, a coherent and realistic doctrinal framework; we did not have that framework in 1965. The question now is, Will we have that broad doctrinal framework in the post–Gulf war era?

Notes

1. It is worth noting that the Germans, after their overwhelming success against Poland in September 1939, judged their combat effectiveness in that campaign as having been severely deficient and then set about creating a massive training program to correct those deficiencies. That analysis, as well as the program to correct the weaknesses, played a critical role in the overwhelming victory that German forces won in May–June 1940. See Williamson Murray, "The German Response to Victory in Poland: A Case Study in Professionalism," *Armed Forces and Society*, Winter 1981, 285–98.

2. I am indebted to Maj Gen Minter Alexander, Headquarters USAF, for this important point.

3. For air doctrine and its development during the interwar period, see—among others—Giulio Douhet, *The Command of the Air*, trans. Dino Ferrari (London: Faber and Faber, 1943); Edward Warner, "Douhet, Mitchell, Seversky: Theories of Air Warfare," in *Makers of Modern Strategy: Military Thought from Machiavelli to Hitler*, ed. Edward Mead Earle (Princeton, N.J.: Princeton University Press, 1971), 485–503; Williamson Murray, "The Luftwaffe before the Second World War: A Mission, A Strategy?" *Journal of Strategic Studies*, September 1981, 261–70; Barry D. Powers, *Strategy without Slide-Rule: British Air Strategy, 1914–1939* (New York: Holmes and Meier, 1976); Williamson Murray, *Luftwaffe* (1983; reprint, Baltimore: Nautical and Aviation Publishing Co., 1985); Thomas A. Fabyanic, "A Critique of United States Air War Planning, 1941–44" (PhD diss., Saint Louis University, 1973); and Barry D. Watts, *The Foundation of US Air Doctrine: The Problem of Friction in War* (Maxwell AFB, Ala.: Air University Press, 1984).

4. John Kenneth Galbraith has been the leader of this school:

> German war production had, indeed, expanded under the bombing. The greatly heralded efforts, those on the ball-bearing and aircraft plants for example, emerged as costly failures. Other operations, those against oil and the railroads, did have military effect. But strategic bombing had not won the war. At most it had eased somewhat the task of the ground troops who did. The aircraft, manpower and bombs used in the campaign had cost the American economy far more in output than they had cost Germany.

John Kenneth Galbraith, *A Life in Our Times: Memoirs* (Boston: Houghton Mifflin Co., 1981), 226. For a more historical example of this argument, see Michael S. Sherry, *The Rise of American Air Power: The Creation of Armageddon* (New Haven, Conn.: Yale University Press, 1987). For another view of the Combined Bomber Offensive's impact on the winning of the Second World War, see Murray, *Luftwaffe*, 282–96.

5. See Wesley Frank Craven and James Lea Cate, *The Army Air Forces in World War II*, 7 vols. (1948–1958; new imprint, Washington, D.C.: Office of Air Force History, 1983).

6. Robert Frank Futrell, *Ideas, Concepts, Doctrine: A History of Basic Thinking in the United States Air Force 1907–1964* (Maxwell AFB, Ala.: Air University, 1971), 101–2.

7. As early as 1924 the British air staff argued in a memorandum that the air forces attacking an enemy

> can either bomb military objectives in populated areas from the beginning of the war, with the objective of obtaining a decision by moral[e] effect which such attacks will produce, and by the serious dislocation of the normal life of the country, or, alternatively, they can be used in the first instance to attack enemy aerodromes with a view of gaining some measure of air superiority and, when this has been gained, can be changed over to the direct attack on the nation. The latter alternative is the method which the lessons of military history seem to recommend, but the Air Staff are convinced that the former is the correct one.

London, Public Record Office, Air 20/40, Air Staff Memorandum no. 11A, March 1924.

8. In particular, see the excellent article by David Alan Rosenberg, "The Origins of Overkill: Nuclear Weapons and American Strategy, 1945–1960," in *Strategy and Nuclear Deterrence: An International Security Reader*, ed. Steven E. Miller (Princeton, N.J.: Princeton University Press, 1984), 113–81.

9. Bernard Brodie and Colin Gray are, of course, exceptions.

10. Here I can speak as both an insider as well as a historian, since I have served over the past six years as an individual mobilization augmentee (IMA) on the Air Staff, attached to the Doctrine Division of the Plans and Concepts Directorate (XOXWD).

11. AFM 1-1, *Basic Aerospace Doctrine of the United States Air Force*, 16 March 1984, v.

12. Army Field Manual (FM) 100-5, *Operations*, 5 May 1986, and Fleet Marine Forces Manual (FMFM) 1, *Warfighting*, 6 March 1989, are more directly connected with the realities of fighting than is the current Air Force basic manual. The Navy has no doctrine, only standard operating procedures.

13. See Williamson Murray, "A Tale of Two Doctrines: The Luftwaffe's 'Conduct of the Air War' and the USAF's Manual 1-1," *Journal of Strategic Studies*, December 1983, 84–93.

14. Quoted in Futrell, 101.

15. Caroline Frieda Ziemke, "In the Shadow of the Giant: USAF Tactical Air Command in the Era of Strategic Bombing, 1945–1955" (PhD diss., Ohio State University, 1989), 53.

16. Ibid., 68.

17. Ibid., 78.

18. Ibid., 106.

19. Quoted in Allan R. Millett and Peter Maslowski, *For the Common Defense: A Military History of the United States of America* (New York: Free Press, 1984), 490.

20. Quoted in Callum A. MacDonald, *Korea: The War before Vietnam* (New York: Free Press, 1986), 228.

21. Ibid., 242.

22. Quoted in Allan R. Millett, "Close Air Support in the Korean War, 1950–1953," in *Studies in Close Air Support*, ed. Richard Kohn, in press.

23. Robert F. Futrell, *The United States Air Force in Korea, 1950–1953*, rev. ed. (Washington, D.C.: Office of Air Force History, 1983), 407.

24. For the most thorough examination, see Millett, "Close Air Support."

25. Quoted in Futrell, *Ideas, Concepts, Doctrine*, 143.

26. As a former maintenance officer in an F-101B Air Defense Command fighter wing from 1965 to 1968, I find the idea of using the F-101B in a daylight arena ludicrous, especially with its pitch-up problems. This aircraft was, however, one of the main frontline American fighters—an aircraft which could get to an altitude swiftly, but which had *no* capability to maneuver as a fighter once it engaged the enemy.

27. Ziemke, 227–35.

28. Quoted in Futrell, *Ideas, Concepts, Doctrine*, 231.

29. Benjamin S. Lambeth, "Pitfalls in Force Planning: Structuring America's Tactical Air Arm," *International Security* 10, no. 2 (Fall 1985): 105.

30. Robert F. Futrell, "The Influence of the Air Power Concept on Air Force Planning, 1945–1962" (Paper presented at the Eleventh Military History Symposium, USAF Academy, Colorado Springs, Colo.).

31. One of the ironies of history and certainly one indication of the complete contempt of most Americans for history (even recent history) was the appearance of Robert McNamara, one of the principal authors of that disastrous strategy, before the congressional hearings in fall 1990 on what American strategy should be used in the Persian Gulf. Certainly, the attention that the former secretary of defense received from both the committees and the media would lead one to conclude that he was regarded as a brilliant practitioner of strategy.

32. See Timothy Travers, *The Killing Ground: The British Army, the Western Front and the Emergence of Modern Warfare, 1900–1918* (London: Allen & Unwin, 1987); and Andrew F. Krepinevich, Jr., *The Army and Vietnam* (Baltimore: Johns Hopkins University Press, 1986).

33. In this regard, see Mark Clodfelter, *The Limits of Air Power: The American Bombing of North Vietnam* (New York: Free Press, 1989), 76–102; and George C. Herring, *"Cold Blood": LBJ's Conduct of Limited War in Vietnam*, The Harmon Memorial Lectures in Military History, no. 33 (Colorado Springs, Colo.: United States Air Force Academy, 1990).

34. Clodfelter, 123.

35. This was a result of the inclinations of the secretary of defense, as well as those of many people within the Air Force community.

36. Art Hanley, "The Great Fighter Shoot Out," *Airpower*, January 1985, 20–45.

37. Lt Gen Charles Boyd, commander, Air University, Maxwell AFB, Ala., conversation with author, 26 February 1991.

38. This represented an issue that British and American ground commanders as well as air commanders had settled in North Africa in *1943*. See Lord [Arthur William] Tedder, *With Prejudice: The War Memoirs of Marshal of the Royal Air Force, Lord Tedder G.C.B.* (Boston: Little, Brown and Co., 1966).

39. The lack of cooperation between the two services was in many respects not only irresponsible, but morally reprehensible. In one case an Air Force forward air controller (FAC) squadron flying over the trail had significantly improved the performance of a new Navy carrier air group (CAG) by sending some of its pilots to fly in the right seat of A-6s, while allowing Navy aircrews to fly in its aircraft to speed up their acclimatization to combat. After an immediate and significant improvement in combat performance by the CAG, Seventh Air Force stepped in and ordered the exchanges stopped. Moreover, it refused a proposal to use such exchanges to improve Air Force fighter-bomber performance with the comment that FACs had nothing to teach fighter pilots.

40. Clodfelter, 128.

41. See John Schlight, *The War in South Vietnam: The Years of the Offensive, 1965–1968* (Washington, D.C.: Office of Air Force History, 1988), 148.

42. The situation around Khe Sanh in spring 1968 is a case in point. But for platoons, companies, and even battalions, close air support was often the difference between survival or annihilation. See S. Lawrence Gwin, Jr., [with Alexander Cochran], "Ambush at Albany," *Vietnam*, October 1990, 42–48.

43. Barry D. Watts, "Unreported History and Unit Effectiveness," *Journal of Strategic Studies*, March 1989, 88–98.

44. For this point I am indebted to Col Thomas Fabyanic, USAF, Retired.

45. Clodfelter, 184–93.

46. The crucial player in winning that argument for the Air Force was Col Robert Gaskin of the Doctrine and Concepts Division, Headquarters USAF (then XOXID, presently XOXWD).

47. John A. Warden III, *The Air Campaign: Planning for Combat* (Washington, D.C.: National Defense University Press, 1988).

Aerospace Forces and Power Projection

Lt Gen Michael A. Nelson, USAF

It is an exciting time for the United States and the US Air Force. As part of a multinational coalition, we went nearly halfway around the world in answer to a cry for help from a beleaguered friend. Air power played a pivotal role in answering that call—in the initial response, the buildup that followed, and the final showdown with Saddam Hussein. Although we recognize the preeminent contribution of air power in this conflict—from the Air Force, the Navy, the Army, the Marine Corps, and our allies—from time to time it is healthy to look at our purpose and, more important, our future.

This essay addresses power projection and the Air Force's role in that mission. It is an important time to be looking at today's capability, and we can benefit by reviewing some of the lessons we have learned in the deserts of Southwest Asia. But we also need to investigate some of the systems and capabilities we are pursuing for the future.

The US military is undergoing the most sweeping revision of its defense planning since World War II. We have relied on a strategy of forward defense for more than 40 years, but now we are pulling back many of our forces to the continental United States. Although our forces will be based closer to home, our interests will remain global. That dichotomy will have significant implications for the Air Force—as we have just seen in the desert halfway around the world.

Air Force actions during the three phases of the Desert Shield and Desert Storm operations—the initial response, the buildup, and the conflict—offer a tremendous example of what we in the Air Force can do best when it comes to power projection. Based on our speed, range, flexibility, precision, and lethality, we can reach out to project power to protect America's interests anywhere in the world within a matter of hours.

Historical View of Power Projection

Power projection is a new term for an old concept. The use of military force to exert national influence goes back thousands of years. In the time of ancient Greece, the Athenians projected power with maritime forces. Sparta employed land forces for the most part, but the Peloponnesian War ended when Sparta was able to project maritime power and cut off Athens's food supplies from the Black Sea.

Gen Norman Schwarzkopf, commander of the coalition forces, likes to cite the example of Hannibal and Hasdrubal at the Battle of Cannae to illustrate the use of envelopment, but one can also use the competition between Carthage and Rome to analyze the need for persistent power projection. Carthage was an economic power and used its naval forces—and its elephants—to project power. In the end, Rome was able to overwhelm Carthage by being able to project *more* power, *farther*. The result was the end of Carthage, several hundred years of Pax Romana, and many more examples of successful Roman power projection through the use of land and maritime forces.

Great Britain also used power projection to obtain and exploit its empire. Its forces operated on land and at sea, and the technology of the day determined the speed with which they could project power. When the Mahdi captured Charles George ("Chinese") Gordon and held him hostage in Khartoum in the late 1890s, it took Gen Horatio H. Kitchener of Great Britain nearly a year to travel by sea and land to arrive at the gates of the city. By that time, Gordon and his men had long been martyrs.

Although the concept of power projection is not new, the means we have to bring it to life are very definitely changing its character. As we showed in early August of 1990, air power offers us the speed to respond quickly enough to affect the outcome of conflict, rather than just recover the bodies of martyrs.

The point of this brief historical review is that technology has always had an impact on the roles and missions of the military. The role of power projection is no different. Just as aircraft have had an immense impact on the battlefield in reconnaissance and close air support—indeed, in all the ways with which we are familiar—so does air power offer us a tremendous opportunity in projecting power.

The United States has been a leader in taking advantage of the air to project power—and not just in the last few months. The Berlin airlift immediately after World War II, the Lebanon crisis of 1958, and the Cuban missile crisis of 1962—in which aircraft from Strategic Air Command (SAC) played a key role—were all successfully concluded in part because of US capability to project power globally with air forces.

Power Projection in the War with Iraq

As mentioned above, the recently completed operation in the Persian Gulf provides an example of successful US power projection. Air power played a critical role in each of the operation's three phases.

Initial Response

F-15s of the 1st Tactical Fighter Wing, supported by airborne warning and control system (AWACS) aircraft and tankers, were in place on Saudi soil and defending Saudi airspace within 38 hours of the president's saying, "Go!" I am quite confident that those airplanes—and the aircraft, men, and equipment that quickly followed—played a key role in stopping Saddam Hussein at the Saudi border.

Buildup of Forces

Military Airlift Command's (MAC) crews and aircraft performed superbly in the buildup of forces that followed the initial response, as did SAC's tankers. The immense effort needed to ferry people, weapons, and planes to the Gulf simply would not have been possible without MAC and SAC.

Conflict

Air power played a decisive role in the conflict against Saddam Hussein and his armed forces. The contributions of Air Force men and women were tremendous. During the 43 days of the war, coalition air forces flew about 110,000 sorties, and the US Air Force flew just under 60 percent of them.

We have, in effect, passed our operational readiness inspection in the "world after East-West confrontation." Can anyone contend that we will not be tested again ere long? The capability that we demonstrated in Desert Shield and Desert Storm—to project lethal force globally—will be necessary for the foreseeable future because, fundamentally, the world is not a safe place.

Formula for Success against Iraq

In 1990 we were euphoric over the spread of democracy and the prospects for peace. We had good reason for our euphoria—the crumbling of the Berlin Wall, the disintegration of the Warsaw Pact, the demise of communism, and the prospects for disarmament. Everything seemed to be coming together to make real the vision of a safer, more peaceful world. Imagine yourself in the world as we knew it in the summer of 1990, suggesting to someone that we needed an Air Force capable of moving 30 squadrons and full gear plus the Army personnel for nearly eight divisions (and keeping them supplied), not to mention conducting 2,000-plus sorties a day in order to push Iraq out of Kuwait. What do you think the reaction to your suggestion would have been? The point is that the world is uncertain and that events develop faster than we are able to build military capability. Doubts about this should have been erased in the week after you made your suggestion. Then came 2 August 1990 and a reminder that we need to maintain the capability to defend our shores and project power in defense of America's interests. But we have had other opportunities to project power—ones in which we were less successful than in Desert Storm. What was different about this operation?

Political-Military Factors

President George Bush was committed to achieving the four objectives he outlined to the American people and the world on 7 August 1990, and the military objectives and means were permitted to match the clarity of the national-level objectives. Rather than the gradualism and politically driven restraint of Vietnam, President Bush was committed to a military victory and communicated his objectives to the military planners very clearly and succinctly, saying to them, "I've told you my objectives. Go plan and execute the campaign." Under the direction of Secretary of Defense Dick Cheney, Chairman of the Joint Chiefs of Staff Gen Colin Powell, and General Schwarzkopf, we were able to do that. We had a plan which we were able to turn into air tasking orders and execute. In addition to the political-military factors, a number of other elements were keys to our ability to execute the campaign.

Training

For instance, our forces were ready for the conflict in January and February of 1991 because of the dollars we spent on training, readiness, and parts in the 1980s. *Training* deserves some elaboration. I do not put it first idly. We were ready in January because we made a commitment in the eighties to realistic training. We put money into training programs, developed realistic training scenarios, built better ranges, and recognized that realistic training includes a degree of risk—but one that is manageable. In fact, better trained aircrews fly more safely—as our accident rates vividly show. We had our best years, from a safety standpoint, during the late 1980s and 1990.

Integration of Air Forces

In addition to the well-trained forces in the Gulf, having a single air commander was another key element in the execution of the air campaign. As the quarterback for all the air players in the Gulf, Gen Chuck Horner was able to pull all the pieces together and employ all the air assets in a single, integrated force in support of a single, integrated air campaign plan. Further, he had the tactical command and control system necessary to execute his plan and fight his forces, responding flexibly when changes were required in the plan.

Technology

Another ingredient in our success in the Gulf was technology that delivered not only precision guided munitions and stealth—as has been repeatedly noted—but also better intelligence-collection capability, better communication, and better use of space assets for a variety of purposes.

Opponent

The fact that we had the right opponent contributed to our success in the Gulf. That is, all of our good features were matched by an almost unbroken string of incorrect decisions on the part of the Iraqis. In fact, it is hard to think of a decision our opponent made—including the original decision to invade Kuwait—that was a good one.

Lessons Learned

In learning our lessons from Desert Storm, however, we must be cautious. It is possible, after all, to learn too powerfully from a victory as well as from a disaster. We need to be realistic about what we learn from the Gulf and how we plan for the future. Specifically, we need to avoid overconfidence and complacency by not assuming that the next war will be like this war. There is much to take away from this conflict, and we would be fools not to take notes. But we need to be alert to the possibility that other places and other circumstances may present different problems. Put simply, 16 January 1991 was the right time, Southwest Asia was the right place, and Saddam Hussein was the right opponent for *this* war. We did have some things go our way: (1) We had five months to build our forces in theater—without opposition. Had we had to fight our way into Dhahran, Saudi Arabia, for example, things would have been much costlier. (2) We were favored by pretty good weather. Although the weather was the worst in years during parts of the campaign, compared to climatic conditions in many parts of the world in the dead of the winter, it was superb. (3) The geography—flat, almost featureless, with no terrain to hide behind and no triple-canopy jungle to operate in—was favorable for this war. (4) Interdiction circumstances were favorable. The source of supply was fairly central and connected to the potential battle area by one railroad and few enough roads and bridges to make a complete cutoff "doable." (5) The countries to which we deployed had the concrete and basic requirements for our beddown.

Such favorable circumstances as the ones mentioned above, however, take nothing away from the tremendous victory that America won in the Gulf. Nothing can diminish the brilliant leadership of President Bush, General Powell, and General Schwarzkopf or the superb performance of all the men and women of the allied coalition. Nevertheless, we must ensure that we take the right lessons away from the Gulf war and be aware that we will not be the only ones to learn from it. Potential adversaries will learn some lessons too—some good, some bad.

First, the good news. Countries around the world—including our allies and potential adversaries—will be reminded that America is standing tall. They will see that we are willing and able to take the leader's role and exert influence when necessary in the national interest. Perhaps some would-be Saddam Husseins in other parts of this world—and there will always be Saddam Husseins—will think twice before "pressing to test" America the next time.

But there is bad news as well. Others will learn from the war in the Gulf. They will learn a variety of lessons about American tactics, technology, and weapons and will adjust their own capabilities accordingly. The *Washington Post* of 27 March 1991 reports that the People's Republic of China plans to increase its military spending by nearly 12 percent in 1991, based primarily on the success of US weapons and technology in the Gulf. China, a major supplier of weapons to the Middle East, saw some of that hardware devastated by the allies. No doubt, there are other countries taking notes about America's military capabilities. We cannot rest on our laurels; rather, we must ask ourselves how we can ensure America's security for tomorrow.

Security Issues

At least part of the answer is that our interests and focus must remain global. We are both a maritime and an *aerospace* nation with a network of economic, political, and military interests around the world. If there ever was a "makeable" case for isolationism, it has been lost in the mists of the past. Far too many of our raw materials come from other parts of the world, and far too many of our markets are outside the US for us to disregard affairs on the world stage. We must be more than interested. We must be able to *participate* with all the instruments of national power, including the military. That means we need to maintain a credible capability to project military power anywhere in the world where American interests are threatened—no simple task. Central to this discussion is the change in focus of American defense planning during 1989–90.

We have had the luxury over the 40-plus years since World War II of relying on a strategy of forward defense and in-place forces in our efforts to deal with a single, most-likely scenario—war versus the Warsaw Pact in central Europe. We were able to deal with this scenario through the basing of heavy US Army units and tactical air forces in-theater—where we expected them to be needed—

supplemented with reinforcement. That luxury of forward defense, for political and economic reasons, is eroding as the world is changing.

The Warsaw Pact is no longer an effective military organization. In fact, the last day of the pact, which I have spent my adult life planning to fight, was 1 April 1991. As a result, war is less likely in central Europe, and the Soviets—were they to invade—would have to fight their way through the countries of eastern Europe to reach our allies. Furthermore, the warning time for war—if it comes—will increase, allowing reinforcement spread over a longer period.

The emphasis obviously has shifted to a less well defined and vastly more unpredictable array of threats, ranging from incidents that precipitated operations such as Just Cause to Desert Shield and Desert Storm. We cannot predict where the next Desert Shield will occur. It could easily be in a place where we have no troops and no infrastructure—no bases or support systems in place. We will have to take with us everything that we need, including shelter, maintenance facilities, hospitals, and food and water. Remembering the lesson of General Kitchener of Khartoum and the unhappy fate of Chinese Gordon, we will need to get it all there within hours if we expect to stop the next Saddam Hussein at the border.

All of this discussion about the uncertainty inherent in this world, the lessons of the Gulf war, and the future of the Air Force leads us to some "certainties" and "probable certainties"—maybe we should call them "semicertainties"—in dealing with the Air Force and its role in power projection.

Future Concerns of Air Force Power Projection

No single nation aside from the USSR will present a *fatal* threat to US interests. Others may force us to action, but only the Soviet Union maintains the capability to incinerate our nation in a matter of 30 minutes. Other nations and extranational groups will threaten US interests in ways requiring military action, but not with the consequences—in the event of US failure—of a danger to our continued freedom or existence.

Nuclear Deterrent

Therefore, the United States must maintain a guaranteed nuclear deterrent to block the only overwhelming threat to its most vital interests. It is interesting to note that our policy of deterrence is based on the threat of overwhelming power projection by strategic forces in the event of nuclear aggression. In my mind that drives the need for the B-2 as part of a vibrant, modernized nuclear triad. The B-2's flexibility, survivability, and capability—the fact that it enhances deterrence while increasing stability in a crisis and the fact that it will possess a strong conventional capability—all argue for its procurement. Nothing we have or expect to have will bring more life to power projection than this platform, which can go anywhere, arrive unannounced, and deliver a powerful message.

Global Projection

Seizing on that point, the US must be capable of bringing conventional force to bear globally. My earlier points—that our forward defense will be eroded and that our forces will be based more in the continental US—take on even more importance when they are framed by the context of the need to "go global" when tasked. This is what makes the C-17 so important to the future of America's national security. Notice I did not say "so important for the Air Force." The C-17 is certainly important for the Air Force, but airlift is a *national* asset (e.g., most of our customers are in the Army). The C-17 is important for *America*.

Strategic Basing

We will require strategically located bases overseas for the foreseeable future. We need operating bases from which to deter, conduct immediate reactions, and offer throughput capacity for action elsewhere.

Mobile Forces

We need mobile, high-impact forces—the strength of the Air Force. We must be capable of—and others must see us as capable of—routine long-range (literally global) surprise, precision, conventional strikes. We also need highly mobile, specialized threat- and mission-driven packages. These long-range packages and specialized packages should train together and be recognized as a well-oiled outfit that could show up on anyone's doorstep with little warning. This shock force would need to be reinforced in some circumstances but should be capable of operating independently. Air Force Chief of Staff Gen Merrill A. McPeak's concept of the composite wing is obviously designed to provide such a capability.

Space Assets

Because we also need to control the high ground, our focus is on space (the high ground of the future) and command, control, communications, and intelligence (C^3I) systems. Smaller force levels and access to fewer forward bases will increase our dependence on space-based force multipliers. Space-based communications, attack warning systems, and surveillance and navigation systems are all increasing in importance to US forces, and the Air Force—which provides most of the Department of Defense's space infrastructure—is working to improve our space capabilities.

We need to keep in mind that we live in an uncertain world. The key to surviving and prospering in that world is flexibility, which is the long suit of air power. In our future planning we need to make sure that we learn the *right* lessons from Desert Shield and Desert Storm.

Conclusion

Perhaps it is appropriate to conclude with a note from a column by Stephen Rosenfeld in the *Washington Post* of 29 March 1991.

Rosenfeld talks about another lesson we may learn from the Gulf war—one that may mitigate my fears about others learning too much about American tactics, techniques, and technology. He had asserted in a previous piece that it was lucky that Saddam Hussein had not read the field manuals in which the American military had written the "new doctrines" of battle it applied against him. Had he taken timely notice, Hussein might have saved himself some grief. A Marine colonel had an illuminating rejoinder: reading the manuals would not have helped Saddam Hussein because only nations with a society and governing system similar to ours can hope to wage war in the American style.

Think about that statement. It goes to the heart of our operations. We *trust* our people and *entrust* them with a great deal of tactical control over their own situations. People who have worn Air Force blue are well aware of the truth of this assertion (our pilots, for example, operate relatively independently). But the same is true to a certain extent in American small-unit tactics. Our men and women are volunteers—not "simple soldiers" who are helpless without direction. They were, and are, Americans. The bane of every commander and the strength of every unit is the American soldier's desire to know why.

Saddam Hussein and other despots cannot afford to entrust their soldiers with responsibility and authority or to answer their whys. Surely, revolution and overthrow would be the result of any attempt to follow the American example. In our case, technology—which reinforces the discretion we allow our soldiers and airmen—was combined with individual initiative and authority to build an effective, flexible fighting force that Saddam Hussein could not withstand.

That is the most important lesson we can learn from the Gulf. I hope that everyone who watched the war sees that the real strength and advantage we enjoyed over Saddam Hussein was the strength of a democracy.

The Relevance of High-Intensity Operations

Lt Gen Glenn A. Kent, USAF, Retired

Four decades after World War II, the European scenario still dominated US planning. This scenario stemmed from the presence of many Soviet divisions on the intra-German border. Military forces were to underline and enforce the stated US national security objectives: prevent the Soviet Union from dominating Western Europe, deter the Soviets from large-scale military aggression against our NATO allies, and prevent the success of such an aggression if it were launched.

The European scenario centered on a key military objective: provide a forward defense. To achieve this objective, the United States deployed forces from the Army and Air Force in the sovereign territory of some of our NATO allies and established a line of defense on the NATO front. These forward-deployed forces were to be rapidly reinforced from the continental United States (CONUS) by deploying tactical aircraft and by airlifting Army troops. These troops were to marry with their tanks, armored personnel carriers, and other heavy equipment previously stored in Germany.

At the same time, US planners were aware that planning should also consider scenarios that were quite different. The United States could be required to insert forces to block an enemy's advance in circumstances where there was no organized line of defense, no basing infrastructure, and no large stocks of prepositioned equipment.

Two historic events have completely changed our concepts about which type of scenario is more relevant: (1) the events unfolding in Europe (the unraveling of the Warsaw Pact and the agreements designed to greatly reduce—if not eliminate—the threat of Soviet military actions against Western European countries) and (2) the events in the Persian Gulf since August 1990. In fact, there is now convergence between Persian Gulf–type scenarios and the new

European scenario. In the latter, the United States—after having withdrawn most of its forces in Europe—might be called upon to deploy a "covering" force to assist the Atlantic Alliance in some now-unforeseen crisis. Although this new European scenario is somewhat similar to a Gulf scenario, planners will understand that Gulf-like scenarios are more relevant and probably more tasking.

The essence of planning the structure and capabilities of future military forces is to grasp a vision of where and under what circumstances military power will be called upon to enforce security objectives defined and stated by the president. The correct approach to such planning is to know what threats we should worry about and how we are to react to such threats. The wrong approach is to try to arrange the world into collectors about conflict—high, medium, and low.

I have always quarreled about a formulation that classifies conflicts (wars) according to intensity, which is defined as the amount of action per unit of space and time. It is not to be confused with scope and duration. Intensity *is* an important concept—but not in the way it is commonly used. Intensity does not depend on the size of the forces or countries; rather, it describes the mode of operation (the rate of action) with respect to a particular mission area within a particular phase of a stated conflict. If the forces and battle control are available in a particular mission area, a commander will surely conduct operations in that mission area at the highest intensity that is appropriate and feasible.

To repeat, intensity has to do with the rate at which a combatant commander conducts particular operations in a particular mission area in a particular phase of an overall campaign of war. The rate may be high for one combatant in a particular mission area during a particular phase and low for the other.

For example, in the Persian Gulf the United States conducted air operations at high intensity to gain air supremacy quickly in order to decrease the duration and scope of the war. The United States had the capability to do so. The Iraqis lacked such a capability and were forced to operate their forces at low or no intensity—much to their detriment.

HIGH-INTENSITY OPERATIONS

Now, back to planning. The vision of a new world order will frame the background of our future planning. Such a vision mandates the objectives of quickly projecting sea power, air power, and ground power to the far reaches of the globe and of being able—once forces are deployed—to sustain high-intensity operations as required. The notion of global reach/global power captures this concept:

- Project effective firepower early on (within a few hours).
- Project massive firepower soon thereafter (hours to days).
- Deploy very capable ground forces (days to weeks).
- Sustain high-intensity combat operations as long as required.

The statements above are generic and sound too much like doctrine. Going through some scenario makes one think more perceptively about the relevance of intensity. The trouble is that scenarios invented by planners are not taken seriously until they happen—and then not for long. To try to pass the test of plausibility, I will build on a scenario that has already happened.

The year is 1999, and we are engaged in a postwar analysis of a scenario that had its beginnings nine years before. On 2 August 1990 Iraq invaded Kuwait. The United States responded and—beginning 18 January 1991—engaged in massive air strikes. On 21 January 1991 Saddam Hussein—much to the surprise of most and chagrin of some—chose a strategic course of saving his forces to fight another day. On that date, he ordered all his forces to withdraw from Kuwait. Saddam achieved a cease-fire by accepting all the United Nations resolutions. His forces in Kuwait were seriously pounded prior to the cease-fire; however, the Republican Guard was still relatively intact.

The president had to appear pleased, Congress was relieved, and the public applauded. However, a few pundits had dire visions of events to come.

Saddam was subsequently relieved of office; after all, the strongman had acquiesced to the Great Satan. There arose a new strongman. The bad news: he had the same expansionist views as Saddam. The worse news: he was much smarter. The worst news: there emerged a tenuous alliance between Iraq and Iran.

Now we shift to 2 August 1998. Iraq invaded Saudi Arabia. The invasion force did not stop to park in the sand at the border but proceeded in a relentless drive to occupy key areas of Kuwait and Saudi Arabia before any effective countervailing military action could be mounted. A major drive was directed at capturing the ports and oil fields in the Eastern Province of Saudi Arabia. Also, a large ground force proceeded toward Riyadh to capture airfields in that area and to unhinge the Saudi government. At the same time, Iraqi aircraft and missiles attacked Saudi ports, airfields, and other assets.

The president of the United States responded immediately and decisively, declaring that this aggression would be halted and reversed. He quickly committed US forces to the region to enforce this objective.

This scenario was more testing than that of Operation Desert Storm. In the new scenario, the United States did not have the luxury of an invading army parking in the desert to allow the president time to form a coalition, to project air power to bases with unscathed infrastructure, and to disembark ground forces at intact ports and without contest. In the new scenario, the commander of allied forces declared it absolutely critical to achieve three operational objectives early on: (1) disrupt the enemy command and control, (2) slow or halt the invading armies, and (3) maintain the viability of the ports and airfields.

Most of the B-2 force, which operated from bases in Diego Garcia and the CONUS, was assigned the first two objectives. Some B-2s were on airborne alert at sea and were over their targets in less than two hours after the presidential go-ahead, which came 30 minutes after border crossing. Those bombers on ground alert in Diego Garcia arrived in six hours—those based in CONUS in 13 hours. Once in the region, the B-2s assigned to attack the moving columns on invasion routes were "controlled" by a director in the back end of the joint surveillance target attack radar system (JSTARS). The JSTARS monitored the movement of enemy forces along the invasion routes and provided general "targeting" to the incoming B-2s. This system was already on hand, since several were owned and operated by the Saudis. The United States had previously seen the wisdom of providing (selling) the Saudis a dozen of these surveillance and control centers. This decision was based, in part, on the previous success of the airborne warning and control system (AWACS). We had come to depend on the JSTARS as a central control element in interdicting mobile and moving forces for air-to-ground operations, just as AWACS became a central control element in engaging enemy aircraft in air-to-air operations.

By virtue of having forces capable of quickly mounting effective attacks, the United States was able to conduct high-intensity counterforce operations early on, and such operations had a decided effect on the duration and scope of the war.

Another critical objective was to defend the two ports in the Eastern Province and the airfields in north-central Saudi Arabia. Initially, the Saudi F-15 force was dedicated to defending these assets against enemy air attacks. This fighter force was now equipped with the "best" of air-to-air missiles—the advanced medium-range air-to-air missile (AMRAAM)—which gave a good account of itself in terms of enemy kills versus friendly losses. But the fate of the ports and airfields hung in the balance.

A number of F-22s—the Air Force's newest fighter—arrived 24 hours after the president's go-ahead. The low observables, high sustained speed, and far-superior air-to-air missiles of this new fighter brought new dimensions to air-to-air combat. The concept of few Blue (friendly forces) on many Red (enemy forces) and many Red on few Blue had no relevance. Each Blue aircraft could engage many Red, but Red aircraft could engage only a few Blue. Lanchester's square law (equations describing the attrition of two opposing units) no longer applied. The fighter pilot's dream had come true: unobserved entry into the battle, many shots with impunity, and disengagement at will. Although outnumbered, the United States could and did operate in the high-intensity mode and stopped the enemy attacks.

Iraq now possessed surface-to-surface ballistic missiles of greatly increased range and accuracy, and these missiles posed a serious threat to the ports, bases, and oil fields. The president, in his state of the union address in 1991, set forth the objective of protecting against limited strikes. In military terms, this became known as "countermissiles" alongside "counterair"—the ability to cover our deployments and operations from enemy attack, whether air or missile.

By avoiding the starts and stops attendant to most programs in the acquisition process, the United States had been able to equip four ships with batteries of long-range interceptors that could protect fairly large areas against attacks by ballistic missiles. We had already deployed two of these ships in the Persian Gulf and two in the Red Sea. These ships, along with extended-range Patriot missiles already in Saudi Arabia and more deployed from the CONUS, proved quite effective.

Some of the F-117As and F-15Es were tasked to accomplish a mission popularly known as "Scud hunting," even though the missiles were no longer Scuds. The concept for countering enemy tactical ballistic missiles had become an operational art. Center stage to the whole operation was JSTARS, with its powerful radar. But the operators and directors in the back end of the JSTARS were the key to success. By correlating and associating the data from many sensors aboard other platforms, including satellites, these operators were able to "target" a good number of the enemy launchers before they fired and target nearly all of them in near real time once they fired. "Shooters" on airborne alert were then directed to the appropriate coordinates to engage and kill. Thus, we were able to conduct very effective counterforce operations against the enemy's launchers. A combination of high-intensity counterforce and active defense against ballistic missiles saved the day—the ports and airfields remained viable.

Most of the remaining USAF combat aircraft were deployed to bases somewhere in the region in the next few days. Although some of the bases had scant infrastructure, this posed no great problem. Beginning in 1991, the Air Force had taken purposeful action to implement concepts of maintenance and supply so that combat aircraft could quickly commence operations at such bases and then sustain operations at high intensity thereafter.

Operating the high-observable aircraft (primarily F-16s and F-15s) demanded the suppression of enemy defenses, especially radar-controlled surface-to-air missiles (SAM). The Air Force now has an EC-X, a system to jam enemy radars from large, standoff distances. The concept of standoff jamming is not new. What is new is that the power of this new jammer is quantum leaps beyond that of previous jammers. Thoughtful planners saw to it that this powerful device was mounted on a long-range aircraft so that rapid deployment was possible.

The JSTARS had also been equipped to control attacks against enemy SAM batteries. Again, the operators in the JSTARS were the key. By correlating and associating data from all other platforms, they were able to "tag" the blobs on their radar screens. The director then declared "tallyho" (indicating that a particular blob is indeed an enemy SAM) and assigned a shooter on airborne alert to attack each located battery.

The essence of the overall concept is captured as follows: Once an enemy radar emitted, it was jammed with enough power so that it could not complete an engagement. Kill of the radar was then ensured—even if the radar turned off—before it could move or move far. By the combination of jamming in real time and implementing real-time battle control to accomplish a sure kill shortly thereafter, Blue aircraft experienced very low attrition from ground defenses—even for the high-observable aircraft. We had the battle control and the forces to engage enemy defenses in the most effective mode—high intensity.

Once we began to achieve air superiority, the ground forces were rapidly deployed to the region by airlift and sea lift. In the ensuing years since 1991, considerable effort had been directed toward the objective of being able to deploy massive ground power in a short time:

- The Army adopted a new measure of merit—"the most combat capability per ton."
- The number of wings of transports (active and reserve) was increased.

- More airlift capability was made available from civilian sources.
- The capability for fast sea lift was much greater.
- More heavy equipment was prepositioned on ships in the Indian Ocean.

I will not elaborate further with respect to this scenario. I am glad to report that all the objectives set by the president were achieved and enforced.

We had superior aircraft that were equipped with superior weapons and piloted by superior pilots. The combat forces were supported by superior battle-control centers operating in real time. Further, we had real-time assessment of damage to targets, as well as a planning system that could respond immediately to this information.

We had it all ways. By virtue of high-intensity operations, we gained air supremacy in a short time. Blue air forces attacked Red ground forces and other assets at will. Conversely, Red air did not—and could not—attack Blue assets. Blue ground forces could move at will, but Red ground forces could not and were forced to dig in.

We had correlation centers (especially AWACS, JSTARS, and the Rivet Joint electronic reconnaissance system) that could correlate and associate data—in near real time—from a myriad of sensors on board other platforms. This capability, coupled with the disruption and destruction of the enemy's structure for command and control, gained command, control, communications, and intelligence (C^3I) supremacy. This meant that Blue knew about Red activity and could act accordingly, but Red could do neither.

Because of all of the above—and especially because of very effective real-time battle control and shooters that could respond to this control—we had the initiative and the wherewithal to engage in high-intensity operations, to unhinge the enemy, and to gain objectives quickly and with minimal casualties. That is the real meaning of high intensity. We see now that intensity is not a sterile descriptor of conflict according to the size of opposing forces. Rather, high intensity describes tactics and operations of the superior force.

Lesser forces are relegated to low intensity or even none. Intensity modifies operations—nothing else.

Now, a brief digression as to the critical role the B-2 force played in slowing the advance of the invading armies.

Very effective weapons were employed on the B-2. Clever engineers had designed a smart submunition that was two things: It was quite small, but at the same time it was quite effective in one-on-one engagements against trucks and transporters and also against armored vehicles. Each B-2 carried several weapons, each weapon containing many of these smart submunitions, for a total of 800 submunitions per aircraft. Planners expected that—in the case of large columns of vehicles on roads—some 500 enemy vehicles would be at risk by each B-2 sortie and that one-third of these vehicles would be damaged or destroyed.

Clever engineers had also designed an extended-range, off-road mine, first conceived in the mid seventies. "Purposeful" planning coupled to a "streamlined" acquisition process had made it possible to put this mine into our operational forces in a little over 20 years. The killing element of this mine is a variant of the same smart submunition referenced above. Each B-2 carried several weapons containing mines, for a total of 500 mines, and—during each sortie—employed them along 25 kilometers of highway. They were activated at the appropriate time by a command from JSTARS. Planners expected the mines from each B-2 to create an ambush involving more than 500 enemy vehicles and, again, to damage or destroy one-third of them. Planners had considered employing these mines along selected highways even before border crossing by the Iraqi force. However, authority to do so was not forthcoming until just minutes prior to border crossing.

The first question: Are the capabilities described above mostly fantasy? The smart (and small) submunitions capable of killing trucks, transporters, and armored vehicles have been demonstrated. What is required is to provide the means of dispensing these submunitions in a somewhat ordered manner over their intended targets so that they can do their thing—engage and kill hot engines in the endgame.

The second question: Why was the B-2 force front and center in delaying the invasion forces early on? One, the B-2 had the range to operate from bases under our control (CONUS, Diego Garcia, and perhaps elsewhere). Two, the B-2—by virtue of low observables—could be used over enemy territory and enemy forces prior to our gaining air superiority. Three, the B-2 force could project enough firepower to make a significant difference in the rate of advance of the invading forces.

Cruise missiles from battleships, submarines, and other bombers were launched within hours against selected targets. However, the total capability provided by these force elements was limited. For example, the total number of smart submunitions carried aboard all the cruise missiles in each battleship was about the same as the total number of smart submunitions carried aboard all the weapons in each B-2 bomber. The capability per submarine was one-half that of each B-2. Also, the number of battleships and submarines "on station" at the beginning was limited. Once these ships completed their sortie (fired out their load of cruise missiles), the turnaround time for the next sortie was several days, compared to one or two days for the B-2s with their weapons and the high-observable bombers with their cruise missiles.

The third question: Why weren't there more ships and bombers with more cruise missiles in the first place? Years earlier someone in the Office of the Secretary of Defense commissioned a cost and operational effectiveness analysis. There were several inputs to this analysis.

First, some operational inputs. Low-observable bombers can operate in the vicinity of a target and, thus, use some form of a gravity weapon (i.e., bomb—a device with no propulsion). Because battleships and submarines cannot operate this way, they must use long-range standoff cruise missiles. Bombers with high observables must also use standoff cruise missiles until defense-suppression operations achieve air supremacy.

Now, some monetary inputs. Bombs—including smart bombs—do not cost much. Long-range cruise missiles cost a lot. Taking into account the number of weapons to be expended and the cost of smart bombs versus that of smart cruise missiles, it turned out that investing in a carrier that could use smart bombs (the B-2) in order to save on the cost of expended weapons was quite cost-effective. The crossover point was a dozen sorties (i.e., after a dozen B-2 sorties, the monies saved by using smart bombs instead of smart cruise missiles paid for acquiring the B-2 bomber in the first place). Besides, the B-2 puts a man on the scene who can react to real-time battle control. Controlling attacks on moving columns with JSTARS is straightforward for the case of the B-2. In contrast, cruise missiles could be targeted only against fixed targets of known status. Also, the B-2's sensors and crew allow the aircraft to accomplish its own targeting.

I have emphasized the relevance of having the "best" so that high-intensity operations are possible. This is somewhat at odds with analyses that focus on measures of merit such as "least cost per kill." Such measures are perhaps relevant if all "costs" are taken into account. Generally, however, the costs taken into account are strictly monetary and neglect the larger costs to the nation.

There may be "opportunity costs." The president might not commit the prestige and might of the United States because he was not confident that the military option was viable if it had to be executed—that is, not viable in the sense that the president was not confident the mean time to success by the military was comfortably shorter than the mean time to failure of congressional and public support. Worst still, the cost may be one of execution. The war could drag on, casualties could mount, public support would erode, and eventually the United States could fail to enforce the objectives stated by the president. In either case—"opportunity cost" or "execution cost"—leadership by the United States erodes, and the new world order becomes a blur.

Fielding forces that can engage in high-intensity operations does not come easily. Almost without exception, all of the so-called high-tech items in the war in the Persian Gulf were—at some stage or another—close to termination.

The AWACS is a case in point. In the early stages, some otherwise respected technical people said that it would not work. Amendments presented on the floor of the Senate to delete the program were only narrowly defeated. Fortunately, wisdom prevailed. Technical people worked diligently to establish proof-of-principle in such a fashion to finally mute the most fervent critics (i.e., to demonstrate it really was feasible to get 58 decibels of clutter rejection so that we could indeed detect and track low-flying aircraft against ground clutter from an airborne platform). At the same time, operators held the vision and concept that AWACS was to be the eyes of commanders around the world and would be central to the control of high-intensity, air-to-air operations in far-distant lands. We hope that such outcomes will be the case for programs in the years before us.

The decision by the president to announce to the world that he was committing the prestige and might of the United States to halt and reverse the invasion by Iraq was not easy. Central to such a decision and commitment and freedom of action was the conviction that if military action became necessary, our forces could achieve and enforce the stated objectives in a relatively short time with minimal casualties.

If the United States intends to play a central role in a new world order, then we must have a planning-and-acquisition process that ensures the president is backed by truly superior forces when aggressors sorely test our resolve in critical regions. If our military forces are not capable of high-intensity operations, the president will not be inclined to assert leadership and to assemble the political and military power to counter these aggressors. The rogues and tyrants will come to know this and act accordingly, much to the detriment of world stability and our own national interests.

Air Power in Low- and Midintensity Conflict

Gen Larry D. Welch, USAF, Retired

The first and most difficult of tasks in addressing this subject is to understand the nature and varieties of conflict. Given an understanding of the nature of the conflict, the task of describing the employment of air power is straightforward. Achieving that understanding is not so straightforward. The conventional wisdom is that economic and political approaches to resolving conflict are good and that military approaches are bad—the lower the level of military involvement, the better. That conventional wisdom persists, though repeatedly proved wrong. Economic and political solutions seldom stand alone, for reasons discussed in this essay. In contrast, appropriate military forces—in the 1980s and into the 1990s—in support of political objectives have produced decisive results. This essay discusses important changes in the nature of conflicts likely to involve the United States. The following summary of trends introduces the subject:

- Emphasis on low-intensity conflict (LIC) over the past 40 years grew out of the US focus on opposing Soviet-sponsored insurgencies. Opposing insurgencies was considered an essential element of underwriting the policy of containment. With the collapse of the Warsaw Pact, together with the Soviet and Chinese preoccupation with internal challenges, communism has been discredited as a viable basis for national modernization. The Soviet Union and China no longer have either the capability or the interest to export revolution.

- Low-intensity conflict solutions have never been particularly effective. Most of the problems addressed as LIC have either been too big—forcing military escalation—or beyond military solution (e.g., essentially internal political or economic problems). Economic and political approaches to dealing with underlying causes of conflict have been neither sustainable nor effective.

- Since the Vietnam War, there has been a tendency in the LIC community to regard special operations forces (SOF) as linked primarily to LIC. US planners need to treat SOF and LIC as the separate entities they are—not as synonymous. Special operations forces are designed and sized for operations across the spectrum of conflict.
- For a variety of reasons, future US military involvement is likely to escalate quickly into the realm of midintensity conflict. There are large and formidable forces in areas where the issues are intense and intractable—the Middle East and South Asia. In other areas, the proliferation of modern weapons will place them in the hands of even politically and economically unsophisticated nations.
- The conventional descriptions of levels of conflict (low, mid, high) are less and less related to the level and sophistication of forces employed. There is an increased US willingness to commit overwhelming forces at any level of conflict to control the level of violence and to resolve the issue quickly.
- There has been a quantum increase in the effectiveness of air power since the Vietnam War. Air power is well suited to the preferred "American way of war": short, decisive, as bloodless as possible for US ground forces, with limited long-term military liability. Air power can move in and out quickly.

The term *air power* is used in its broadest sense. It includes the air assets of the four services, including armed helicopters; strategic and tactical airlift; space and airborne surveillance; command, control, and communications; and other air-support assets.

Evolving United States Policy

The most basic US policy calling for air power capabilities in low- and midintensity conflict situations rests on a commitment to a community of free nations with open political systems. For more than 40 years, US policymakers perceived the Soviet and Chinese Communist systems to be the principal threats to free nations and open political systems. Consequently, fear of Soviet and Chinese expansion shaped the US policy toward low- and midintensity conflict.

After 18 months of observing Soviet expansion following World War II, the United States sought a countervailing policy. The Truman Doctrine, proclaimed in 1947, was intended to contain expansion to the south. While the Marshall Plan served broader objectives, an important element was containing expansion to the west. United States policymakers saw evidence of a monolithic strategy of communist expansion in the defeat of the Chinese Nationalists, revolutions in Southeast Asia, and the invasion of South Korea. Finally, as the true nature of Castro's government in Cuba emerged—followed by revolutions in Latin and Central America—containing communism became a global American policy.[1] The Eisenhower Doctrine rounded out the policy to include a joint resolution of Congress in 1957 declaring that the independence of Middle Eastern nations was vital to American interests.[2] The 1957 resolution "'authorize[d]' the President to use American armed forces 'as he deems necessary' to defend the Middle East nations 'requesting such aid against overt armed aggression from any nation controlled by international Communism'."[3] The 1957 resolution rounded out the policy and the basis for appropriate forces to underwrite the policy of meeting aggression across the scale of conflict.

It would be difficult to overstate the degree to which containing communism dominated US attitudes toward insurgencies and revolutions. A 1986 speech by Secretary of Defense Caspar Weinberger illustrated the continuing preoccupation with the Soviet menace as the justification for US interest in LIC. He declared that "tonight, one out of every four countries around the globe is at war. In virtually every case, there is a mask on the face of war. In virtually every case, behind the mask is the Soviet Union and those who do its bidding."[4]

This preoccupation with communism as the predominant force behind insurgency can obscure the reality that revolts, coups, and insurrections are as old as history. There is also the danger that overstating the Soviet role in LIC and insurgencies could eliminate US interest in other causes of LIC in the face of a receding Soviet empire. The sheer number of conflicts would demand continuing attention. The Department of Defense (DOD) estimates that there have been some 1,200 conflicts since World War II, with about 80 percent classified as low intensity.[5] Most of the rest qualify as midintensity.

The Definition Challenge

History has confirmed the wisdom of Clausewitz's advice that "the first, the supreme, the most far-reaching act of judgement that the statesman and commander have to make is to establish . . . the kind of war on which they are embarking; neither mistaking it for, nor trying to turn it into, something that is alien to its nature."[6] Unfortunately, the terms *low-intensity conflict* and *midintensity conflict* do not promote understanding of the kind of war under consideration. While it is neither possible nor useful to settle on a precise definition of low-intensity conflict, there needs to be at least a description of the relevant characteristics. The official definition describes LIC as a

> political-military confrontation between contending states or groups below conventional war and above the routine, peaceful competition among states. It frequently involves protracted struggles of competing principles and ideologies. **Low intensity conflict** ranges from subversion to the use of armed force.[7]

Others would define LIC by various limits. Sam Sarkesian and others suggest defining limits on geographic area and number of participants, with political-psychological dimensions predominating over tactical considerations. He goes further to suggest that low-intensity conflicts are usually limited wars or revolutionary or counterrevolutionary wars. He also expresses a strong preference for special operations forces over conventional forces.[8]

In attempting to define the kind of war being considered, one may find it equally useful to say what LIC is not. LIC does not equal SOF.

Further, special operations is not a mission; rather, special operations forces provide capabilities in support of a variety of missions. US special operations forces are sized and equipped for roles across the spectrum to include a major role in high-intensity conflict. In the most recent midintensity to high-intensity conflict in the Persian Gulf region, SOF played major roles in supporting or supplementing the air campaign. One of those roles was locating and designating targets for attack by precision guided conventional weapons.

Conversely, conventional forces have predominated in recent LIC situations: the counterterrorist strike against Libya, the 1987 crisis in the Persian Gulf, the rescue operation in Grenada, and the operation in Panama. Some of the most sophisticated conventional air power capabilities in the US forces—two carrier battle groups, F-111F fighter aircraft, precision guided bombs, EA-6B jamming aircraft, KC-10 tanker aircraft, and so forth—were used to carry out the limited raid against Libya.

Nor is LIC necessarily low in the intensity of military violence or the severity of military consequences. Those consequences are likely to be asymmetrical. In the operation against Panama—from the US viewpoint—only modest forces were employed, with little long-term effect on those forces. In contrast, for the Panamanian Defense Force, the operation eliminated their capability and role as a military force. In the Vietnam conflict—in contrast to the US low-intensity view (some would say midintensity)—Gen Van Tien Dung, commander of Hanoi's final offensive, believed that his purpose was to destroy the enemy's political and military system—a dual purpose of clearly high-intensity proportions.[9]

LIC extends into at least midintensity levels of force and military violence. Unconventional warfare and employment of SOF stretch across the spectrum from low- to very high-intensity conflict. So LIC is not adequately characterized by the forces involved, the geographic area encompassed, or the level of violence.

To define the kind of war represented by LIC, then, one finds that the most useful distinction may be the primacy of political considerations in both the purposes and execution of operations—

whatever their size and scope. Furthermore, a country may wage LIC without employing military force, relying—at least for a time—on political, economic, and diplomatic means, as well as the coercive power of the threat of military force.

In contrast to LIC, describing midintensity conflict has received short shrift from most writers addressing the spectrum of conflict. For purposes of this essay, I describe midintensity conflict as conflict between significant opposing military forces short of a superpower confrontation. Midintensity military operations are conducted to achieve a political end by destroying or neutralizing a significant part of the opponent's military force or other assets he values.

Military forces, at all levels of conflict, are employed to achieve political ends. In contrast to LIC, military considerations in midintensity conflict are at least coequal with political considerations and can predominate in the actual conduct of military operations.

Special Operations Issue

In response to the abiding confusion on the roles of SOF, it is useful to stress those roles again. The proliferation of sophisticated military capabilities and the trend toward higher levels of conflict and violence increase the need for the specialized capabilities of SOF. Still, the record of support for those capabilities has not been a good one, and there remains a need for continuing special emphasis.

Concerned with perceived apathy toward SOF, Congress enacted the Cohen-Nunn Amendment in 1987. The purpose of the law was to mandate attention to the funding, structure, and readiness of SOF. Specifically, that legislation requires (1) an assistant secretary of defense of special operations and low-intensity conflict, (2) a unified combatant command for SOF, and (3) a board for low-intensity conflict within the National Security Council. The bill also suggested the creation of a deputy assistant to the president for national security affairs for low-intensity conflict, which was not implemented.[10]

There was immediate concern expressed about the Cohen-Nunn Amendment by opposite constituencies—people who opposed elevating the status of special operations and LIC and people most interested in expanding the capabilities of SOF across the spectrum of conflict. The title of the new assistant secretary was seen as adding to erroneous perceptions that SOF is a mission instead of a set of capabilities; that SOF is somehow more closely linked to LIC than to midintensity and high-intensity conflict; and that LIC can be pursued without employing sophisticated conventional forces.

In testimony to the Senate Armed Services Committee in January 1987, before enactment of the amendment, Gen Paul Gorman reminded the committee that special operations forces have missions across the spectrum of war. Both US and Soviet SOF were conceived for the apocalyptic contingencies of high-intensity conflict in central Europe and the western Pacific. Most special operations forces have little to do with countering guerrillas or terrorism.[11]

In spite of these difficulties, the assistant secretary and the unified command fill important needs. Consistent, institutional advocates for special operations capabilities now have a voice in the highest DOD councils. The unified command leverages the capabilities of service SOF components with better joint training and cooperation. The result has been a significant improvement in focus on needed special operations capabilities. The assistant secretary also provides a more effective focal point for DOD to work with the Departments of State, Treasury, Justice, Transportation, and Commerce, as well as the Drug Enforcement Agency, US Information Agency, Central Intelligence Agency, and other agencies to coordinate the political, economic, and military dimensions of LIC.

United States Strategy and Experience in Low-Intensity Conflict

The national security strategy statement of January 1987 relates a basic objective of the US, with regard to countries facing LIC:

When it is in U.S. interest to do so, the United States:

- Will take measures to strengthen friendly nations facing internal or external threats to their independence and stability by systematically employing, in coordination with friends and allies, the full range of political, economic, informational, and military instruments of power. Where possible, action will be taken before instability leads to violence.

- Will work to ameliorate the underlying causes of instability and conflict in the Third World by pursuing foreign assistance, trade, and investment programs that promote economic development and the growth of democratic social and political orders.[12]

Help from Economic Support and Security Assistance

The basic policy and strategy statements stress the need to help address internal economic causes of instability. It is equally clear that it is in our national interest to help strengthen the military capabilities of friends and allies facing external military threats. Still, even when there was a high propensity to consider insurgencies important to US national interests, the US record in delivering economic and security assistance has not supported the declaratory strategy that emphasizes such help. The United States has not been successful in buying stability with economic or security assistance.

There are few questions about the continuing potential for instabilities resulting from economic desperation. Almost one-half of the population of sub-Saharan Africa and South Asia and over one-third of the population of Latin America live in absolute poverty.[13] Per capita income is shrinking in sub-Saharan Africa and Latin America and is stagnant in Eastern Europe.[14] The Agency for International Development currently characterizes some 46 countries as recent problem nations. That group posted an average economic growth of 2.3 percent per year from 1972 to 1979 and an average decline of 1.74 percent from 1978 to 1987.[15] Long-term debt, a source of both economic difficulty and Southern Hemisphere resentment of their Northern counterparts, is also a growing problem. For the 46 nations mentioned above, long-term debt grew from $93 billion in

1975 to $549 billion in 1987. Debt service now demands over 45 percent of Argentina's export income and over 25 percent of the export incomes of Brazil, Colombia, Mexico, and Turkey.[16]

The US response to these growing needs has been economic and security assistance that is more restrictive and less generous.[17] The report of the House Committee on Appropriations of the 100th Congress succinctly describes Congress's attitude toward helping friends and allies with security assistance:

> Basically, the reductions to foreign assistance programs reflect the relative priorities of Congress given the overall budget constraints. The Administration has consistently failed to acknowledge this reality and last year responded to Congress' reductions . . . by skewing the country allocations and submitted a $1.2 billion supplemental budget request. . . . However, the . . . submission of a large supplemental request at a time when domestic spending programs are suffering continued drastic reductions shows a failure on the part of the Administration to acknowledge the implications of the passage of the Gramm-Rudman-Hollings legislation.[18]

The skewing referenced in the House report is the large share of the security-assistance budget earmarked for Egypt, Israel, Greece, Turkey, and Pakistan—leaving very little for the rest of the globe. In aggregate—since 1985—bilateral assistance to all countries has been cut by 21 percent. Assistance to nations facing LIC threats has declined by almost 45 percent.[19]

It seems then, that however desirable and sensible the strategy of addressing root economic and political causes may be, it is a forlorn hope. It is just possible that buying the third world out of its economic quandary is beyond the means of even the most generous and affluent nations. Given the fact that we must maintain strong military capabilities for other reasons, the marginal cost of their use may be more affordable—though less satisfying—than adequate economic aid. In any case, there is a greater likelihood of a continuing—perhaps expanding—need to support US political aims with military forces appropriate to the level of conflict.

Help from Military Forces

The preferred role of military forces in addressing any level of conflict is deterrence. But historical experience shows that the effectiveness of the deterrent strategy varies roughly with the level of conflict. It works well at the high end of the scale but poorly at the low end.

The consequences of a failure of deterrence are also proportional to the level of conflict—at least in the near term to midterm. Further, the predictability of consequences is also proportional to the level of conflict. Failure to deter strategic nuclear conflict is immediately and inevitably disastrous. In contrast, the consequence of failure to deter or even respond quickly to low-intensity situations is neither immediate nor predictable. Expanding, interlocking future events drive long-term results. For example, the US failure to win a military victory in Vietnam had serious domestic consequences but did not, over the longer term, seriously affect US international interests (the economic consequence of the approach to financing the war is another matter). Furthermore, the US failure did not provide lasting benefit to the principals—the Soviet Union and China—who supported the adversary.

The decision to commit US military forces—in other than advisory roles—to help friendly governments that are resisting insurgency or revolution is a complex matter. The need for such a decision results from failure to respond effectively to the political and economic causes of insurgency and revolution. Given such failure, US history gives little cause to expect that low-level assistance from US military forces will turn the tide.

The longer, fuller British and French experiences would further lower expectations of success. David Charters points out that between the end of World War II and the end of 1982, British forces had carried out 94 operational commitments worldwide. Of these, only three—Korea, Suez, and the Falklands—involved combat in conventional, if undeclared, wars. Some involved significant forces—two and one-half divisions in Palestine and 21,000 troops in Northern Ireland in 1972.[20] With rare exceptions—Malaysia, for example—

most of these experiences, along with the French experiences in Indochina and Algeria, were no more successful than our experience in Vietnam.

In November 1984 Secretary of Defense Caspar Weinberger indirectly suggested that the heavily political nature of such conflict often precludes successful commitment of US military forces. He set forth the following conditions for committing military forces:

- Existence of a particular engagement or occasion deemed vital to our national interest or that of our allies.
- Wholehearted commitment, with the clear intent of winning.
- Clear definition of political and military objectives.
- Forces capable of doing the job.
- Reassessment and adjustment of committed forces to meet combat requirements.
- Reasonable assurance of support of the American people and Congress.[21]

Those conditions are likely to be incompatible with a long-term commitment to patient—often frustrating—military operations, carefully integrated with political approaches. Yet that commitment is required if one is to prevail in countering insurgencies and revolutions. Again, without a vigorous accompanying political and economic commitment, the probability of sustaining those conditions falls to near zero.

Shift from Counterinsurgency to Broader Interests

In spite of the frustrating history of involvement in counterinsurgency, the commitment to containment continued to sustain a high propensity to become involved. However, accelerating events—increasingly apparent since the mid-1980s—leading to the complete collapse of the Warsaw Pact have fundamentally altered the situation. The perception of a monolithic—or even fragmented—communist world promoting wars of liberation and otherwise threatening the stability of free nations has very nearly disappeared. Internal matters increasingly occupy Soviet attention. Cuba, with the loss of much of its earlier Soviet support, is much less inclined to foreign adventures. The need for economic modernization and internal stability consumes the attention of the government in Beijing. Communism has been widely discredited as a political and economic system. In view of these events, containment seems a far less relevant task—a situation that challenges the legitimacy of what has been almost automatic US opposition to many insurgencies.

Even so, without Soviet agitation, economic and political pressures will continue to foment threats to stable, open governments throughout the third world. In the Middle East and Persian Gulf regions, Islamic fundamentalism, uneven oil wealth, historical animosities—those directed toward former colonial powers and those within the Arab world—and the Arab-Israeli conflict will continue to generate high tensions. Recent events show that, even when the Soviets cooperate with moderate governments, these regional tensions will continue to threaten the stability of friendly governments. In Latin America, there has been a gratifying movement to representative governments. Still, heavy debt, stagnated economies, and deteriorating quality of life make the region highly unstable. The African continent continues to seethe with insurgency and economic failure, all of which suggests that the US cannot leave the outcome of LIC situations to divine providence. However, the policy and the capabilities required to deal with those and other conditions extend well beyond most definitions of LIC.

Changing Conditions of Conflict

Over the past decade, conflict that threatens friends and allies has tended to polarize toward extremes. At the low end, international, state-sponsored terrorism has been an important feature. Terrorism is particularly resistant to the strategy of deterrence or the effective employment of military forces. The Israelis have followed a policy of rapid retaliation to deter terrorist attacks for almost 40 years but continue to suffer frequent acts of terrorism.

The US has devoted significant resources and attention to forces designed to counter acts of terrorism; these include a well-trained, well-equipped hostage-rescue team. Yet, there remains only a scant likelihood of a successful US hostage rescue on foreign soil. Friendly governments involved are usually unwilling to accept visible assistance from US forces. The retaliatory air attack on Libya seems to have been somewhat more effective in discouraging Libyan-sponsored terrorism. Still, that single experience is not sufficient to draw any general conclusions.

None of this suggests that we can forgo providing the most effective achievable counterterrorist capability, including special operations air support. It does suggest that preventive measures and law enforcement agencies are probably more effective in combatting terrorism than are military forces—even well-conceived and well-trained special forces.

At the other end of the low- to midintensity spectrum, there are at least three trends that shift the likely nature of conflict toward higher levels. These trends will also tend to raise the potential level of military violence and the need to involve more sophisticated air power. They are as follows:

- A lower propensity to engage in counterinsurgency for all the reasons stated earlier.
- The tendency of the proliferation of high-technology weapons to drive the level of military violence into the midintensity category. (This tendency will persist even when political objectives dominate—a common criterion for LIC.)
- The growth in quantity and quality of regional military forces in the hands of belligerent governments.

The increased lethality of available conventional weapons is a major factor in the likely escalation of the level of conflict and military violence. The Exocet missile in the 1987 Persian Gulf crisis and the Stinger missile used by Afghan rebels had major impacts on the nature of those conflicts. The easy manufacture of chemical weapons, coupled with expanding third-world access to short- to medium-range ballistic and cruise missiles, adds the prospect of new levels of escalation in third-world conflicts. Nor is there any likelihood of reversing this trend. The US, the Soviet Union, and

Western Europe are the principal suppliers, and there is some—though remote—possibility of an agreement among these powers to curtail proliferation. Yet Brazil, Israel, China, India, and Argentina are also major suppliers, and all are committed to both the technological and economic benefits of high-technology arms industries beyond that required to satisfy national needs.

To illustrate the level of arms-transfer activity from 1982 to 1989, one may note that Saudi Arabia and Iraq each spent over $40 billion and that India imported $18.5 billion, in addition to its internal production. Iran, Syria, Cuba, Vietnam, Afghanistan, and Angola each exceeded $10 billion in military imports. The total in transfers to major buyers reached almost 11,000 tanks and self-propelled guns, some 21,000 artillery pieces, and almost 34,000 surface-to-air missiles.[22] From 1968 to 1990, the Iraqi army grew from 70,000 men and 600 tanks to 1 million men and 5,500 tanks. Syria grew from 50,000 men and one mechanized division to 300,000 men and over 4,000 tanks.[23]

Given the abiding issues and the proliferation of military capabilities, conflicts in Southwest Asia/the Middle East are likely to escalate quickly to the high end of the midintensity conflict scale. There is also the constant risk of escalation to weapons of mass destruction. Chemical/biological weapons are already in the hands of third-world military forces. It seems only a matter of time before nuclear weapons and the means to deliver them are also in the hands of some unstable third-world nations. United States Army technology planners project that early in the twenty-first century, some 20 countries could have chemical/biological weapons; between 10 and 20 could have tactical nuclear weapons; and 15 will be able to produce ballistic missiles.[24]

Air Power in Support of Low- and Midintensity Operations in the 1980s

The role of military forces in addressing low- and midintensity conflict is to persuade nations with interests divergent from those of the US to change course to more compatible approaches. If that fails, the purpose is then to compel those nations whose actions threaten the US and its friends to adopt a course of action compatible with the interests of the US and our allies.[25] While deterrence has not been particularly successful in precluding conflicts that threaten US interests, continuing the deterrent theme to various levels of coercion holds more promise. The objective is to employ political, economic, and military means to raise the cost of continuing action contrary to US interests and to lower the cost of cooperating with US interests.

Ideally, diplomatic, political, and economic coercion could preclude the need for use of military force. Even so, the threat of using military force is likely to greatly enhance diplomatic and political pressure. However, the urgency of the objective—often driven by domestic politics or international alliances—drives the degree to which the nation can afford to wait for the impact of nonmilitary forms of coercion. For example, the Libyan-sponsored attack against Americans resulted in almost immediate escalation to the retaliatory strike against Libya.[26] In the recent Gulf crisis, the coalition applied the full range of coercive pressures to persuade Iraq to leave Kuwait. But domestic and international pressures precluded giving diplomatic and economic coercion time to prove itself either effective or ineffective.

Finally, when clear national interest satisfies Secretary Weinberger's first premise—an occasion deemed vital to the US—and when other forms of coercion fail, US policy is to follow the other four precepts articulated in Secretary Weinberger's 1984 speech.[27] Similar concepts guided the development and training of forces and characterized the four principal uses of military force in the past decade. In each case, the forces decisively achieved the goals of the military operation.

The Minimum-Force Issue

The writings of the past two decades are replete with admonishments about the need for minimum force in LIC situations, emphasizing instead the need to win hearts and minds with minimum use of violence. These writings often oppose any introduction of conventional forces into LIC situations. In this respect, many highly vocal critics of conventional thinking have themselves become victims of stagnated thinking. Minimum violence should not be presumed to result from the use of minimum force. Experience has shown that the "number of troops required to control a given situation goes up as the amount of force which . . . is politically acceptable . . . goes down." [28]

Public patience—particularly the public patience of Americans—can also strongly drive the demand for forces to rapidly resolve the situation. Long-suffering approaches are not an American strong suit. Where US involvement is warranted—at any level of conflict—both the American psyche and experiences over the past decade argue for overwhelming—not minimum—force to control the level and duration of violence.

The demonstration of precise and devastating air attacks in the 1990 Panama operation and the 1991 Persian Gulf war adds a new dimension to the minimum-force issue. Air power can be used across the spectrum to apply maximum force to an objective of any size—from a single building to a massive army—with minimum risk of domestic political fallout and minimum collateral damage in the target area.

Grenada and Panama

Political considerations were overriding in the Grenada and Panama situations and dictated the objectives and the constraints on the employment of military forces. Yet, in contradiction to the LIC concepts of prior decades, the clear need for carefully measured force and minimum violence did not translate to either minimum forces or to a gradual buildup of forces. In both cases, conventional and special operations airlift delivered clearly overwhelming ground forces. In Panama, AC-130 gunships, A-37s, and F-117 fighter aircraft supported both conventional ground forces and SOF. That combined strength quickly overwhelmed opposition, with minimum military losses on both sides and minimum damage to the civilian community.

The Panama experience illustrates the likelihood that low-intensity conflict will escalate before resolution. After a decade of low-intensity political, economic, and occasionally military activity, Manuel Noriega's response was increasing arrogance. That arrogance translated to increased frequency and scope of officially sanctioned harassment and violence against US forces in Panama.

Unfortunately, conditions in Panama since Operation Just Cause also provide another example of failure to leverage successful military operations with a continuing commitment to economic and political support. Thus, the underlying obstacles to stable representative government are not addressed. The government of President Guillermo Endara continues to struggle with little tangible support from the US and with little prospect for a lasting, robust representative government in Panama.

In both the Grenada and Panama operations, special operations played key roles in supporting conventional operations. In both cases, success depended on closely integrating special operations with conventional operations under a single commander and operating within a single command-and-control structure.

1987 Persian Gulf Crisis

The 1987 Persian Gulf crisis demanded a new dimension in joint Navy and Air Force air power employment. Political sensitivity on the Arabian Peninsula precluded basing US land-based combat aircraft to meet the need for air coverage to help protect sea-lanes. Geography made it impractical for carrier-based air to provide the necessary coverage without support of land-based air-refueling tankers. The combination of carrier-based combat aircraft supported by land-based tanker and surveillance aircraft provided the solution. The combination clearly conveyed US capabilities and commitment to both belligerents. The US presence protected shipping and significantly lowered the level of violence on Gulf waters. Although the situation was resolved at low-intensity levels of violence, it required midintensity force levels and high-intensity air power capabilities.

The 1990–91 Persian Gulf War

While some people would argue that the Persian Gulf war went beyond even midintensity conflict, it passed through almost every stage from diplomatic and economic coercion to various levels of armed conflict. That conflict provides several important lessons about dealing with low- and midintensity conflict situations. At each level—beginning with the April 1990 Arab League meeting in Vienna—there was a perceived opportunity to use coercive power short of military action, first to protect and then to liberate Kuwait without further escalation. In retrospect, coercive power was not credible to Saddam Hussein. He clearly did not perceive that his invasion of Kuwait would be of vital interest to the US and Saudi Arabia.

It is probably futile to attempt to divide the Gulf war into low-, mid-, or high-intensity phases. Iraq opened the conflict with total war against Kuwait and pursued that total-war policy until the retreat on 28 February 1991. The coalition response initially employed the tools of LIC—the coercive power of diplomatic, political, and economic actions and the threat of military force.

With the failure of diplomatic efforts to forestall armed conflict, US over-the-horizon presence needed rapid upgrade to highly visible capability on the scene. Air Force tactical fighter squadrons and light Army forces that can be quickly airlifted, as well as Marine expeditionary forces afloat in the area, provide the worldwide capability to do that. Carrier air provides additional firepower on arrival in the area.

By the fall of 1990, there was little belief in the near-term effectiveness of measures short of armed conflict. That led to the decision, announced on 8 November 1990, to raise the ante to overwhelming military forces in place in Saudi Arabia and environs.

By then, most participants and observers had concluded that at least midintensity combat was very likely. Still, even after the onset of a massive air campaign, some hoped that the coercive power of formidable ground forces—poised for action—would lead Saddam Hussein to conclude that the cost of continuing to occupy Kuwait would be unbearable.

The 38-day air campaign concentrated land-based tactical fighter forces, carrier-based air, and long-range bombers in an intense campaign to destroy Iraq's ability to fight effectively. Following the air campaign, coalition ground forces completed the defeat of a 42-division force in about 100 hours with fewer than 300 Americans killed and wounded. In the face of this overwhelming success, it is easy to overlook the lack of other options. Air power had to buy time to continue to deploy, position, and prepare ground forces for the ground campaign. Only air power—rapidly deployable land-based and carrier air present in the area—can be ready to engage in intense combat at a moment's notice. As in this case, air power may initially be employed with apparent autonomy. Further, air power can be decisive in that it could assure the eventual outcome. Even so, the end objective is most likely to be to shape the battlefield for an eventual ground campaign to control the resolution of the conflict. It is difficult to imagine that Saddam Hussein failed to see that the Iraqi army would become weaker and weaker while the coalition forces became stronger and stronger. Still, he did not capitulate until his forces were physically overrun by ground forces.

Some would blame the escalation on a mutual miscalculation by both sides that somehow could have been avoided through diplomatic and political means. But after the invasion on 2 August 1990 it is not clear that miscalculation strongly drove the developing situation. The coalition nations could never accept a world in which Saddam Hussein dominated the Persian Gulf region. Feeding on oil riches, he could have increasingly intimidated neighboring states, eventually dominating the Middle East. At the same time, there may have been no way out for Saddam Hussein that was less costly than near-term loss of power. In such circumstances wherein vital interests are in such opposition, conflict is likely to escalate to the limit of the weaker side's capabilities.

The lesson is that it is dangerous to assume—in the face of failure at the political level—that important situations can be resolved with military force at the LIC level. The more general lesson from the conflicts of the past decade is the likelihood of the demand for a full range of air power capabilities. The overarching US policy to promote the growth of free and open societies is likely to invoke that demand from the low end of LIC to the high end of midintensity conflict. Midintensity conflict stretches to levels of force and violence characterizing twentieth-century conflicts in the Middle East/Persian Gulf regions. Therefore, the ability to distinguish sharply between levels of conflict is less important than ensuring the appropriate spectrum of strategies and force capabilities.

Command and Control of Low- and Midintensity Forces

There have long been troublesome questions about who is in charge when military forces are involved in low- and midintensity situations. The answers tend to be the most complicated at the lower levels of conflict. Who, for example, is responsible for supporting the national effort in Central America: CINCSOUTH? CINCLANT? The regional assistant secretary of state? An interdepartmental task force? The National Security Council? Individual ambassadors heading country teams? The lack of unity at the national and regional levels makes a difficult task far more difficult.[29]

The command-and-control challenge for LIC includes the need for military forces to be effectively integrated with political and economic aims. It also includes the need for unconventional operations to be effectively integrated with conventional forces. At the lowest end of the scale, political and economic factors dominate. As the intensity of conflict moves up the scale, military considerations become more important. The difficulty is that some—the most consequential—modern-day conflicts run the gamut, over time, from political and economic dominance to military dominance. Further, modern-day conflicts involving US military forces employ both SOF and conventional forces. Therefore, the command-and-control arrangement must accommodate the spectrum of forces.

The Vietnam War experience burned important military-political lessons into the souls of today's senior military leaders. Many of these officers were battalion, squadron, and ship commanders during that conflict. Among the overarching maxims taught by that war are the following:

- No one can intelligently plan and direct combat operations from Washington, D.C. (or any place removed from the theater of operations). President Lyndon Johnson's reported boast that "not even an outhouse" was struck in Vietnam without his personal involvement was an indictment of his relationship with his military commanders.
- Combat operations call for the best equipment and training that the nation's technology can produce. The most demanding tasks demand optimized systems.
- There is no place in combat theaters for parochial service interests. The theater commander must have the authority to subjugate perceived service interests to the larger theater objectives.
- To be effective, an air campaign must be a well-coordinated effort responding to the direction of the theater commander through the air-component commander. The same need applies, though less dramatically, to the ground campaign.

Three out of the above four maxims demand that, once significant military forces are committed, there be an unequivocal answer to the question, Who is in charge? Presidents Reagan and Bush have provided such an answer in the 1980s and extending into the 1990s. Civilian leaders set the objectives, define the constraints, approve the forces to be employed, and hold military leaders accountable. But a single military commander is in charge of the combat operations of US forces. The theater commander has full authority over component commands and forces. That authority was contested in the 1987 Persian Gulf crisis. Fortunately, the result was an unmistakable demonstration that component commanders answer to the theater commander. In both the Panama and the 1990–91 Persian Gulf crisis, there was clear unity of command under a single theater commander.

Given the renewed dedication to that long-proven military principle, the combatant command role of US Special Operations Command could create confusion. Fortunately, it does not cause difficulty in practice. The services remain responsible for organizing, training, and equipping SOF. The unified command ensures that worldwide requirements receive proper attention by the services and advocates those requirements to the services and the Office of the Secretary of Defense. The unified command also ensures that component-command capabilities meet the standards required for global demand. However, for other than very special and limited missions, SOF objectives and operations are integrated with theater forces and are under the command of the theater commander. It cannot sensibly be otherwise.

Summary

From the mid-1950s to the mid-1980s, the policy of containing communism fed preoccupation with the causes and consequences of insurgencies. By the late 1980s, that concern had receded with the decline of Soviet and Chinese interest in wars of national liberation.

Even in the days of maximum concern over insurgencies, the US found that the preferred economic and political approaches to dealing with underlying causes were neither sustainable nor effective. Nor has the consequent resort to low-level military means provided satisfying results. There is nothing to suggest any near-term renewed commitment to adequate political and economic means. There is much to suggest that causes of conflict will continue and intensify. Abiding tensions and genuine conflicts of interest will continue to breed the conditions for low- to midintensity conflict in the Middle East, Southwest Asia, Africa, and South Asia.

There has been an unwarranted tendency to regard special operations forces as linked primarily to low-intensity conflict. Special operations forces—always designed and sized for operations across the spectrum of conflict—will need to continue to provide specialized capabilities from the lowest to the highest levels of conflict. The challenge of focusing attention on needed special capabilities will continue to require special emphasis.

The conventional descriptions of levels of conflict—low, mid, high—are almost unrelated to the level and sophistication of forces employed and less and less related to the level of military violence. The proliferation of modern weapons and growth of regional military forces are likely to lead to rapid escalation of the level of conflict and an increased level of military violence at all levels of conflict. The US will increasingly need to size and configure US air power for midintensity levels of conflict and high levels of violence.

There is an increased US willingness to commit overwhelming forces to control the level of violence and to resolve the issue quickly. Minimum-force approaches and gradualism have been thoroughly discredited in the eyes of both political and military leaders.

Too many of our conceptions of how to use air power are based on experience that is no longer relevant. There has been a quantum increase in the effectiveness of air power since the Vietnam War. Saddam Hussein discovered too late that the power of the triad of modern, conventional combat air forces—heavy bombers, land-based tactical air, and aircraft carrier-based forces—is devastating. Air power will still be used to shape the battlefield for ground forces. In most cases, only ground forces can complete a clean and full resolution of the military situation. Although the basic role of air power in low- to midintensity conflict may not change, its decisiveness has already changed the nature of war.

Notes

1. Sam C. Sarkesian, "The American Response to Low-Intensity Conflict: The Formative Period," in *Armies in Low-Intensity Conflict: A Comparative Analysis*, ed. David A. Charters and Maurice Tugwell (London: Brassey's Defence Publishers, 1989), 22–24.

2. Ibid., 25.

3. Paul Y. Hammond, *Cold War and Détente: The American Foreign Policy Process since 1945* (New York: Harcourt Brace Jovanovich, Inc., 1975), 124.

4. Caspar W. Weinberger, secretary of defense, "The Phenomenon of Low-Intensity Warfare," speech to the Conference on Low-Intensity Warfare, National Defense University, Washington, D.C., 14 January 1986.

5. R. Lynn Rylander, deputy director for special planning, International Security Affairs, "Tools of War/Skills of Peace: The US Response to Low-Intensity Conflict," speech to the Ninth Air University Air Power Symposium, Maxwell AFB, Ala., 11 March 1985.

6. Carl von Clausewitz, *On War*, ed. and trans. Michael Howard and Peter Paret (Princeton, N.J.: Princeton University Press, 1976), 88.

7. Joint Publication 1-02, *Department of Defense Dictionary of Military and Associated Terms*, 1 December 1989, 212.

8. Sam C. Sarkesian, "Organizational Strategy and Low-Intensity Conflicts," in *Special Operations in US Strategy*, ed. Frank R. Barnett, B. Hugh Tovar, and Richard H. Shultz (Washington, D.C.: National Defense University Press, 1984), 263–89.

9. Stanley Karnow, *Vietnam: A History* (New York: Viking Press, 1983), 660.

10. The Cohen-Nunn Amendment to the National Defense Authorization Act for Fiscal Year 1987.

11. "Military Strategy for Low-Intensity Conflicts," in *National Security Strategy: Hearings before the Committee on Armed Services, United States Senate*, 100th Cong.; 1st sess.; 12–14, 20–21, 27–28 January; 3, 23 February; 25, 30 March; 3 April 1987; 749–801.

12. Ronald Reagan, *National Security Strategy of the United States* (Washington, D.C.: The White House, January 1987), 33.

13. The World Bank, *World Development Report 1990* (Oxford: Oxford University Press, 1990), 5.

14. Ibid., 9–11.

15. Alan Woods, *Development and the National Interest: U.S. Economic Assistance into the 21st Century* (Washington, D.C.: Agency for International Development, 1989), 3–6.

16. Ibid., 131, 144.

17. Ibid., 12–17.

18. House Committee on Appropriations, *Report to Accompany H.R. 3186*, 100th Cong., 1st sess., 1987, 8.

19. Michael W. S. Ryan, "Foreign Assistance and Low-Intensity Conflict," in *Low-Intensity Conflict: The Pattern of Warfare in the Modern World*, ed. Loren B. Thompson (Lexington, Mass.: Lexington Books, 1989), 168.

20. David A. Charters, "From Palestine to Northern Ireland: British Adaptation to Low-Intensity Operations," in *Armies in Low-Intensity Conflict*, 171.

21. Caspar W. Weinberger, "The Uses of Military Power," speech to the National Press Club, Washington, D.C., 28 November 1984.

22. Richard F. Grimmett, *Trends in Conventional Arms Transfers to the Third World by Major Supplier: 1982–1989* (Washington, D.C.: Congressional Research Service, Library of Congress, June 1990), 66–67.

23. Department of the Army, *Army Technology Base Master Plan* (U), vol. 1 (Washington, D.C.: Department of the Army, 7 November 1990), I-2. (Unclassified version)

24. Ibid.; see also Charles W. Taylor, *A World 2010: A Decline of Superpower Influence: Final Report* (Carlisle Barracks, Pa.: Strategic Studies Institute, US Army War College, 10 July 1986).

25. For a further discussion, see Col Howard Lee Dixon, *A Framework for Competitive Strategies Development in Low Intensity Conflict* (Langley AFB, Va.: Army–Air Force Center for Low Intensity Conflict, 1988), viii.

26. For a more complete discussion, see Tim Zimmerman, "The American Bombing of Libya: A Success for Coercive Diplomacy?" *Strategic Review*, Spring 1987, 200.

27. Weinberger speech, "The Uses of Military Power."

28. Frank Kitson, *Low Intensity Operations: Subversion, Insurgency, Peace-keeping* (Harrisburg, Pa.: Stackpole Books, 1971), 90; and Charters, in *Armies in Low-Intensity Conflict*, 171.

29. See "Executive Summary," in *Joint Low-Intensity Conflict Project: Final Report*, vol. 1, *Analytical Review of Low-Intensity Conflict* (Langley AFB, Va.: Army–Air Force Center for Low Intensity Conflict, 1 August 1986), iii.

PART III

Air Power: Deterrence and Compellence

Introduction

In the midst of the changes taking place in the international security environment, it is necessary to reassess long-standing strategic concepts and doctrines that were codified during the cold war era. This reassessment includes the question of alliance relationships, as well as the reliance on deterrence as our central strategic principle. In this section, the two authors raise a host of questions and make intriguing observations about American defense doctrine and strategy and the place of air power in the new security paradigm that has yet to be fully defined.

In his essay, Dr Richard H..Shultz, Jr., poses four salient questions regarding US defense posture in the years ahead:

- What are the continuities and discontinuities between the cold war and post–cold war international security environments?
- Will the preeminent US strategic concept of the cold war—deterrence—remain so in the years ahead, or will a different concept be equally or possibly more relevant in this new environment?
- Is *compellence* [coercive force] a more appropriate strategic concept for the 1990s?
- Can air power . . . contribute to the adroit use of compellence . . . as a strategic concept?

As for discontinuities, Shultz points to an especially grave trend toward nuclear proliferation in the third world, as well as the stockpiling of chemical and biological weapons. Conventional armament will also progress as it has in the past—toward heavily armored, mechanized, and increasingly "smart" weapons. He warns of the "growing importance of regional security environments" as opposed to the traditional fixation on the European theater, and of an upsurge in political instability due to noncommunist ideologies and movements such as fundamentalist religious sects, secessionism, irredentism, and other "extreme forms of nationalism."

Following this discussion, an inquiry into the historical roots of American national security policy identifies three elements—defense, deterrence, and compellence. Shultz then focuses on compellence as the element most likely to be employed by future administrations, given the aforementioned new international security environment. Rather than use deterrence, the US may have to employ military power to halt an enemy operation, reverse a completed action, or initiate an action at variance with the adversaries' stated goals. Compellence becomes necessary, asserts Shultz, because of the loosening of restraints on third-world states, which is occasioned by the attenuation of the superpower military rivalry and the aforementioned proliferation of arms. In the future, compellent military actions will be a necessary option for defending vital US interests.

According to Dr Shultz, air power offers

> a resolute and decisive military instrument for situations requiring the compellent use of force. If diplomacy and other means have proven inadequate, air power provides a highly sophisticated capability to persuade opponents to alter their political and military behavior.

Dr Shultz believes that the current operational reorganization plans envisioned by the Air Force are ideal for prosecuting a compellent strategy. Gen Merrill A. McPeak, Air Force chief of staff, has called for dual operational structures—nuclear and conventional commands. This arrangement, Shultz argues, will be the theoretical basis for the ability to project power to compel globally. Air power's unique attribute is its ability to project itself to great distances with the all-important ingredient of surprise, as well as precision. Thus, air power now provides policymakers with even more options from which to choose.

Dr Jacquelyn K. Davis agrees with Dr Shultz and most of the contributors to this volume that

> the Gulf war . . . has demonstrated that air power is an indispensable element of a strategic concept that is designed to destroy enemy logistical infrastructure and counterforce capabilities in a timely and decisive fashion before—if possible—the beginning of ground-force operations.

Dr Davis asserts that the importance of air power in a future campaign will depend on three variables:

> (1) the nature and level of capabilities that are fielded by both friendly and adversarial forces; (2) the extent and quality of each side's logistics; and (3)

more and more importantly in the last years of the twentieth century and into the next—from a political as well as from a military perspective—the synergism between US and allied air power assets, including offensive and defensive, active and passive capabilities.

It is clear to Dr Davis that in the years ahead, the United States will require a national security strategy that is committed to the defense of allies in Western Europe, although this commitment "will assume a new character, based upon a drawdown of the forward-deployed American presence in Europe and in the context" of the collapse of the communist political order in Eastern Europe and the Soviet Union. Major spending cuts and force-structure reductions arising from these new political factors "underline the importance of mission rationalization and allied interoperability." Dr Davis foresees an upswing in the roles and missions of the US Air Force and other services' air components, given "the increased incidence of 'burden sharing' by most NATO allies and their attitude relating to out-of-area contingency planning."

Dr Davis notes the concern of the US over the steady shrinking of its "access to overseas bases and logistical infrastructure." This trend will soon present the US with the need for longer-range aircraft "based in the [United States] and refueled in flight," in order to carry out power projection missions. In the future, Dr Davis argues, the US must make hard choices about the contingencies to which it will commit itself, and thus must make equally hard decisions about force structure and acquisition. She believes that, from this point forward, forces "will have to be developed and optimized according to more exacting criteria that maximize force survivability and systems flexibility in a variety of complex military environments."

Compellence and the Role of Air Power as a Political Instrument

Dr Richard H. Shultz, Jr.

With the end of the cold war, many of the existing assumptions about conflict, the role of force, and military power have been called into question. Prior to the Gulf war, a lively debate took place in the US foreign policy and national security communities over the likelihood of violent conflict in the future and the extent to which military power had a role to play in a post–cold war world. Some experts forecast ever-increasing stability, global cooperation (especially in economic affairs), and an end to the use of force.[1] Others disagreed with such predictions and argued that the accelerating rate of change was likely to be accompanied by various forms of instability.[2]

However, with the Iraqi invasion of Kuwait and the war that ensued, the debate over the utility of military power has shifted. The questions now are, What kind of military capability will the US require in the years ahead? and What overarching strategic concept should guide its employment? Within this context, the following four issues are addressed:

- What are the continuities and discontinuities between the cold war and post–cold war international security environments?
- Will the preeminent US strategic concept of the cold war—deterrence—remain so in the years ahead, or will a different concept be equally or possibly more relevant in this new environment?
- Is *compellence* (a term coined by Thomas C. Schelling to denote the counterpart of deterrence[3]) a more appropriate strategic concept for the 1990s?

- Can air power, as employed strategically and tactically in the Gulf war, contribute to the adroit use of compellence by the United States as a strategic concept?

Continuities and Discontinuities in a Post–Cold War World

The international security environment, as it existed from the late 1940s to the late 1980s, has undergone some fundamental changes. Below, we will highlight several of these developments. Before doing so, however, we find it equally important to recognize the continuity that exists in the past, present, and likely future with respect to the utility of military power as an instrument of foreign policy.

Clearly, the dramatic changes in Eastern Europe—and, to a lesser extent, in the Soviet Union, as well as the upsurge of democratically inspired movements in parts of the third world—are all significant new trends in international politics. But they do not signify, as some believe, the dawn of a new world order of global cooperation. Interestingly, the end of war—whether hot or cold—engenders among American intellectuals and academics the presumption that international relations is entering a golden age. This is a recurring vision that has taken hold at least three times in the twentieth century, most memorably following both World War I and World War II. Yet, contrary to those forecasts and confidence in the peacekeeping capacity of international organization, states continued to compete—and some to dominate—through the use of military force and coercion.

Similarly, Iraq's invasion of Kuwait and its bid for hegemony in the Gulf region demonstrated that the end of the cold war likewise did not alter certain enduring historical realities. In the years ahead, those nations threatened by similar adversaries will still have to make the necessary provisions for their security, with military power remaining the central component. Even with the end of the cold war, we are not yet entering a Kantian epoch in which national interest gives way to greater harmony and mutual understanding. While some states may eschew the use of force in the name of higher principles, the efficacy of military power remains the final arbiter when states disagree. Despite the development of new rationales and new modes of using force, the resort to military power—as Clausewitz observed long ago—will remain an instrument of statecraft.

That being said, what are the discontinuities that will differentiate the cold war and post–cold war international security environments? Although several factors stand out, the focus here is on seven developments that are likely to contribute to increasing regional instability and conflict.

First, and most worrisome, is the proliferation of mass-destruction weapons. The cold war was marked by essential nuclear bipolarity, with a limited number of other stable states possessing nuclear capabilities. The years ahead will see increasing nuclear multipolarity, with proliferation by states seeking regional hegemony. Iraq is a case in point. Additionally, the proliferation of chemical and biological weapons will continue. It is estimated that during the 1990s, 16 states will acquire both a chemical/biological capability and the means to deliver these weapons through ballistic missiles. With respect to the latter, Janne E. Nolan has observed that "in the late 1980s, ballistic missiles became the currency of a new international security environment, as a number of developing countries heralded their entry into the missile age." She points out that most of the countries that are acquiring this capability are "in regions of chronic tension."[4] Furthermore, as the Iran-Iraq war demonstrated, there is a high probability that these weapons will be used during conflict.

Second, the international security environment of the 1990s will likewise continue to experience the proliferation of conventional arms. The buildup during the 1970s and 1980s has allowed at least 15 third-world nations to develop large, modern conventional armies based on a concept of heavy armored divisions. In the Middle East, for example, this group includes Egypt, Iraq, Israel, Libya, Saudi Arabia, and Syria.[5] Each of these powers also has modern combat aircraft including F-4s; F-14s; F-15s; F-16s; Mirages; Tornados; and MiG-23s, -25s, and -29s. Additionally, many third-world regimes have in their inventories a range of "smart" weapons such as the Exocet cruise missile. This is simply one of a class of precision guided munitions (PGM) which are appearing in the arsenals of third-world states. It will be recalled that it was an Exocet that demolished the HMS *Sheffield* during the Falklands War and damaged the USS *Stark* in 1987.[6] During the Soviet-Afghan War, as one specialist has observed,

> the Stinger was the war's decisive weapon—it changed the nature of combat. Stinger directly attacked the Soviet military center of gravity—airpower—and demonstrated that control of the air environment is as vital in low intensity conflict as in higher intensity warfare.[7]

In the aftermath of the Gulf war, it appears that the acquisition of smart weapons will accelerate as the nations of the Middle East embark on a new phase of the arms race.

Third, several third-world states have progressed to the point where they can domestically design and produce one or more of the following major categories of weapons: armored vehicles, aircraft, naval vessels, and missiles. "Eight Third World countries," as Andrew L. Ross noted, "are now able to design and produce all four types." These include Argentina, Brazil, South Korea, Taiwan, South Africa, India, Israel, and Egypt. He also points out that "eight more countries are producing at least two or three of the four types of conventional arms: Chile, Colombia, Indonesia, Mexico, North Korea, Pakistan, the Philippines, and Thailand."[8] This will only contribute to the diffusion of power to various regions of the developing world and make the resort to force, even in the face of opposition from major powers, a more attractive option for these emerging military powers.

A fourth discontinuity has to do with the growing importance of regional security environments (especially the Middle East/Persian Gulf, South and Northeast Asia, and Latin America). This development is already being reflected in US international security planning. During the cold war, the focal point for the United States was Europe. In the years ahead, Europe will remain important but not to the exclusion of other regions. Two reasons account for this change: (1) the US has numerous economic and political interests in the regions identified above and (2) these areas will continue to experience various forms of conflict that will be exacerbated by the previously mentioned arms buildup. Although the US was, at times, concerned with conflicts in the third world during the cold war, these incidents were seen through East-West lenses and viewed as secondary national security issues.[9] This will not be the case in the 1990s and beyond.

Fifth, low-intensity conflict (LIC) will now be seen as endemic to various third-world regions, with the number of states involved on the rise. The Reagan administration, in its 1987 statement on the *National Security Strategy of the United States*, set forth the dimensions of LIC in the following terms:

> Low Intensity Conflicts may be waged by a combination of means, including the use of political, economic, informational, and military instruments....
>
> Major causes of Low Intensity Conflict are instability and lack of political and economic development in the Third World. . . . These conditions provide fertile ground for unrest and for groups and nations wishing to exploit unrest for their own purposes....
>
> An effective U.S. response to this form of warfare requires . . .
>
> the use of a variety of policy instruments among U.S. Government agencies and internationally. Responses may draw on economic, political, and informational tools, as well as military assistance.[10]

This definition is instructive for the following reasons: One, LIC is characterized as a political-military confrontation short of conventional war between either contending states or a group/movement and a state. It can range from covert subversion to a paramilitary insurgent conflict. Two, the instruments utilized in these conflicts include political, psychological, economic, informational, and military means. According to two specialists, these activities

> might be described as parapolitical. . . . The ultimate objective is political and the political stakes and risks are frequently high. But the intermediate objectives and the chosen instruments range from political into the military and paramilitary fields.[11]

Three, LIC involves strategies of conflict that are both indirect and unconventional in approach. Finally, among the societal factors that underlie or cause LIC are discontentment, injustice, repression, instability, and political, economic, and social change. These conditions are generally found in the third world, where most LICs occur. In fact, LIC describes an environment or situation in which conflict or instability can take one of several forms. This will place regional LIC higher on the security agenda of the US in the years ahead.

Sixth, the ideological causes of instability will continue to expand in the post–cold war world rather than contract, as some commentators suggest.[12] During most of the period since 1945, destabilizing messianic ideologies were confined to various forms of Marxism-Leninism, with strategic links to the Soviet Union and its global aspirations. Today and in the future, these ideologies will expand to include Islamic and other kinds of religious fundamentalism, ethnicity in the form of radicalized secessionism and irredentism, and—possibly—extreme forms of nationalism. Furthermore, these groups and movements will be better armed.

Finally, ethnic-based LIC may not be confined to the third world. Variations of it could occur in Eastern Europe and the Soviet Union. Indeed, in the years ahead these regions may experience instability initiated by movements following the previously mentioned messianic ideologies. The Soviet Union, in particular, is likely to find itself embroiled in tense and violent internal disputes with diverse ethnic and nationalistic movements.

How will the above developments affect US national security policy and strategy? The short answer is that they will present decision makers with diverse, complex, and uncertain forms of instability and conflict in regions of the world that we have not understood very well in the past. Additionally, they call into question whether or not the preeminent US strategic concept of the cold war—deterrence—will remain so in the years ahead or whether other concepts will be equally or possibly more relevant in this new environment.

The Preeminence of Deterrence during the Cold War

During the latter half of the 1950s and the early 1960s, American strategic specialists devoted considerable attention to the functions or roles that military power could serve as an instrument of foreign policy. While wide-ranging and diverse, these conceptual efforts share common themes. A review of these concepts supports the following assessment by Robert Art:

> Although the goals that states pursue range widely and vary considerably from case to case, there are four categories that analytically exhaust the functions force can serve: defense, deterrence, compellence, and swaggering [or show of force].[13]

In effect, these were the choices available to support policy objectives. Here we will be concerned with defense, deterrence, and compellence.

What follows is a brief examination of each of these functions and an explanation of why deterrence emerged as the central strategic concept for the United States during the course of the cold war. This phenomenon should not be surprising, given the fact that a great deal of attention was paid to the development of nuclear weapons and the requirements for deterrence. Such a concern can be seen both in the works of US strategic thinkers and in the nuclear policy and strategy of post–World War II administrations. It also explains why, as Alexander George and Richard Smoke have pointed out, "there has been a marked tendency for theorists to employ strategic deterrence as a paradigm case for thinking about deterrence in general [i.e., across the spectrum of conflict]."[14]

Defense

From a conceptual perspective, "the defensive use of force employs military power to accomplish two things: to ward off an attack and to minimize damage to oneself if attacked. . . . The defensive use of force may involve both peaceful and physical employment."[15]

Although defense has long been a part of military planning and strategy (Clausewitz described it as "the stronger form of waging war"[16]), its relevance at the nuclear level came into question during the formative period of American strategic thinking.

This debate concerned the question of whether defense was possible against a Soviet nuclear attack. During the early 1960s, there was extensive disagreement over this issue.[17] However, this situation changed, as Secretary of Defense Robert S. McNamara adopted a doctrine of mutual assured destruction (MAD) and rejected the possibility of defense. Thus, at the nuclear level the historical linkage between deterrence and defense was decoupled.[18] So powerful was McNamara's influence and so accepted was the logic underlying his MAD doctrine that not until the second Nixon term was MAD challenged by Secretary of Defense James R. Schlesinger. However, it was only in the Reagan administration that the concept of defense was reconsidered within the context of nuclear doctrine. Thus, beginning in the early 1960s, deterrence moved to the forefront in US strategic thinking and policy formulation.

Deterrence

The analytic assumptions of deterrence are straightforward, as George and Smoke point out:

> In its simplest form, deterrence is merely a contingent threat: "If you do x, I shall do y to you." If the opponent expects the cost of y to be greater than the benefits of x, he will refrain from doing y; he is deterred. Rarely in the real world does deterrence actually work in this simple a way. But strategic deterrence can approach it. Assured Destruction is nearly this: if the Soviets launch an atomic attack upon the United States, the nuclear destruction of the Soviet Union will be assured. . . . The logic of the threat is straightforward.[19]

The concept of deterrence—convincing an opponent that the risks of a course of action outweigh any possible gain—is not new. It can be found in the oldest works on statecraft and military power. However, in the nuclear age, deterrence took on certain assumptions that made a difference. The requirements for it were developed within the context of two superpowers armed with nuclear weapons, and these requirements depended upon the idea of perfect rationality. The methodology of those who devised it was dominated by the cost-benefit or economic-utility model.

In the literature and at the policy level, the deterrence of nuclear war received the greatest attention. Furthermore, the simplicity of the abstract definition of deterrence as a contingent threat seemed to hold at the strategic level. The factors that generally complicate the process of making it operational—subjective and cultural differences between the actors involved over such issues as objectives, means, commitment, and so forth—did not seem to apply. Both the US and the Soviet Union, it was argued, followed the assumptions and logic of the cost-benefit/rational-actor model of behavior. Fundamental political and philosophical differences between the two superpowers did not seem to matter because of the level of destructiveness involved. Indeed, these significant differences were seen as extraneous.[20]

Compellence

The purpose of compellence is to employ military power to affect an adversary's behavior in the following ways: (1) halt an activity that is under way, (2) undo a deed already accomplished, or (3) initiate an action that is undesirable. The concept received its initial and most detailed consideration in Thomas C. Schelling's *Arms and Influence*. He asserted that "compellence . . . usually involves *initiating* an action . . . that can cease, or become harmless, only if the opponent responds. The overt act, the first step, is up to the side that makes the compellent threat [Schelling's italics]."[21] Thus, to be credible, "the compellent threat has to be put in motion . . . and *then* the victim must yield [Schelling's italics]."[22]

For Schelling, compellence almost always involves the use of force. Furthermore, it entails attention to where, what kind, and how much military power is to be used in order to convince the adversary to comply. Compellence is offensive and action oriented.

The distinction between deterrence and compellence is apparent. The former uses force passively to prevent an action from taking place, while the latter employs force actively and involves a sequence of actions and reactions. Unlike deterrence, compellence is easier to demonstrate or verify because it requires something to take place. However, it is precisely because of this criterion that it is more difficult to achieve. In the case of deterrence, the adversary has the veil of plausible denial. This is not true for compellence, which requires a state to alter its behavior.

As a strategic concept, compellence was never developed beyond the level of abstraction that characterized Schelling's work. It failed to pay attention to the impact of different political cultures and regimes. By framing his discussion in terms of nations "A" and "B," Schelling obscures the political dimensions of conflict. For example, if nation A seeks to compel nation B to do its will, it is important to know whether nation B is committed to a doctrine of holy war. This would have an important impact on its level of commitment and resolve. It does not mean that such a regime is impervious to compellence—only that one must develop a strategy based on a clear understanding of an opponent's beliefs and commitment. Unfortunately, compellence never appears to have received this kind of conceptual enrichment from the defense community. When such a concept is employed without attention to cultural and contextual complexities, the results can be disastrous.

The Functions of Force in the Post–Cold War World

Previously, authorities argued that in the international security environment of the 1990s, military power would remain a central instrument of statecraft. However, although each of the functions described above will have a role to play in support of US foreign policy objectives, at least in the near term it would appear that—for several reasons—compellence will be particularly important. The rationale for this assertion is derived from our outline of the parameters of the post–cold war international security environment.

Over a period of time in the old bipolar structure, the superpowers had worked out a set of unwritten arrangements that placed limits on the direct and indirect instigation of instability and the use of force. This was true not only for direct US-Soviet confrontations, but also for the use of force by their allies and clients. By curbing such incidents, the US and Soviet Union were able to prevent regional conflicts from turning into superpower confrontations. In other words, the power balance and modalities that were worked out over the years between the two superpowers had a spillover effect into those critical regional areas of the world troubled by long-standing disputes and emerging new ones. Although regional conflicts occurred, on several occasions the superpowers were able to limit the extent of hostilities by exerting their influence over their allies.

This is not likely to be the case in the 1990s. Rather, the frequency and intensity of regional conflicts may be greater due to the increasing diversity of interests, disagreements, and demands of states in these subsystems, and the absence of the moderating effect of the bipolar structure. As Geoffrey Kemp has argued, the decline of the superpower struggle is likely to serve to fuel regional tensions for three reasons: (1) superpower retrenchment will create a vacuum that regional powers will move quickly to fill, (2) the sources of conflict in key regions of the world have not diminished, and (3) little political incentive exists for participants in regional conflicts to work for a reduction of tension.[23] Thus, the US is likely to find itself in situations where regional powers have already employed military force in ways that threaten one or more of our vital interests. In order to return to the status quo, the aggressive regional power will have to undo whatever its force has achieved. In such situations, the compellent use of military power must be an arrow in the quiver of instruments available to American policymakers.

Regional powers not only will be less constrained or motivated to avoid conflict, but also they will be much better armed to conduct war in support of political objectives. As we noted earlier, various regional powers carried out a dramatic buildup in arms during the 1980s. The most disturbing aspect of this activity has been the proliferation of weapons of mass destruction, the danger of which is self-evident. Imagine how the recent war with Iraq would have been complicated if Baghdad had possessed nuclear weapons. It is not likely that in the hands of leaders like Saddam Hussein nuclear weapons will have the moderating or restraining influence that some people have suggested.[24] His use of other mass-destruction weapons during the war with Iran is evidence of this fact.

Will international pressures and legal constraints deter future leaders like Saddam from procuring nuclear weapons? Although one must pursue every effort of this kind, the record of such attempts is not a happy one. Hopefully, the future will be different. If this is not the case, then one must consider the compellent use of force to undo such situations. As difficult as it might be to come to grips with what might be termed the "Israeli solution" (i.e., Israel's destruction of Iraq's Osirak nuclear reactor in 1981), one should not reject it out of hand. The coercive use of force was the only way to undo the situation, although Iraq was not dissuaded from trying again.

Numerous third-world nations have also developed armies based on the concept of the heavy armored division and have purchased modern air forces and ballistic missiles. Although Iraq may be the extreme example, its invasion of Kuwait demonstrated a willingness to use these capabilities to achieve regional political objectives. In this case, any conception of American deterrence was irrelevant even though it was apparent that an Iraqi use of force would threaten several of our interests. The US and its coalition partners faced a classic compellence situation. To force the Iraqis to undo what occurred on 2 August 1990, the coalition had to apply coercive military power. This kind of situation will not be the exception in the years ahead, although one could argue that it is the most extreme case. Certainly, one must consider every effort to establish regional security arrangements to forestall such situations, but one should nevertheless retain the compellent use of force as a policy option.

We observed above that various forms of low-intensity and indirect conflict—including insurgency, terrorism, and narcotics—are also likely to continue to increase in the years ahead. Additionally, states will persist in supporting groups that carry out these actions. Indeed, over the last 15 years several states have come to see this as a normal instrument of statecraft and have aimed these indirect forms of attack at the US and several of its allies and friends. One lesson the United States should derive from the 1980s is that responding to such indirect forms of attack—whether initiated by a terrorist or insurgent group on its own or on behalf of a state patron—is extremely difficult. Apparently, deterrence has not been very useful in countering such challenges. In effect, compellence may be more germane in these cases.

Finally, each of the above forms of emerging and ongoing conflict and instability will take place in those regions of the developing world that are of increasing importance to the US in the post–cold war era. Although Europe will remain prominent, in the years ahead the Middle East/Persian Gulf, South and Northeast Asia, and Latin America will continue to grow in significance. However, these regions will also contain threats that may be difficult to respond to by relying on strategic concepts of the cold war. This is why compellence may be of increasing importance. However, the use of military power to compel adversaries to undo actions already accomplished or to take steps they would prefer not to take will remain difficult. In light of the fact that these situations arise in those regions of the world where our understanding of culture and tradition has been lacking, we will have to base the compellent use of force on a sophisticated knowledge of these factors. To achieve the desired objective, we must therefore pay attention to cultural and contextual complexities.

The Role of Air Power as an Instrument of Compellence

Modern air power, as possessed by the United States and employed during the Gulf war, has several attributes that make it a resolute and decisive military instrument for situations requiring the compellent use of force. If diplomacy and other means have proven inadequate, air power provides a highly sophisticated capability to persuade opponents to alter their political and military behavior. For example, one might seek to compel an adversary to reduce political objectives, withdraw military forces, accept a cease-fire, or give up/destroy critical military capabilities. What these policy objectives have in common is that they stop short of the complete defeat and unconditional surrender of an opponent's military force. Across the spectrum of conflict—particularly at the conventional level and below—if compellence is the policy goal, modern air power has emerged as one of the primary military instruments to accomplish it.

This raises two questions: (1) What are the attributes of modern air power that make it suitable to compellence situations? and (2) How did the Gulf war demonstrate this suitability? The answer to the former lies in the following dimensions of modern air power, the first of which can be discerned from the new paradigm of air power that the senior Air Force leadership is currently refining. According to Gen Merrill A. McPeak, Air Force chief of staff, in the Air Force of today the old paradigm that distinguished between Strategic Air Command (SAC) and Tactical Air Command (TAC) has blurred:

> It no longer is the case that one is nuclear and the other is conventional. Tactical forces have been nuclear capable for many years, and SAC has . . . conventional missions. . . . So strategic and tactical no longer mean short versus long range; they no longer have much to do with payload. . . . I no longer know what the division between tactical and strategic is. It seems to me that the categories maybe never made much sense when applied to aircraft, and certainly are less and less relevant.[25]

On this basis, General McPeak asserts that the US Air Force of the future should be divided into a nuclear command and a conventional command. The latter, which McPeak has labeled the Operational Air Command, can be employed for missions at the conventional level and below. Regardless of the location of the conflict, the Operational Air Command could (1) carry out independent or solo missions, (2) support an ally by providing varying degrees of air power, and (3) conduct fully integrated joint operations with the other US armed services. Thus, as Maj Gen Robert Alexander (USAF) has pointed out, "The new paradigm that is emerging is an Air Force that is fully integrated institutionally, organizationally, intellectually, and culturally to resolutely and decisively apply air power . . . across the spectrum of conflict."[26]

Although this new paradigm is applicable to each of the functions of military force, it is particularly suited to compellence, providing the theoretical basis for projecting power to compel on a global scale. Indeed, General McPeak takes this so far as to envisage a "composite wing" in the Air Force of the future, "the purpose of which would be to go to any spot on the earth quickly and conduct immediate air operations."[27] This power projection capability is the first and most important attribute for the employment of modern American air power in compellent operations. Furthermore, this capability will grow in importance if the US continues to lose regional bases for forward-deployed forces. In the future, we will increasingly achieve forward presence through power projection.

A second important attribute of modern air power is the ability to achieve surprise. As we will discuss below, stealth proved itself in the war with Iraq. The ability of the F-117 to avoid detection is reflected in the fact that none were lost to Iraqi air defense systems. Reportedly, it was the only aircraft to fly inside Baghdad. In the future, the ability of the F-117, F-22, and B-2 to achieve operational surprise through stealth will enhance the ability of the US to employ air power as a compellent across the spectrum of conflict.

The third attribute of modern air power that enhances the US capacity to carry out compellence missions is precision, which contributes greatly, for example, to General McPeak's concept of a composite wing. In conjunction with the ability to arrive quickly, achieve surprise, and rapidly begin operations, PGMs allow for immediate strikes against the critical or strategic assets of an adversary. The shock effect of such strikes enhances compellence.

Beyond rapid power projection, surprise, and precision, the flexibility of American air power as a compellent force is also enhanced by its ability to configure the appropriate force package to meet the requirements of diverse missions. This can range from the rather small force employed against Libya (Operation El Dorado Canyon) to the massive deployment in Operation Desert Storm. At the operational level, the ability to maneuver forces that span such a wide range provides compellence flexibility across the spectrum of conflict.

With respect to the second question posed above, these attributes of modern air power played a decisive role in the Gulf war and reflected the suitability of air power for compellent missions. For instance, the deployment to the Gulf demonstrated the capacity of the USAF for global reach and power projection. Fighter units deployed from the US to Saudi Arabia and were ready to conduct operations within 34 hours of receiving orders. Within five days, five fighter squadrons were in place, and in 35 days a fighter force numerically equal to that of Iraq had arrived. By the late fall, a tremendous air armada was in the theater of operations and ready to fight. This included an array of sophisticated combat aircraft including the F-117, F-15, F-15E, A-10, F-111, EF-111, F-4G, F-16, B-52, airborne warning and control system (AWACS) aircraft, and joint surveillance target attack radar system (JSTARS) aircraft. This buildup of aircraft was aided by the availability of a sophisticated airfield infrastructure in Saudi Arabia. With respect to airlift, Military Airlift Command moved 482,000 passengers and 513,000 tons of cargo over 7,000 miles.

The five primary objectives of the air campaign sought to paralyze the Iraqi regime, avoid civilian casualties, and compel Saddam Hussein to withdraw from Kuwait. The specific objectives included isolating and incapacitating the Iraqi political and military leadership, achieving air superiority, destroying all weapons of mass destruction, eliminating offensive military capabilities, and forcing the Iraqi army out of Kuwait. The latter two objectives were to be accomplished through fully integrated joint and combined air, land, and sea operations.

The flexibility of air power allowed the US to isolate and bypass the Iraqi army and shut down its air defense and air force. In turn, this permitted immediate strikes at the center of the regime—the civilian and military leadership—and then at other strategic targets. During the war the USAF flew 65,000 sorties (59 percent of all sorties flown by the coalition) to reach and destroy many of these targets.

In addition to power projection and global reach, the other attributes of US air power noted above contributed to the rapid achievement of the objectives of the air campaign. The F-117 provided the critical element of surprise and helped assure air superiority by destroying command and control capabilities and related strategic assets. Stealth likewise allowed the F-117 to operate in a heavily defended environment. Before the Iraqis detected it, a massive raid led by F-117 stealth bombers so overwhelmed and largely blinded Iraqi command, control, communications, and intelligence (C^3I) that the latter never recovered the initiative.

Precision munitions and missiles likewise made a strategic contribution to achieving the previously listed objectives. Vital civilian and military leadership centers, military equipment, and infrastructure across the width and depth of Iraq and Kuwait were struck with devastating effects. Command bunkers, aircraft shelters, and other protected targets were penetrated and destroyed with surgical accuracy. PGMs also had a deterrent effect in that they kept the Iraqis from using their operable radars and control centers.

Finally, the flexibility of American air power was reflected in its ability to configure, deploy, and sustain the appropriate force package to meet the requirements of this mission. In addition to the previously discussed air armada, a wide variety of space and intelligence assets was utilized to enhance the planning and conduct of the air campaign. These assets augmented the coalition's ability to carry out effective night operations that denied the enemy sanctuary and kept him under constant pressure around the clock. Additionally, they gave the coalition theater-wide situational awareness on a real-time basis. Equally important was the joint-force component commander, who provided unity of command under a single air tasking order. This avoided the problems that plagued the use of air power in the Vietnam War.

The results of the air campaign were impressive. First, it paralyzed the leadership capacity of Iraq's national command authority. Second, the Iraqi air defense system was completely disabled and never recovered, while its air force was so intimidated that it tried to hide in hardened shelters, fled to Iran, or was dispersed inside Iraq. These actions opened the door to other strategic targets throughout the theater. Several nuclear and biological weapons research and production facilities were destroyed, along with chemical weapons facilities and storage sites. Likewise, defense production capabilities were severely damaged. Nevertheless, in the aftermath of the war we learned that a significant amount of Iraq's mass-destruction capabilities survived. How much still exists is unclear. However, the shortcomings of US intelligence are troubling. We knew much less than we thought.

Finally, air power greatly weakened Iraqi forces in Kuwait before the coalition ground offensive began. Over half of the tanks and artillery in the Kuwait theater of operations was destroyed by air attack. Iraq's army was cut off as air power destroyed railroad and highway bridges, storage depots, and the movement of supplies to forward-deployed forces. Furthermore, the terrifying and constant bombardment by coalition aircraft greatly demoralized Iraqi troops, a fact reflected in their high rate of desertion. As an offensive threat to the region, the Iraqi armed forces suffered a serious setback, as these figures demonstrate. However, enough survived—when coupled with forces in Iraq—to put down the postwar internal insurrection.

In sum, the air power campaign was central to compelling Iraq to pull its army out of Kuwait. As an instrument of compellence, modern air power proved to be quite effective in this situation. Indeed, a by-product of the campaign against Iraq may be the strengthening of deterrence against similar actions by future Saddam Husseins.

Notes

1. John E. Mueller, *Retreat from Doomsday: The Obsolescence of Major War* (New York: Basic Books, 1989); and Francis Fukuyama, "The End of History?" *National Interest*, Summer 1989, 3–18.

2. Eliot A. Cohen, "The Future of Force and American Strategy," *National Interest*, Fall 1990, 3–15; and Robert J. Art, "A Defensible Defense: America's Grand Strategy after the Cold War," *International Security*, Spring 1991, 5–53. During the early 1970s, similar predictions were put forward about the growing disutility of military power and rise in global cooperation. A stinging critique of those arguments that has direct relevance today can be found in Adda B. Bozeman, "War and the Clash of Ideas," *Orbis*, Spring 1976, 61–102.

3. Thomas C. Schelling, *Arms and Influence* (New Haven, Conn.: Yale University Press, 1966), 71.

4. Janne E. Nolan, "Missile Mania: Some Rules for the Game," *The Bulletin of the Atomic Scientists*, May 1990, 27. See also W. Seth Carus, "Missiles in the Middle East: A New Threat to Stability," *Policy Focus*, The Washington Institute for Near East Policy, Research Memorandum no. 6, June 1988.

5. See United States Arms Control and Disarmament Agency, *World Military Expenditures and Arms Transfers* (Washington, D.C.: Government Printing Office, 1989); Ruth Leger Sivard, *World Military and Social Expenditures, 1989* (Washington, D.C.: World Priorities, 1989); Rodney W. Jones and Steven A. Hildreth, *Modern Weapons and Third World Powers* (Boulder, Colo.: Westview Press, 1984); and Shlomo Gazit, ed., *The Middle East Military Balance, 1988–1989* (Boulder, Colo.: Westview Press, 1989).

6. For a discussion of the transfer of smart weapons to third-world states, see Paul F. Walker, "High-Tech Killing Power," *The Bulletin of the Atomic Scientists*, May 1990, 23–26.

7. Maj William McManaway, "Stinger in Afghanistan," *Air Defense Artillery*, January–February 1990, 3–8.

8. Andrew L. Ross, "Do-It-Yourself Weaponry," *The Bulletin of the Atomic Scientists*, May 1990, 22.

9. During the post–World War II period, the Kennedy and Reagan administrations were most concerned with third-world conflict and Soviet involvement in it. There is extensive literature on the subjects. On the Kennedy years, see Douglas S. Blaufarb, *The Counterinsurgency Era: U.S. Doctrine and Performance, 1950 to the Present* (New York: Free Press, 1977). With respect to the Reagan years, see Richard H. Shultz, Jr., "Discriminate Deterrence and Low-Intensity Conflict: The Unintentional Legacy of the Reagan Administration," *Conflict* 9, no. 1 (1989): 21–43; and Sam C. Sarkesian, *The New Battlefield: The United States and Unconventional Conflicts* (New York: Greenwood Press, 1986). With respect to Soviet involvement, see Richard H. Shultz, Jr., *The Soviet Union and Revolutionary Warfare: Principles, Practices, and Regional Comparisons* (Stanford, Calif.: Hoover Institution Press, 1988).

10. Ronald Reagan, *National Security Strategy of the United States* (Washington, D.C.: The White House, January 1987), 32–33.

11. Maurice Tugwell and David Charters, "Special Operations and the Threat to United States Interests in the 1980s," in *Special Operations in U.S. Strategy*, ed.

Frank R. Barnett, B. Hugh Tovar, and Richard H. Shultz, Jr. (Washington, D.C.: National Defense University Press, 1984), 34.

12. See Fukuyama.

13. Robert J. Art, "The Role of Military Power in International Relations," in *National Security Affairs: Theoretical Perspectives and Contemporary Issues*, ed. B. Thomas Trout and James E. Harf (New Brunswick, N.J.: Transaction Books, 1982), 27.

14. Alexander George and Richard Smoke, *Deterrence in American Foreign Policy* (New York: Columbia University Press, 1974), 46. The spectrum of conflict is a framework frequently employed in the US national security community to categorize conflict/war into a three-level classification.

15. Art, "Role of Military Power," 27.

16. Carl von Clausewitz, *On War*, ed. and trans. Michael Howard and Peter Paret (Princeton, N.J.: Princeton University Press, 1976), 359. This issue is treated extensively by Clausewitz in Book 6.

17. Glenn H. Snyder, *Deterrence and Defense: Toward a Theory of National Security* (Princeton, N.J.: Princeton University Press, 1961), 8–9.

18. For a discussion of the change, see Lawrence Freedman, *The Evolution of Nuclear Strategy* (New York: Saint Martin's Press, 1981), 227–56.

19. George and Smoke, 48–49.

20. It should be noted that while these assumptions dominated the defense community, there were several specialists who disagreed. For strategic thinkers like Colin S. Gray, the arguments presented above amounted to an "Americanizing" of the Soviet Union. This was highly ethnocentric and ignored the impact of tradition and political culture on Soviet thinking about nuclear weapons and military strategy. See Gray, "National Style in Strategy: The American Example," *International Security*, Fall 1981, 21–47. If doubts existed about the transferability of the cost-benefit logic of deterrence at the nuclear level, problems quickly appeared when the US sought to apply this concept to conventional and low-intensity situations. Varying cultural and contextual factors created uncertainties and complexities that were not clearly understood and limited the application of American deterrence logic. The results were predictable, Vietnam being the most obvious example.

21. Schelling, 72.

22. Ibid.

23. Geoffrey Kemp, "Regional Security, Arms Control, and the End of the Cold War," *Washington Quarterly*, Autumn 1990, 33–51.

24. On this point, Kenneth N. Waltz has argued that the possession of nuclear weapons infuses a state with a greater sense of responsibility and sobriety, thus decreasing its willingness to cause instability or start a war. He bases his argument on the experience of the superpowers. See Waltz, *The Spread of Nuclear Weapons: More May Be Better*, Adelphi Papers, no. 171 (London: International Institute for Strategic Studies, 1981). Others disagree with Waltz and argue that the factors that

brought stability to the superpower nuclear confrontation are not present in those regions of the world which are experiencing proliferation. In their opinion, the greater the number of states possessing nuclear weapons, the more probable is their use. See Karl Kaiser, "Non-proliferation and Nuclear Deterrence," *Survival*, March–April 1989, 123–36.

25. Gen Merrill A. McPeak, Air Force chief of staff, address to the Air Force Association Tactical Air Warfare Symposium, Orlando, Fla., 31 January 1991.

26. Maj Gen Robert M. Alexander, "The World Is Rapidly Changing and AF Must Keep Up," *Air Force Times*, 11 January 1991.

27. McPeak address.

Reinforcing Allied Military Capabilities in a Global-Alliance Strategy

Dr Jacquelyn K. Davis

For the United States and its allies, Operation Desert Storm holds important lessons for air power and its future employment in support of US global and allied theater and "out-of-area" interests. Even though many of the attributes of Desert Storm are unique to that specific conflict, the Gulf war nevertheless has demonstrated that air power is an indispensable element of a strategic concept that is designed to destroy enemy logistical infrastructure and counterforce capabilities in a timely and decisive fashion before—if possible—the beginning of ground-force operations. Just how decisive the contribution of air power may be to an integrated air-land-naval battle campaign in the future will depend on (1) the nature and level of capabilities that are fielded by both friendly and adversarial forces; (2) the extent and quality of each side's logistics; and (3) more and more importantly in the last years of the twentieth century and into the next—from a political as well as from a military perspective—the synergism between US and allied air power assets, including offensive and defensive, active and passive capabilities. Each of these three generic elements played a decisive role in the success of the Desert Storm campaign, and in future potential military operations they are likely to take on increased significance—especially if prospective budget cuts and the force restructuring that follows the Conventional Forces Europe (CFE) treaty reduce US and allied (NATO) defense assets to lower operational inventories, manpower deployments, and infrastructure levels.

In the years ahead, US geostrategic interests will still require a continued commitment to the defense of allies in Western Europe through the framework of the Atlantic Alliance. Yet, for a variety of reasons, our security guarantee to NATO Europe will assume a new character, based upon a drawdown of the forward-deployed American presence in Europe and in the context of the dramatic changes that have altered the European security landscape over the last several years. As NATO moves to bring the force posture and military concepts of the alliance in line with the new strategic realities of the European theater, the operational flexibility inherent in air power assets lends greater importance to its role, both in terms of the traditional context of NATO planning against the possible reemergence of the Soviet Union as a threat to Western Europe and with regard to new missions to protect allied interests against risks that may emerge within Europe or—more likely—outside NATO's traditionally defined perimeter. Both in terms of power projection in a crisis and in the context of articulated NATO military guidance, air power remains fundamental to an allied defensive posture that embraces an operational concept for deep strikes against Soviet infrastructure and force dispositions, as well as for counterair, special operations, and close air support.

At the same time, in the closing years of the twentieth century, US interests and global strategy dictate renewed emphasis on contingency planning for military operations outside traditional US alliance frameworks and in support of nations with which we may not necessarily have formal defense treaties, but with which we have parallel security interests—such as Kuwait and Saudi Arabia. Thus, even though we may not be able to fall back upon a preestablished, integrated alliance structure that is legally binding—such as exists in NATO—operating within a broader-based coalition framework may be a necessary prerequisite to building political consensus in support of military operations outside of NATO, especially in security environments where the Soviet Union may support an opposing set of interests. But in this circumstance—as with NATO planning—the military efficacy of any future military operation rests on an ability to obtain agreement on a unified strategy and the establishment of a single, integrated operational command. For future operations in which the United States is actively involved, this probably means American leadership—both at the political and military levels. In the case of Desert Shield/Desert Storm, it is instructive to realize that the United States deployed (with Navy and Marine assets) up to 73 percent of the coalition's air power and 62 percent of the ground forces.[1] With its overwhelming leadership role, the United States accomplished the intricate and challenging task of holding together a coalition force composed of a diversity of cultures and languages. In certain selected contingencies, however, the United States may opt to defer its leadership role to a US ally which has a tradition or experience in a specific region, as happened in the early 1980s when US forces supported France in Chad.

Any future operation in a theater distant from the continental United States (CONUS) that involves a coalition of forces—including a NATO contingency—will require no less effort in this regard, suggesting that prewar operational planning must explicitly spell out leadership roles and mission responsibilities. As was the case in Desert Shield/Desert Storm—and in the future—strategy, tactics, rules of engagement, and the operational deployment of forces must be agreed to by the political leadership of coalition partners before their actual employment. Failing such agreement, coalition planning could be put at risk, opening opportunities for adversary forces to exploit what could be regarded as a weak link in the coalition. Prior to the outbreak of war in the Gulf, the possibility existed that French forces would not allow themselves to be placed under the operational control of the United States. This uncertainty, which contributed to the resignation of Jean-Pierre Chevènement, French minister of defense, led some US planners to question the contribution of French ground forces (Operation *Daguet*) and air power in the execution of Desert Storm. (The French ground forces were to be deployed in Southwestern Iraq with a brigade of the US 82d Airborne Division, while French aircraft were to be deployed against counterforce targets—largely fixed—in Kuwait.) Ultimately, French military leaders, with the support of President Francois Mitterrand himself, committed French forces to the operational control of the United States. This enabled US planners to count on French assets to perform specifically identified missions which, in the latter phases of the air war, included strikes against the Al Salman airfield in Iraq to cut off the potential of Republican Guard units either to retreat to Baghdad or to disrupt the logistical train of the flanking US VII Corps forces. In the final analysis, the military commitment of French forces to the Desert Storm operation may not have been indispensable. However, from a political perspective, in terms of allied unity it was essential. It may also prove important to the postwar situation in the Middle East, based on France's unique legacy of engagement with the countries of the region.

For France, as well as for other NATO allies of the US, Desert Storm revealed force-posture deficiencies that relate to NATO military planning as well as to out-of-area contingency planning. Notably, in this regard, a sizable percentage of the NATO allied forces that were deployed to the Gulf region demonstrated a lack of sufficient flexibility for operations over desert terrain and under adverse climatic conditions. On more than one occasion, bad weather forced coalition aircraft to return to their operating bases fully loaded because of an inability to acquire targets. Even though US military planners have emphasized that weather conditions over the Kuwaiti theater of operations (KTO) were the worst for at least the last 14 years, the coalition was able to adapt by employing new tactics and reformulating the components of the designated strike packages. But in addition to the climatic factor, in many cases non-US coalition forces (e.g., French Jaguar bombers) lacked appropriate night-fighting technologies and were forced to operate only in the daylight hours. These shortfalls also posed some limitations on campaign strategy and placed a much greater burden on US air power assets, as did other allied force-posture deficiencies. For example, despite France's previous military interventions in Chad, French force-posture deficiencies included inadequate lift, intelligence, and electronic countermeasures capabilities, the latter in part the result of French transfers of advanced military technologies to Iraq during its war against Iran. (In fact, during the opening stages of the air war, French Mirage F1-CR reconnaissance planes and C-version fighters could not be employed over Kuwait for fear of creating identification, friend or foe [IFF] problems with Iraqi Mirages.) Consequently, France's experience in the Gulf war has occasioned a serious debate over force structure and acquisition priorities—as has occurred in other NATO European countries—which will not be easily resolved, given the legacy of Gaullist planning that had emphasized nuclear "dissuasion" as the keystone of French defense planning. Likewise, in the United Kingdom, where the Options for Change study had been driving the British toward reduced force-structure sizing[2] and greater relative emphasis on force mobilization—a concept toward which the United States intends also to move—debate is emerging over the lessons of the Gulf war. In the context of planning for operations in the European theater—still a major focus of US global strategy—NATO's multinational forces concept, together with the projected drawdown of US and allied forward-deployed assets, suggests that in the future the need for closer coordination of allied efforts—from weapons acquisition to logistics and the development of a unified strategic concept—is enhanced, not diminished. This holds true even in the European theater, where the strategic environment has changed so dramatically over the last two years, and the temptation is to be as self-sufficient nationally as possible.

Paradoxically, however, defense-spending cuts and force-structure reductions underline the importance of mission rationalization and allied interoperability. In the instance of air power and NATO force restructuring, the role and missions of US Air Force, Army, Navy, and Marine Corps air assets are likely to be reinforced due to the increased incidence of "burden sharing" by most NATO allies and their attitude relating to out-of-area contingency planning. In the emerging security environment in Europe, this may prove to be an extremely difficult task as the NATO nations scramble to redefine and thin out their own respective force structures in anticipation of the yet-to-be-realized "post–cold war peace dividend." Yet, as Western countries reduce their defense structures, the requirement for more flexible forces is enhanced, leading to a new emphasis on air power in the planning and execution of military campaigns.

It is current conventional wisdom to suggest that the threat in Europe from the Soviet Union has been reduced due to the announced withdrawal of remaining Soviet forces from Eastern Europe and the force reductions to which the Soviets have agreed, both as part of the CFE treaty and on a unilateral basis. Although the current situation in the Soviet Union itself is characterized by instability and uncertainty with regard to the future direction of Soviet domestic policy, it is generally conceded that the Soviet military threat directed against Western Europe has changed so dramatically that NATO members can safely reduce and restructure their respective theater force structures without endangering the security or stability of the Continent. For the United States, this means a reduced forward-deployed presence in Europe, with about five wings or 360 aircraft and associated personnel remaining in theater (as compared to the eight wings that were deployed on the Continent before Desert Shield/Desert Storm). With this reduced in-theater presence, the United States and NATO will be forced to rely on a mobilization-based structure, much as the US did during the Gulf war. As in the Desert Storm operation, the time lines for reinforcement and mobilization of reserve personnel and the reassignment of active units from the CONUS to the theater take on increased importance, especially in Europe, where the Soviet Union could be expected to be a more formidable adversary than the surprisingly and relatively poorly trained and inexperienced pilots and air defenders in Iraq. Mobilization timeliness, together with in-flight refueling and long-range capability, is a prerequisite for US Air Force operations in each of the "two-half-war" contingencies against which Pentagon planners are today directing their attention. This means that US reserve-force components must be just as well trained and equipped as their active duty counterparts. In addition and just as significant will be a future acquisition strategy that balances reserve-force procurements and modernization programs with those of active forces.

For many observers of Desert Storm, the air campaign predetermined the war's outcome, and from this lesson they derive the view that in the future, the role of the tactical air force should be less dedicated to fighting a European war and instead should offer a multifaceted capability for use in a variety of situations. The latter would include different types of single-mission raids as well as a full-blown operation in a high-intensity conflict environment that would be characteristic of a war in Europe. Planning for this range of contingencies requires reliance upon "surgical" strike assets, using weapons that have pinpoint accuracies and produce minimal collateral damage. To obtain allied military objectives through the use of indiscriminate capabilities, resulting in high levels of civilian losses, may in the long run create as many problems as it solves. Stated differently, the postwar peace process—certainly in a well-defined theater such as Europe, the Middle East, or Northeast Asia—may depend on whether the United States (and its coalition partners) is perceived to be concerned about the condition of the adversary's population and homeland (territorial integrity). As a consequence, US and allied force inventories must be planned within political parameters that relate ends to means and resource constraints to acquisition priorities. For many of the possible contingencies in which US air power may be used in support of allies, this implies a need to concentrate resources on the development of standoff-range, low-collateral-damage weapons which may be interoperable with a variety of aircraft platforms, including the European fighter aircraft, which is currently under development. Conversely, in many of the conceivable scenarios about which we can speculate—including those which may involve the Soviet Union or a "proxy" force—a penetration capability will continue to be important for the United States and its allies, especially in the interdiction of relocatable ballistic-missile assets (a role for which the B-1 has been designed, although its dedication as a strategic nuclear carrier—together with its engine's developmental problems—has limited consideration of its mission orientation in this area). Certainly, stealth characteristics are critical in this regard, and even though its cost is considerable, procurement of a "stealthy" strategic/tactical bomber force appears to be essential to the global strategic-planning requirements of the United States.

Additionally, the fundamental importance of deploying surgical-strike capabilities is matched by the need to establish a well-protected and well-provisioned logistical stockpile (of spare parts; petroleum, oil, and lubricants; and ammunition) and infrastructure. For the variety of contingencies which may engage US forces in the future, logistics remains, as always, the key to military success. Yet, we are living in an era when US access to overseas bases and logistical infrastructure is steadily shrinking. More and more, therefore, the ability to sustain US overseas operations will depend on autonomous support systems and longer-range capable assets that could be based in the CONUS and refueled in flight. Conversely, if politically possible for Europe, as well as for other potential theaters of operation, the United States should as a matter of course assign—as a priority element of its political-diplomatic initiatives—activities and agreements designed to retain or negotiate access to in-theater facilities and/or collateral operating bases in a crisis prior to the outbreak of hostilities. But to do this, there is the clear political prerequisite to bring US allies on board an operation before the hostilities actually begin. In regions other than Europe, this may often require the support of the United Nations as a "legitimizing" agent to pave the way for the establishment of a logistical infrastructure to support an air campaign. In Europe, for the time being, this means NATO and/or Western Europe Union or European Community support for US access, in a crisis, to operational bases and collateral facilities. Thus, US access to forward operating bases for aircraft should be inextricably tied to the retention of some agreed level of US forces in Europe and defined precisely within the context of NATO operational planning. In this sense, while we can expect local political authorities to attempt to place constraints on the tempo and nature of air operations in peacetime, it must be clearly established that the continued presence and peacetime operation of US forces—including dual-capable aircraft (DCA) assets—are fundamental to American forward deployments and their readiness for use in a crisis deployment or wartime contingency. Although the European allies have been sending mixed signals over the last several years regarding US forces deployed on the Continent, the uncertainties inherent in contemporary European politics have moved even less-compliant allies to state publicly their support for retaining at least some defense connection with the United States, thereby offering the US a bargaining chip in its negotiations on access to bases and facilities and overflight rights.

Another lesson that appears to be emerging from the Gulf war and which has implications for US reinforcement of allies in its global war strategy relates to the fact that technology, while critical to a force's operational effectiveness, nevertheless is not a substitute for innovative tactics and a sound strategy. Even as Desert Storm illustrated the importance of such new and advanced technologies as cruise missiles, precision guided munitions, stealth, and the joint surveillance target attack radar system (JSTARS), it was the way in which the coalition forces were deployed and coordinated that more than any other factor determined the outcome of the conflict. While it is certainly true that new and emerging US (and other Western) technologies contributed significantly to the low number of allied casualties in the Gulf war, of greater importance was the employment of tactics of deception, outflanking maneuvering, and the disruption of logistical infrastructure based on around-the-clock air operations that culminated in the defeat of the Iraqi armed forces. By interdicting the bridges across the Tigris and Euphrates rivers, coalition air forces eliminated logistical reinforcement from the north and a retreat of Iraqi forces to Baghdad as viable options for Iraq. More than this, however, the use of air power to interdict Iraqi command, control, and intelligence nodes effectively made counterattack an incredible option for the Iraqis who, blinded and confused over coalition dispositions, were caught completely by surprise by the allies' flanking offensive in the brief ground war.

The Iraqis' surprise was compounded by their decision to dig in and reinforce ground-force positions along a static defensive line. This strategy, which was used successfully during Iraq's eight-year war with Iran, failed against the tactical employment of allied air power in close air support (CAS) and battlefield air interdiction (BAI) roles and, later, long-range artillery (multiple launch rocket system—MLRS) barrages (that were directed on target by combat air patrol aircraft). In a future contingency in a high-density conflict environment as was the KTO (or was assumed to portend, based on the fact that Iraq deployed the world's fourth-largest land army) or one that is characterized by more advanced air defense networks (as Syria could be, for example), the need to interdict enemy intelligence assets and communications nodes early in the campaign will be critical to the ability of the United States and its allies to blind enemy forces quickly in a war and—preferably—before ground operations begin. This means that, among other things, allied forces must have access to timely and accurate intelligence about enemy communications networks, (fiber optic) nodes, and critical switching points. In this sense, the Gulf war—which represented for the United States the first "space war"—demonstrates the importance of sensor, satellite, and mapping technologies, especially because such capabilities contribute greatly to target acquisition and forces interdiction.

In allied countries, as in the United States, there is great debate over the precise composition of future air force deployments. As resources become scarcer, competition among military sectors means that fewer platforms will be purchased—especially given the high cost associated with modern air power platforms—and systems characteristics will likely be altered to emphasize multipurpose capability. Thus, as with the current European debate over the new-generation European fighter aircraft, controversy over mission orientation may lead to compromises in design that could result in operational deficiencies which would, in wartime, have to be offset by US air power. In addition to the fact that the United States leads in the deployment of advanced capabilities, such as stealth, that would prove to be indispensable in a European contingency, it may be necessary for the United States to assume mission responsibilities that should have been—but could not be—assigned to the allies, given the technology limitations of their air power assets. Once the euphoria of the success of the Desert Storm operation had passed, allied leaders found themselves faced with questions about weapon procurements and system deficiencies. In Britain, for example, the Royal Air Force (RAF) was confronted with the embarrassing situation in which it had to incorporate vital pieces of electronic equipment on British Tornado aircraft before they could be deployed to the Gulf. The British air assets were configured to operate in the more sophisticated air defense environment of the European theater. Moreover, when the RAF Tornados were first deployed to the KTO, their pilots were locked into the low-level flying tactics that were better suited to the European theater. But the tactics and capabilities that would be required to implement a European air-interdiction campaign were clearly different from the contingency planning for the KTO (and would likely also be for other out-of-area operations). To facilitate the Tornados' usefulness in Desert Storm, the British had to rush a number of vital weapons and electronic countermeasures systems into service or purchase them from Britain's allies to allow the RAF crews to perform their missions. The need to "borrow" technologies was accompanied by a need for the RAF to deploy aging Buccaneers to the Gulf as target designators to facilitate the Tornados' employment of Paveway "smart" munitions. Even after the Tornados' thermal energy and laser designation system arrived in the Gulf and was installed on the aircraft platforms, the Buccaneers remained indispensable, in part due to the fact that only four trial pods were available for operational use.

In addition, some of the requirements for new systems were recognized only when the low-flying tactics adopted by the RAF for its NATO role in central Europe proved redundant against Iraqi air defenses. The comparatively high number of Tornados that were lost during Desert Storm (as compared to other allied aircraft) led British commands to try to adapt their tactics by ordering the aircraft to fly over Iraq at medium altitudes. But this could be done only after Rockeye cluster bombs were obtained from US Air Force stocks. The main weapons employed by the RAF's Tornados and Jaguars normally are the JP 233 airfield-denial system and the BL 755 cluster bomb, both of which were built to be delivered at low level. Had standoff versions of these capabilities been available, RAF pilots could have performed their missions flying at low levels but without "flying down the teeth of enemy defenses."[3] Although Prime Minister John Major has said that the lessons of the Gulf war would be fully reflected in the Options for Change review of British forces and their structuring, a severe fiscal crisis threatens to undermine planning objectives for all the services over the next several years. As a result—as in the United States—hard choices will face British planners, who will have to decide whether Britain's future force-structure options should be tailored to European contingency planning or optimized for use in so-called out-of-area operations. Apart from France, which retains some global commitments and interests, most other alliance nations have only limited capabilities for "extra-NATO" operations, and few are even willing to discuss the employment of their national or NATO-assigned forces to contingencies outside of Europe. Even during the Gulf crisis, the debate in NATO over the assignment of elements of the Allied Command Europe (ACE) mobile force to Turkey—a NATO member—was divisive, although eventually even the Germans permitted the stationing of 18 Alpha Jet aircraft and their support personnel on Turkish soil, but not before extremely limiting rules of engagement were agreed to by NATO.

As part of the NATO Strategy Review, the future role of alliance military forces is being shaped to meet the new risks and threats of the dynamic European security environment. Integral to the development of the political concept by which the potential employment of NATO military power will be driven is the notion that air power can contribute fundamentally to the deterrence of war in Europe through the continued in-theater stationing of allied DCA for—if appropriate, under national auspices—extratheater operations to project power and indicate the resolve of US and allied leaders. Particularly with regard to the European theater—but in other areas where the United States has interests, notably Northeast Asia and now the Middle East—the modernization of US (and, where applicable, allied) assets to incorporate a new-generation nuclear-tipped tactical air-to-surface missile (TASM) will be critical to a credible deterrence posture. While support for such "substrategic" weapons has diminished in the US—as well as in the Air Force itself—and in NATO Europe, the political (i.e., deterrence) symbolism that is manifested in the deployment of forward-based, "tactical" nuclear systems should not be underestimated, especially in the context of a strategic calculus which includes a broader global diffusion of nuclear-weapons capabilities. In this context, it is uncertain whether, in the course of the Gulf war, Iraq refrained from launching a crude chemical-warhead device on a Scud missile because of fear of a possible US nuclear reprisal. In this instance, the uncertainty of the nature of a US response to the Iraqi chemical threat may have been one factor (the others being warhead fusing problems and climatic conditions) that deterred Iraq's use of chemical or biological weapons against Israeli population centers, especially in the early days of the air war before the fixed Scud sites were identified and destroyed.

In fact, it is ironical in this regard that the United States and some of its principal allies are questioning the nature of deterrence as a viable political-psychological-military construct at a time when additional states are acquiring the means of mass destruction. The Soviet Union, notwithstanding the politics of the post–cold war period, continues to modernize its theater and strategic nuclear-force structure and to reformulate and update its deterrence concepts (to match its technological options). Many other states are now on the brink of developing their own nuclear capabilities, which may be used to blackmail US allies overseas or hold hostage vital American interests. In Europe, the prospective drawdown of US Army and allied ground forces' nuclear assets (i.e., Lance missiles and nuclear artillery shells), together with the decision of the NATO summit in May 1990 not to go forward with modernization of the follow-on to Lance (FOTL) surface-to-surface missile system, has made the acquisition and deployment of TASM critical to the delicate deterrence balance in Europe. Among the allies, Britain and France—which maintain their own nuclear forces—recognize the importance of updating Western DCA assets and are planning to procure their own version of TASM, regardless of what the United

States does. Whatever the precise system derivative that ultimately is chosen by the allies (i.e., Britain and France) for their DCA modernization, the endorsement by the alliance of a generic, nuclear-tasked TASM deployment on European soil will be essential to the alliance's deterrence concept for the years ahead.

For the United States, TASM modernization meets other important requirements—military as well as political. In the Asian-Pacific theater, DCA modernization with TASM will provide an important deterrence asset for balancing North Korean military capabilities. It could also prove critical in helping to stem the tide of proliferation in the region, especially in the Korean context where both North Korea and South Korea possess a technical capability to develop and produce nuclear weapons. In point of fact, proliferation on the Korean peninsula threatens to be one of the most serious issues that may face US planners in the years ahead. To the extent that it is possible for the United States to bolster its deterrent presence in the Asian-Pacific region, we may be better positioned to control the proliferation of nuclear and chemical weapons technologies in the area. Without a strong US deterrent presence in the region, the chain reaction that a North Korean proliferation is likely to unleash would profoundly affect regional stability and raise the prospect that Japan could develop its own nuclear force as well.

Quite apart from its political uses, TASM has important military characteristics that contribute to its deterrence credibility, especially against hardened, fixed targets behind enemy lines. As NATO moves to adapt a new defensive concept, TASM could be fundamental—conceived as a weapon of last resort to test enemy intentions and to warn of a prospective strategic response. Outside of Europe, the capacity to deploy nuclear weapons—whether or not they are actually loaded on a DCA—nevertheless continues to perpetuate the notion of uncertainty that has been and continues to be central to the deterrence calculus, certainly in the Asian theater and perhaps elsewhere.

However, if deterrence should fail in Europe, for example, the twin requirements of the allied air forces to win air superiority and subsequently to conduct operations against enemy territory, as well as in support of allied troop movements on the ground, will require more advanced coordination and target-identification capabilities. The type of capability that is represented in the airborne warning and control system (AWACS) will be all the more important for midintensity to high-intensity conflict environments in the future, both to coordinate the flow of friendly air traffic and to help identify and/or interdict enemy ground-force deployments. With the battle-management task supported by AWACS technologies, a typical air force BAI strike package in a midintensity to high-intensity conflict environment of the future could optimally include advanced standoff precision-delivered weapons platforms; associated air-to-air fighters for protection, with electronic-warfare platforms supported by radar-suppression assets; and an air-refueling capability. Depending on the specifics of the warfare contingency itself, US air power typically can be expected to contribute the bulk of such a force—except perhaps in Europe, where allied air power may include elements of each of these generic types of capabilities, and through NATO, where the experience of ACE mobile-forces planning can supplement (as British and French air forces did in the KTO) US operational capabilities.

As was the case during Desert Storm, the US Air Force can expect to use its capabilities in a number of new and important ways, from the interdiction of Soviet-built ballistic-missile launchers to target acquisition and the timely destruction of ground forces. It is unlikely that in Europe—or indeed in any theater of operations in which the Soviet Union may be actively engaged in support of its interests—air power by itself will be able to achieve the dramatic results that it did during the six weeks of bombing in the Kuwaiti theater. Even in the Gulf war, a cease-fire was negotiated only after the ground war began. Nevertheless, the deep-strike assets that were used so effectively in the strategic air campaign over Iraq would be vital to operations in Europe, where Soviet surface-to-air missile networks incorporate more advanced technologies. In point of fact, however, the concept of strategic bombing that was first articulated by such air power pioneers as Giulio Douhet in Italy and Gen Ira C. Eaker and

Gen Carl ("Tooey") Spaatz in the US was made possible by advances in technology that are at the foundation of current US Air Force thinking about contingency planning for the European theater. These advances also underlie the concepts for operations beyond NATO Europe, as in Korea or in the Middle East, where the destruction of enemy territory and infrastructure is considered vital to a possible reconstitution or forces-regeneration effort. For this task in particular—but also in support of tactical air missions (especially battlefield air interdiction)—the use of advanced intelligence capabilities (space-based, AWACS, and the Tactical Information Broadcast System—TIBS) will play an even more decisive role in helping to isolate and defeat frontline forces.

In less-intensive conflict environments, there has been discussion of US air power in support of counterinsurgency operations. Whether this represents the optimal use of US fixed-wing air power assets is questionable, especially if new-generation rotary-wing gunships (Apache and light helicopter) and perhaps even Harrier-type aircraft are available. In these types of contingencies, airfield availability and security would be a greater problem for fixed-wing aircraft than would the relative systems vulnerability of a platform itself as it performs its mission. In the final analysis, however, it is likely that the cost and technological sophistication of new-generation fixed-wing platforms will work against their employment in counterinsurgency environments, although certainly in terms of lift assets an aircraft like the C-17 could contribute to reinforcing allied capabilities in a counterinsurgency operation. In general, however—short of a limited-duration engagement, such as a raiding mission or the operations in Grenada or Panama—the capabilities of high-technology, sophisticated aircraft would probably not be cost-effective for employment in most counterinsurgency-type operations, although a long-range stealth bomber could be useful if employed in a limited fashion to interdict clearly designated enemy staging areas or logistical depots. Normally, by their nature, insurgency campaigns do not lend themselves to the type of target array that would be optimal for fixed-wing air power employment in a CAS or BAI role. Our experience in Vietnam seems to support these conclusions, although the lack of an integrated coalition command structure—coupled with the preference of successive US administrations to interfere with the theater operational planning—certainly limited the effectiveness of both the strategic-bombing campaign in North Vietnam and the CAS/BAI interdiction effort in South Vietnam. In lower-intensity conflict scenarios and counterinsurgency environments, US special operations forces and intelligence assets may contribute to supporting US global interests, provided that there is a political commitment to do so and, if necessary, to sustain operations if a one-time-only mission is not possible (to obtain or satisfy US/allied political objectives).

As in all US planning for the reinforcement of allied interests in specific contingencies, it is axiomatic that the political will and bipartisan consensus must exist in the United States prior to the commitment of American forces overseas. Perhaps it is unfortunate, but the deployment of US forces in support of American global strategy is more easily done in the context of contingency planning against a well-defined, visible adversary force. Saddam Hussein made it relatively easy for the Bush administration to gain congressional and American public support for the Desert Storm operation, which included the unprecedented "peacetime" mobilization of US reserve and National Guard forces. Saddam Hussein also facilitated the actions of the United Nations, which legitimized the organization of the coalition of forces that ultimately were used against Iraq. In the future this will be a very important aspect of coalition-building activities in support of contingency planning for specific conflict scenarios.

If, in the future, great thought must be given to identifying the contingencies to which the United States should commit itself militarily in order to safeguard its global strategic interests, US planners must also be deliberate about facing the hard force-structure and acquisition choices of the future. In an era of constrained defense spending, shrinking logistical infrastructure, and manpower limitations, equipment-acquisition programs will have to be developed and optimized according to more exacting criteria that maximize force survivability and systems flexibility in a variety of complex military environments. Last, it will remain important to remind ourselves that the multidimensional nature of air power facilitates its use in a global-alliance strategy. This will be no less true in the emerging context of forward deployment, power projection, and US interests in the complex world of the future than it was in the earlier years of this century.

Notes

1. Figures are derived from the following sources: *Times* (London), *Financial Times*, *Wall Street Journal*, *Washington Post*, *The Economist*, and *New York Times*.

2. Before the Gulf war, this study envisaged manpower cuts in Royal Army strength from 160,000 to 120,000 over five years; Royal Air Force (RAF) reductions from 89,000 to 75,000; and 5 percent cuts in the Royal Navy and Marines—from 63,000 to 60,000. Equipment cuts for the RAF included four Tornado squadrons in the British Army of the Rhine and one United Kingdom-based Tornado squadron. In addition, the planned order of 33 new Tornado interceptors was cancelled in 1990.

3. Michael Smith, "RAF 'Locked' into European Tactics," *Daily Telegraph*, 9 March 1991.

PART IV

Designing Aerospace Force Structures

Introduction

During the Gulf war, Secretary of Defense Dick Cheney observed that, given the budgetary and fiscal constraints envisioned for the US military over the next several years, had Saddam Hussein waited five years to invade Kuwait (or Saudi Arabia), the United States would have been unable to respond in the successful manner that it did. The Gulf conflict has had the important side effect of demonstrating the critical contribution of mobile forces and long-range lift capacity in responding to threats to US interests around the globe. The following specialists seek to define what shape the future force structure might take, given the anticipated massive cuts to military service budgets.

Maj Gen Robert M. Alexander presents an informative sketch of Air Force restructuring to be effected over the next several years. The impetus behind this move to transform force structure is the realization that "we have witnessed monumental shifts in the paradigms that we traditionally use to plan our force structure. The national military strategy is changing." The changes in the security environment, especially with regard to the Soviet threat, have propelled the movement toward cutting the budget and downsizing the US military. As Secretary Cheney has stated, the cuts are so deep that there must be not only reductions, but also restructuring to achieve maximum effectiveness from smaller forces. Citing Chairman of the Joint Chiefs of Staff Gen Colin Powell and Under Secretary of Defense Paul Wolfowitz, General Alexander sees the future shape of the US military coalescing around the following four "packages": (1) a strategic force, (2) an Atlantic force, (3) a Pacific force, and (4) a contingency force. Each of these packages will require a number of supporting elements from the Air Force. First, there will be the need for an air fleet capable of transporting forces to thwart an aggressor. A second support element will be space systems, including modernized versions of current space capabilities, new constellations of satellites, and advanced launch systems. A third support element will take the form of America's "shrinking defense industrial base [that] will affect reconstitution as well as research and development."

General Alexander provides us with some numbers for the future force structure of the Air Force. Following the Strategic Arms Reduction Talks (START) treaty, strategic forces will amount to 266 bombers and 550 intercontinental ballistic missiles. The number of active duty tactical fighter wings will drop to 15 from the present 24, with another 11 wings in the Guard and Reserve. And strategic lift will be modernized but "stay relatively constant at around 340 aircraft." On the operational side, the Air Force is planning some interesting restructuring. Such measures will involve a change in the way the Air Force organizes its wings. For example, there will be new "composite" wings that will have various packages of aircraft and will have specific roles to play in military action: "One [wing] will be capable of deep-strike attack. Another will provide direct support to the Army. And the third will focus on special operations."

Lt Gen John B. Conaway provides a thought-provoking look at the future of the Air National Guard (ANG) mission. Given the significant scaling down of active duty units, Guard and Reserve units in all the services will take on an increasingly critical role in US national defense. According to General Conaway, although the relationship of the ANG and the Air Force "illustrate[s] the Total Force policy at its best," the cuts in the Air Force's budget will also seriously affect the Air Guard.

Given that the new security environment requires an Air Force that can respond quickly to crises around the world, it follows that the restructuring and realigning of US forces should be done with an eye toward an "effective and viable force mix." General Conaway believes that the National Guard "must continue to maintain its high state of readiness commensurate with its wartime tasking." As the Air Force diversifies and expands its missions, the Air Guard will be an important element in this process. General Conaway envisions that such missions as counternarcotics and forward training will be growth areas for the Air Guard. Additionally, the "'burden shifting' being studied by the DOD may suggest missions in Europe that could be transferred to the Guard and manned on a rotating basis."

Lt Gen Thomas S. Moorman, Jr., presents an enlightening picture of what the US Air Force's space assets and missions will look like in the next decade and beyond. Pointing out that the Air Force Space Command was a product of the late 1970s—a time characterized by a deficit in operational space commands—General Moorman informs us that under the Space Command's direction, the Air Force has reached its full potential in the all-important security arena of space. In the years ahead, he acknowledges, this potential will be challenged by budget cuts and force contractions that will invariably affect the Air Force's terrestrial support systems. Yet, space systems amply demonstrated their importance to tactical and strategic operations during the Gulf war. He mentions several space systems that performed well during the conflict: (1) the global positioning system, (2) the Defense Satellite Communications System, and (3) the Defense Meteorological Satellite Program. As General Moorman puts it, "the importance of Operation Desert Storm as a catalyst for accelerating the future development of tactical space applications cannot be overstated."

In the years ahead, the diverse military benefits accrued from space systems—communications, navigation, weather data, surveillance—will become available to many nations. It is of critical importance, General Moorman warns, that the US develop the capability to control the space battlefield of the future, just as it controlled the ground battlefield during the Gulf war.

Force Structure for the Future

Maj Gen Robert M. Alexander, USAF

It is a wonderful time to write about air power. As a result of Operation Desert Storm, there seems to be a much better understanding of air power and the contribution it can make to our nation's defense. At the same time, we must look to the future. We must understand not only the role air power played in our history but also the role it will play in meeting future security needs. In order to do this, we must think about the future security environment and plan our forces accordingly.

We have witnessed monumental shifts in the paradigms that we traditionally use to plan our force structure. The national military strategy is changing. This is a result of changes in the national security strategy and the still-emerging strategic environment. Those changes, in turn, are affecting in fundamental ways the structure of the United States Air Force. This essay addresses the nature of these shifts: how recent events may totally redefine the security environment in which we operate; how the secretary of defense and the chairman of the Joint Chiefs of Staff (JCS) are translating this new environment into a new security agenda; and how the Air Force is complying with their direction.

It seems that each day brings even more dramatic changes in the world. It was no April fool when the military component of the Warsaw Pact went out of business on 1 April 1991. The Soviet Union has already agreed to withdraw its troops from Czechoslovakia, Hungary, and Germany and is negotiating a withdrawal from Poland. The Soviets' ability to project power into Europe is fading, and they cannot turn this around without giving us months—maybe years—of warning time. The surge of free elections in Eastern Europe has been astounding. Germany is now united within NATO—something that was only a dream a very few years ago. Outside of Europe, the people of Nicaragua have given Daniel Ortega the boot, and Albania, perhaps the most conservative of European communist nations, held free elections. Cuba and North Korea are becoming more isolated from the global community of nations. The remarks of Gen George Lee Butler, commander in chief of Strategic Air Command, concerning these events are well taken:

> The emerging post–Cold War environment is dominated by six new and historic forces that are largely reshaping the global strategic environment: (1) Soviet retrenchment and the end of the Cold War, events so consequential they are akin to a virtual second Russian Revolution; (2) German reunification and its impact on the European security agenda; (3) the emerging prospects for a 21st century Concert of Europe; (4) the intensification of intractable, regional strife and conflict, exacerbated by impatient populations and the proliferation of high technology weapons; (5) catastrophic failures in the human condition due to economic and political disintegration; and (6) the rise of new centers of power with either hegemonic or strongly competitive goals. Taken together, these forces represent a volcanic upset of longstanding strategic calculations and call for a sweeping reassessment of traditional views and approaches.[1]

At the same time, American power is resurgent. Our military has gained confidence and has earned renewed respect. Our political leadership is first-rate. There is a world perception that only the United States could have put the Desert Shield coalition together and led it to the overwhelming defeat of Iraq.

There is another factor that the defense planner must consider—the budget. President George Bush has told us that the cold war is over, and his defense budget reflects this policy. The administration has agreed to cut defense spending to less than 4 percent of the gross national product—the lowest percentage since 1939 and one-third of its 1985 high.[2] The cut for the Air Force is even more dramatic: we expect Air Force purchasing power to decline 45 percent from its 1985 level.[3]

As a result of all this, the president has called for more than simple reorganization: "What we need are not merely reductions, but restructuring."[4] As a consequence, Secretary of Defense Dick Cheney directed that we shift "the focus of defense planning from countering the global challenge posed by the Soviet Union to responding to threats in major regions."[5] The planners' yardstick for building military force structure is no longer the European scenario that escalates to global war.

In response to changes in the security environment and the resulting changes in our strategy, Gen Colin L. Powell, chairman of the JCS, is restructuring and redistributing our military forces while carefully defining the minimum force structure required to meet emerging security needs. He envisions four basic military force packages (strategic, Atlantic, Pacific, and contingency) designed to provide deterrence and defense, regional presence, and crisis response. These force packages will be backed by four supporting capabilities (transportation, space, reconstitution, and research and development).[6] Let me caution that none of this is in concrete.

The planned strategic forces retain the triad of ground-based ballistic missiles, manned bombers, and ballistic missile submarines. We anticipate continued progress in arms control while we continue to modernize our forces and work on the Strategic Defense Initiative. Atlantic forces will maintain our peacetime engagement in Europe and Southwest Asia. They will also form the bedrock of our reconstitution capability, should the need arise. Pacific forces will provide presence and deterrence throughout the Pacific region. Contingency forces are the "tip of the spear," providing rapid crisis and contingency response throughout the world. They will include active duty conventional and special operations forces.

Each of these force packages, however, will depend on supporting elements. Transportation is critical to our ability to project power. The airlift fleet will replace the retiring C-141 with the C-17.[7] Another support element—space—is vitally important. As Adm David E. Jeremiah, vice-chairman of the JCS, recently told Congress, "Space technologies will impact, more than any other, the accomplishment of the military mission. Space will be the key to deterrence."[8] We will institutionalize and modernize current capabilities, add constellations of satellites, and pursue advanced launch systems. A third supporting element—our shrinking defense industrial base—will affect reconstitution as well as research and development. Although outside the scope of this essay, this topic is receiving serious attention from planners at the Deputy Chief of Staff for Plans and Operations, Headquarters USAF.

General Powell's restructuring and redistributing will require a much smaller force. As mentioned previously, none of this is in concrete; however, it gives us a good idea of the structure of our future force. According to Amb Paul Wolfowitz, the under secretary of defense for policy, our strategic force structure following the Strategic Arms Reduction Talks will include 266 bombers and 550 intercontinental ballistic missiles.[9] General Powell's force packages will cut active duty tactical fighter wings from the present 24 wings to 15, with another 11 wings in the Guard and Reserve.[10] Strategic airlift will be modernized but will probably stay relatively constant at around 340 aircraft. The global security environment has changed; the dollars available for defense have dropped by a third; the president has called for restructuring; and the secretary of defense and the chairman of the JCS are directing new strategies, command relationships, and force structures.

What will the Air Force do? On the operational side, it will do some restructuring. We will attempt to match the evolving national strategy with air power's unique capabilities of speed, range, flexibility, precision, and lethality. These are outlined in more detail in Secretary of the Air Force Donald B. Rice's white paper *The Air Force and U.S. National Security: Global Reach—Global Power*.[11] We will seek to maximize these capabilities to project power rapidly and do this in some innovative ways. To quote Secretary Rice's 1991 report to Congress,

> Internal restructuring focuses on streamlining the Air Force to increase organizational efficiency from the flight line to Air Force headquarters. One innovative initiative is the creation of composite wings that include—at one base, under one commander—all the resources needed to form composite force packages. One wing commander will have all the necessary resources to execute "mission type" orders, significantly reducing command, control, and communications (C^3) problems.[12]

The key concepts here are management streamlining and a new approach to the way we organize wings. The Air Force is moving out in both areas. In management streamlining, we have already reorganized the Air Staff, announced the consolidation of Logistics Command and Systems Command into Materiel Command, continued to cut staffs in the field, disbanded a number of air divisions, consolidated laboratories, and changed the group structure within flying wings.

The secretary's comment on composite wings has gotten high-level attention lately. The subject deserves some elaboration. First, composite wings are a test-bed. There is no decision to implement the concept Air Force wide. However, the rationale behind the organization is revealing. Composite wings may not have been appropriate in the past, but they are ideally suited to the way our senior leadership sees the new world order. If one understands why Gen Merrill A. McPeak, Air Force chief of staff, and Secretary Rice are considering composite wings, one can better understand where the Air Force is going. Second, the long pole in the tent on composite wings has always been logistics. We thought that putting multiple aircraft in one wing would drive the support costs through the roof. When General McPeak was in the Pacific, he asked the Rand Corporation to study the logistics side of composite wings. Rand concluded that at any number above a half-dozen or so aircraft of each type, the added costs are marginal—less than 2 percent. The Proven Force operation out of Incirlik Air Base, Turkey, during Desert Storm seems to support Rand's analysis, so we are pressing ahead to test the waters. Third, we are at a unique point in time that is fertile for this idea. Composite air strike forces are not new. Gen Henry P. Viccellio wrote about this idea in 1956.[13] Strategic Air Command, with its squadrons of B-52s and KC-135s, has had composite wings for years. But today, there is a convergence of factors that make composite wings more appropriate: the change in the global environment; a corresponding new military strategy; technological advancements in command, control, communications, intelligence, and space; and improvements in maintainability and reliability.

Consider composite wings A, B, and C. Each wing will be structured to bring different facets of air power to a fight. One will be capable of deep-strike attack. Another will provide direct support to the Army. And the third will focus on special operations.

Wing A is ideally suited for a contingency such as Desert Shield. It would be primed for immediate deployment. The wing would train together and deploy together. It would have capabilities for air defense, deep strike, air refueling, airborne warning and control system (AWACS), and suppression of enemy air defenses. Just like a Navy carrier air wing, it would have its command structure in place. In terms of aircraft, this wing could have F-15Es for deep strike, F-15Cs for air defense, F-16s for interdiction, KC-10s/135s for air refueling, and AWACS aircraft for surveillance and command, control, and communications. Its missions would be rapid response and power projection, and the wing staff would form the tactical air control center. Command and control would be easier because everybody would be at the same base. The wing would have the punch to strike deep and still protect itself. In other words, it could deploy quickly and operate independently. This wing could also have B-52s. In a recent speech, General McPeak spoke of the "blurring distinction between tactical and strategic," noting that

> the difference between the tactical and strategic is very fuzzy. . . . Strategic and tactical no longer mean nuclear and conventional; they no longer mean short versus long range; they no longer have much to do with payload. . . . So I no longer know what the division between tactical and strategic is.[14]

If aircraft are no longer tied to a specific mission, their link to a specific command is cut. That is a huge departure from the way we currently think about air power. But it is totally in synch with power projection, quick response to regional crises, and strategic air power. This is why composite wings reflect a fundamental shift in our national security environment—one to which our Air Force must adapt.

Wing B will be designed to work directly with the Army. Its mission would be to support a land campaign. Assuming a permissive air environment, the wing would concentrate on close air support and maneuver and would work closely with Army planners. One should think in terms of Operation Just Cause in Panama for this wing. It could have A-10s and F/A-16s for close air support, AC-130s for armed reconnaissance, OA-10s for forward air control, and C-130s for tactical airlift. General McPeak wants a wing ready to provide immediate support to the Army, with the command element in place and exercised. This wing would concentrate on AirLand Battle, while wing A focuses on the strategic air campaign.

The last type of composite wing already exists. The 1st Special Operations Wing at Hurlburt Field, Florida, has MC-130 Talons, AC-130 gunships, Pave Low helicopters, and HC-130 tankers. It has all the systems that it needs to operate independently or as part of a larger operation. Because special operations will continue to get high visibility, we will fold it under the composite wing umbrella.

In summary, our chief and secretary are taking an innovative approach. Both men believe that the new defense strategies and budgets dictate a fundamental restructuring of our Air Force. They are developing ways to make the Air Force of the future more responsive and capable.

Notes

1. House, *Statement by General George Lee Butler to the Defense Subcommittee of the House Appropriations Committee*, 102d Cong., 1st sess., 20 March 1991, 969.

2. Secretary of Defense Dick Cheney, Walsh lecture, Georgetown University, Washington, D.C., 21 March 1991.

3. Senate, *Statement by Secretary of the Air Force Donald B. Rice to the Senate Armed Services Committee*, 102d Cong., 1st sess., 20 March 1991, 461, figure 1.

4. President George Bush, address to the Aspen Institute, Aspen, Colorado, 2 August 1990.

5. Dick Cheney, *Report of the Secretary of Defense to the President and the Congress* (Washington, D.C.: Government Printing Office, January 1991), v.

6. House, *Statement by General Colin L. Powell, Chairman of the Joint Chiefs of Staff, to the House Armed Services Committee*, 102d Cong., 1st sess., 7 February 1991, 48.

7. Senate, *Statement by Admiral David E. Jeremiah, Vice-Chairman of the Joint Chiefs of Staff, to the Senate Armed Services Committee*, 102d Cong., 1st sess., 11 April 1991, 574.

8. House, *Statement by Admiral David E. Jeremiah, Vice-Chairman of the Joint Chiefs of Staff, to the House Armed Services Committee*, 102d Cong., 1st sess., 12 March 1991, 286.

9. House, *Statement by Under Secretary of Defense for Policy Paul Wolfowitz to the House Armed Services Committee, Subcommittee on Procurement and Military Nuclear Systems*, 102d Cong., 1st sess., 20 March 1991.

10. House, *Statement by Admiral David E. Jeremiah*, 275.

11. Secretary of the Air Force Donald B. Rice, *The Air Force and U.S. National Security: Global Reach—Global Power* (Washington, D.C.: Department of the Air Force, June 1990).

12. *The United States Air Force Report to the 102nd Congress of the United States of America, Fiscal Year 1992/93* (Washington, D.C.: Government Printing Office, 1991), 2.

13. Brig Gen Henry P. Viccellio, "Composite Air Strike Force," *Air University Quarterly Review* 9, no. 1 (Winter 1956–1957): 27–38.

14. Gen Merrill A. McPeak, Air Force chief of staff, address to the Air Force Association Tactical Air Warfare Symposium, Orlando, Fla., 31 January 1991.

The Air National Guard Today
Looking to the Future

Lt Gen John B. Conaway, National Guard Bureau

> The world security environment has undergone a major transformation, and the risks to U.S. security interests are greatly reduced, especially in Europe. This is due largely to a change in East-West relations brought about by the failure of communism and a successful strategy of deterrence by the West over the past 40 years. The extent of the changes, and particularly the elimination of the threat of a massive, short warning invasion of Europe, has enabled the Department to work towards refining a strategy for the emerging world security environment and has mandated a reassessment of many of the imperatives that have shaped our defense strategy for the past four decades.
>
> —Secretary of Defense Dick Cheney
> *Annual Report to the President and the Congress* (1991)

The world as we have known it since the end of the Second World War has been literally transformed. Nations, once divided, today unite in a common pursuit of economic and political freedom. We who serve in the United States military should feel fortunate to be a part of our world as it stands at the threshold of dramatic and historic transformation.

As Americans enter the 1990s, they see a world quite different from the one they have known virtually all of their lives. The echoes of democracy can be heard across the continents as countries once held in the grip of communist domination get their first taste of what it means to be free. Americans feel great hope as they witness the dramatic events taking shape throughout the world. In light of the new realities in Europe, the US military is undertaking the tremendous task of restructuring and realigning its forces to best meet the unique and uncertain challenges of the coming century. Whereas the 1980s marked an era of growth and expansion in missions and force structure, the 1990s will usher in a period of drastic reductions in defense spending. Such budgetary realities and the fact that tomorrow's Air Force will be leaner while remaining both flexible and responsive will no doubt affect the Air Force's vital arm—the Air National Guard (ANG).

Since the creation of the first federally recognized National Guard aviation unit—the First Aero Company of the New York National Guard—in 1915, National Guard aviation has augmented active duty forces in times of crisis and in the interest of national security goals. ANG units have been called to federal active duty or to otherwise augment active forces in virtually every major crisis of this century, including World War I, World War II, the Korean War, the Berlin crisis, the *Pueblo* crisis, the Vietnam War, Operation Urgent Fury (Grenada), Operation El Dorado Canyon (Libya), Operation Just Cause (Panama), and—most recently—the Desert Shield and Desert Storm operations.

The Air Force and the ANG illustrate the Total Force policy at its best—a mutually beneficial relationship which has evolved over the years from the Total Force policy "blueprint" of the 1970s. Since the inception of this defense policy, the Air Force leadership has enthusiastically embraced the idea of teaming active, Guard, and Reserve units together to capitalize on the strengths and unique qualities of each. In many ways, the Air Force has been a leader in putting the Total Force theory into real-world practice.

As fiscal constraints became a major controlling factor in shaping military policy after Vietnam, the Guard and Reserve became more attractive alternatives to providing a cost-effective deterrent force capable of meeting the nation's security requirements in an emerging era of limited resources. Inspection results and participation in real-world contingencies validated the wisdom of the Air Force leadership's decision to invest in the Air Guard as an equal partner in guarding America's skies.

Over the years, the ANG has earned its wings as an efficient and cost-effective, well-trained and fully capable, ready and responsive resource to augment the active component. The most recent example of how smoothly the Total Force policy can work was the Air Guard's performance in operations Desert Shield and Desert Storm.

The ANG supported Desert Shield and Desert Storm as tasked—in most cases for 60–90 days without requiring mobilization. The number of volunteers ready to deploy on behalf of their nation was truly astounding. Within the first crucial days of the largest military operation since the Vietnam conflict, more than 10,000 National Guard volunteers freely stepped forward, ready to assist their active duty counterparts in every imaginable combat and combat-support specialty. By February 1991, 81 Air Guard units and close to 10,000 Air Guard men and women had been mobilized, with many more guardsmen serving in a volunteer status.

When mobilized, units responded and executed their tasking. The interface with both deployed and active forces based in the continental United States (CONUS) was easy and successful. The secret to this smooth interface between the active component and the ANG has been the Air Force's pioneering steps toward a functional Total Force policy.

From the birth of the Total Force policy during the post–Vietnam era, the Air Force has led the Department of Defense (DOD) in modernizing the reserve component, sharing missions, and training for combat. The combat tasking of flying and ground squadrons in the ANG is virtually identical to that of their active counterparts. For the ANG, when combat calls, units deploy to fight the way they train—and they fight well. Operation Desert Storm has provided an excellent measure of both the credibility and viability of the Total Force policy.

About 60 percent of the members of the average Air Guard unit have prior military service; most of them are former Air Force personnel. This composition combines with the stability of the "hometown" members to yield top-quality people, unit integrity, and an experienced, seasoned baseline. The result is high-quality units that work well together, sustain high morale, and represent a unique "value added" aspect to America.

Fiscal constraints may continue to pressure the DOD to scale back forces. As Secretary of the Air Force Donald B. Rice pointed out in his June 1990 white paper *The Air Force and U.S. National Security: Global Reach—Global Power*, rapid global change guarantees a period of intense political instability, serious economic dislocation, and a broad dispersion of military strength. With the collapse of the Warsaw Pact, the likelihood of a massive invasion into Western Europe has diminished considerably. As the DOD refines and defines the strategic threats of the twenty-first century, we see our national defense strategy shifting focus to containing major regional threats in other areas of the world. With a renewed focus comes the necessary restructuring and realigning of US forces to determine the most effective and viable force mix in the post–cold war era. A complete reevaluation of the philosophy and paradigms that define our military structures is in progress. Just what this will mean to the ANG of the future is unclear at this juncture. New missions and new roles could emerge. But as has been demonstrated time and again, the Air Guard is no stranger to weathering the stormy winds of change.

What we do know is that as our rethinking and restructuring proceed, we must retain a convincing global deterrent capability—a power capable of maintaining our superpower status. As the recognized leader of the free world, our nation today bears a unique responsibility to maintain a strong, credible defense posture in order to reinforce the international laws which guarantee human freedom, enforce US and allied interests, and safeguard our children's birthright of a democratic society.

As Congress and our national leaders labor under severe fiscal pressure to balance the budget, meeting these national security goals in the 1990s may mean that even more missions are placed in the reserve component. The ANG's wartime mission and commitments have continued to grow under the Total Force policy. Today, the Guard has about 117,000 members and provides the Air Force with a significant share of the Total Force in most mission areas. Through the economy of a fully capable, immediately available, ready, and reliable Air Reserve component, we exploit the benefit of a force in reserve. But we are already carrying a heavy load in some areas, even though other missions offer room to help out. For example, by fiscal year 1993 the Air Guard will represent

- 100 percent of the fighter interceptor force
- 100 percent of tactical reconnaissance
- 45 percent of tactical air support
- 40 percent of tactical airlift
- 31 percent of the tactical fighter force
- 30 percent of strategic air refueling
- 30 percent of rescue and recovery
- 6 percent of strategic airlift
- 6 percent of electronic warfare

Of the approximately 1,140 ANG mission-support units, 150 provide manpower and resources to Air Force Communications Command. Air Guard combat communications, as well as engineering and installations units, constitute about 70 percent of their respective areas in the entire Air Force. In fiscal year 1993, 99 percent of the early-warning capability and about 60 percent of the tactical air control requirement will be in the ANG. On the other hand, only 12 percent of the medical capability rests with the Guard, and its 39 weather flights account for about 14 percent of the entire USAF weather force. But the latter figure—modest as it seems—represents over 50 percent of the total wartime weather support for the Army. Further, ANG civil engineering units (priority improved management effort [PRIME] base emergency engineering force [BEEF]; PRIME readiness in base services [RIBS]) represent 27 percent of the total requirement, while rapid engineer deployable, heavy operational repair squadron, engineer (RED HORSE) represents 34 percent of the total requirement. Our 10 aeromedical evacuation units account for 26 percent of the Air Force capability, and our 23 aerial port units account for 13 percent of that area.

Units in these mission areas participate in annual training deployments to overseas locations where Guard personnel work hand in hand with their active counterparts. Where we share missions, the Guard is identical to the active force in terms of capability and execution. In Panama, ANG A-7s on year-round alert duty were

THE FUTURE OF AIR POWER

called upon to support US operations during the liberation that played a key role in helping to restore that country's legitimate democratic government. The Panama alert is now being covered by Air Guard F-16s and F-15s. Closer to home, Guard F-15s, F-16s, and KC-135s cover 24-hour alert year-round in support of air defense and single integrated operational plan (SIOP) alert requirements.

The flexibility of ANG ground and air forces helps form the fabric of national air sovereignty through the ANG's air defense mission. The ANG's versatile air defense fighter and support forces are also supporting President George Bush's domestic and international thrusts in the war on drugs. They fly frequently in the CONUS in support of law enforcement, as well as pull around-the-clock drug alert in Panama to aid the effort to choke off the southern sources of illegal drugs. The Guard has led the way through state-sponsored efforts in drug eradication and interdiction and will continue to work closely to bring our country one step closer to becoming drug free.

The 54 state and territory drug plans are a testimony to the Guard's role as a barometer of national will to fight illegal drugs with every tool available. But fighters and radar systems in the Caribbean Basin are only two ways the Guard has been meeting the requirement for forward presence to support our national policy.

Another program unique to the ANG is its foreign military sales F-16A/B training program at Tucson, Arizona. As the sole US operator of the F-16A/B aircraft, the ANG has assumed an increased responsibility for training international pilots. The Dutch were the first in what may eventually become a larger "customer group" for this complete fighter-training program. As with other international programs, the customer pays for the training, and the program does not degrade the Guard's combat capability. More may be done in this vital area of military assistance.

Other military assistance activities worldwide are a natural for the Air Guard. Engineers, communicators, medics, and others have found a warm reception outside the CONUS from military leaders impressed with the capability of the militia and from the local nationals, who share a common ground with the citizen-soldier.

Engineering and services units have been strong players in humanitarian/civic-action activities in US Southern Command. Bolivian hospitals; Honduran medical facilities, schools, and clinics; Costa Rican schools, community centers, and clinics; and Jamaican and Panamanian hurricane-damage repair and new construction are part of an extensive list of projects done for training. They have the added benefit of winning the hearts of disadvantaged and helpless humans.

To our foreign friends and allies, the presence of air guardsmen on their soil represents the positive will and shared human interests of the general population of the United States. To other nations, the military capability and global reach of the Guard as part of the total Air Force represent an indelible statement by the American people that we—as a nation—care and are committed to supporting and sustaining the growth of world freedom and democracy. Recent events have proven that we are not afraid to use our military power under sanction of the United Nations.

When superpowers were locked "nose to nose," stability was memorialized in concrete and steel: the Berlin Wall. Both competition in the marketplace and the minds of men and women were won decisively by democratic ideals. The wall crumbled. What will fill the vacuum left in the wake of confrontation is as yet unclear. We can be sure of one thing: The "freedom way"—citizens acting on their own behalf to determine their government and to steer their society toward freedom and justice—will be the vision that dominates the balance of the twenty-first century. The citizen-soldier is a perfect image for projecting the will of America and for being the role model of the emerging European frontier.

In the 1990s the Guard must continue to maintain its high state of readiness commensurate with its wartime tasking. ANG units are ready now to do their jobs at bargain prices. This high state of readiness is a perishable national asset that should be safeguarded. Continued use of our personnel in ways best suited to optimize the benefits of a stable, high-tech, lethal combat force is important. But the nature of the militia—with its citizen-soldier core—must also be guarded.

The essential team spirit of the well-managed Total Force policy will continue to provide the balance required for the best air offense and defense for America, and the Air Guard will continue to play its important part at home and abroad. At home, continued sophistication and expansion of Guard counterdrug operations provide a natural growth industry for the next decade. Other forms of military assistance will expand as the Air Force diversifies its global reach.

We see a renewed effort to use our military capability and training to serve American citizens in time of disaster and emergency. State and community service are important commitments made by men and women of the Guard when they take the dual oath to protect and preserve both state and nation. Rapid response is a hallmark of the Guard's state mission, and tough training in realistic environments keeps the Air Guard up for the most challenging circumstances.

Often overlooked is the value of state mission service to the enhancement of federal mission capability. The skill, training, discipline, coordination, and cohesion demonstrated during the performance of state missions directly contribute to the Guard's wartime mission capability. The past era of 48 unit-training assemblies (drill periods) per year and two weeks "in the summer" has been largely overtaken by expanded requirements, resulting in a better trained, highly motivated, and fully capable ANG.

Deployed training will also continue to provide an expanding role for the Air Guard in sharing the load of forward presence with the active component. The "burden shifting" being studied by the DOD may suggest missions in Europe that could be transferred to the Guard and manned on a rotating basis. We have had outstanding results using this concept with the Army Guard's Aviation Classification Repair Activity Depot facility in Brussels, Belgium, and our equipment maintenance center in Kaiserslautern, Germany. Other opportunities to be considered may include transportation, medical, civil engineering, aerial port, fighter, tanker, and airlift missions.

One of our longest experiences with sustained presence in Europe has been the Creek Party deployment program. During the 1960s and 1970s, Air Guard tankers provided 70 percent of the European air refueling requirements. In addition, the operations in Panama with C-130s and fighters have been sustained since the mid-1970s.

Guard training must be clearly guided to take in not only the environment of future battle but also the organizational structure for employment. Wing structures and combat unit dispositions need to be logically reviewed to prepare us for the future battle.

The ANG has also been looking toward the newest frontier of space, where the Guard's stability and high retention rate could pay substantial dividends in such a high-tech environment. ANG participation in the areas of control, radar, and communications offers promise.

Because 99 percent of all Air Guard units are mission capable, protecting the quality of the fighting force retains extraordinary value for Total Force partners. The resources to do the job and the opportunity to serve are all that an American warrior needs, regardless of service or component.

Exciting missions, equipment modernization, significant participation in worldwide training exercises and operational deployments, coupled with exemplary performance in inspections and competitions, make today's ANG a proud, prepared, and professional component of the total Air Force.

In looking to the future, we cannot predict with precision just where tomorrow's threats will be. The volcano of events which have recently taken place illustrates how quickly the geopolitical landscape can shift and change. As Secretary of Defense Dick Cheney outlined in his annual report to Congress and the president, the many factors which have shaped our defense strategy since the close of the Second World War no longer drive our overall military strategy. Regional instability and the proliferation of nuclear, biological, and chemical weaponry rank among the many threats facing continued global security and stability. As we prepare for tomorrow, we know that flexibility, both in our responsiveness and in our approach to defining the appropriate Total Force balance, will be a key element in building an effective, viable military deterrent which will help take our nation into the next century and beyond.

Space: A New Strategic Frontier

Lt Gen Thomas S. Moorman, Jr., USAF

This essay considers how the unique medium of space can help meet the challenges facing our nation. The subject is timely in that space operations are finally coming into their own—specifically, the application of space assets to support Air Force missions. The essay's title may be a misnomer, for space systems are not really very new but clearly will become more important to the Air Force and to the nation during the remainder of the 1990s and beyond. For over 30 years, the Air Force has evolved its space capabilities to provide national decision makers and operational commanders on the battlefield with information critical to the maintenance of deterrence and to the prosecution of hostilities should deterrence fail. Since the formation of Air Force Space Command in the early 1980s, the space community has been working hard to develop the requisite policy, strategy, acquisition, and operational underpinnings to meet the challenge of a range of military conflicts. However, it was not until Operation Desert Storm that space systems were able to make broad, critical contributions to the outcome of a conflict. To better appreciate what the future holds for space in the Air Force, one must review how our presence in space evolved to this point.

Evolution

With the launch of Sputnik I in 1957, the United States—particularly the US Air Force—was galvanized into action to meet the threat posed by the potential Soviet domination of space. Because the new medium had uncertain operational applications, the research and development (R&D) community took the lead in acquiring and operating our space programs. Our launch vehicles were, by necessity, converted intercontinental ballistic missiles (ICBM), and a wide range of space-based capabilities were developed. Satellite systems pushed the state of the art and were understandably technology-driven.

The early satellites focused on meeting strategic missions. For example, a missile warning system known as the missile defense alarm system (MIDAS)—the forerunner of our currently deployed Defense Support Program—became one of the first "operational" Air Force satellites in the early 1960s. To provide detailed meteorological data to strategic users, the Defense Meteorological Satellite Program (DMSP) became operational in the mid-1960s. A host of military and civil communications satellites were developed, especially on the civilian side, spawning an enormously profitable industry within the United States—one which still leads the world.

Early space pioneers such as Gen Bernard A. Schriever built systems which pushed the technology barriers. To keep abreast of the rapidly expanding technology base, scientists incorporated the latest in the state of the art in each new satellite, making each one slightly different from its predecessor. A number of experiments also grew into major satellite programs. Institutionally, the Air Force space community during this time was essentially guided by Air Force civilian leadership.

The nature of the Air Force space business began to change in the mid- to late 1970s due to a variety of factors. One of the most important was that US military forces were gradually becoming more dependent upon space systems as applications were developed from new or evolving satellites. More and more communications traffic was being moved from terrestrial systems to satellites such as the Defense Satellite Communications System (DSCS). The Vietnam War proved the utility of DMSP weather satellites, and the early morning aircraft weather scout became a thing of the past. Visionaries were already looking to a time when satellite-based navigation using the global positioning system (GPS) would revolutionize navigation and weapons delivery. Finally, the tactical utility of data from space programs began to be explored.

With the expansion of space missions came corresponding increases in the size of the Air Force space budget. Space-related funding climbed from 2 percent of the total Air Force budget in the 1960s to 6–7 percent in the 1980s. Another important and related figure is that the Air Force was spending about 75–80 percent of the Department of Defense's (DOD) space budget and also possessed about 85 percent of the space manpower in DOD. Air Force leadership naturally began to pay more attention to a $6-billion space budget.

The space threat posed by the USSR was also expanding. The Soviets fielded the world's only operational antisatellite (ASAT) system and a full complement of reconnaissance and communications satellites. Further, the Soviet Union—year in and year out—demonstrated an extraordinarily robust space-launch capability, including the ability to launch satellites rapidly. Compared to Air Force systems, Soviet military space systems were not as sophisticated, technically capable, or as long-lived; nevertheless, the Soviets were beginning to integrate them into their overall force posture.

Air Force Space Command

These factors led the Air Force to begin studying ways to improve its organizational structure for prosecuting space operations. A series of studies in the late 1970s and early 1980s led to the conclusion that the time had come for a more comprehensive and operational focus on Air Force space programs. This decision was based upon the belief that an operational space command was required for the Air Force to expand its potential in space. Thus, Air Force Space Command was established in the fall of 1982. A year later, Naval Space Command was created, followed in 1985 by United States Space Command and in 1988 by Army Space Command. These organizations now serve both as the advocates for space systems within their respective services and as the operators of these systems, once they are developed and deployed.

In the course of its relatively brief existence, Air Force Space Command has gradually grown in responsibility and resources. At the outset, its mission was confined to operating missile-warning satellites and sensors, and conducting space-surveillance activities. In 1985 it assumed satellite command-and-control responsibilities. In 1990 the space-launch function, as well as the responsibility for associated launch facilities and down-range tracking sites, was transferred to Air Force Space Command from Air Force Systems Command.

Air Force Space Command and the space mission also received significant impetus with the enunciation of Air Force space policy by Secretary of the Air Force Edward C. Aldridge, Jr., and Air Force Chief of Staff Gen Larry D. Welch in December 1988. Two key tenets of the policy were that (1) the future of the Air Force is inextricably tied to space and (2) space power will be as decisive in future combat as air power is today.[1]

Another key tenet of the space policy was that the Air Force made a solid corporate commitment to integrate space throughout the Air Force. This direction resulted in a number of initiatives: incorporating space into Air Force doctrine; establishing personnel policies to stimulate the cross flow of space-trained people between Air Force Space Command and other combatant commands; and expanding space education in the Air Force professional military education curriculum. This policy and the commitment inherent in these statements have far-reaching implications.

A Changing Environment

As we look to the challenges of the 1990s and beyond, the essential ingredients that lead to an expanded role for space are coming together. The Air Force has clearly stated an aggressive space policy to guide its actions; technology has matured to the point that the tactical benefits of space systems can be readily available to our combat forces; and we have in place the organizational structure—a rapidly maturing operational command for space (Air Force Space

Command)—to provide the stimulus and advocacy for new space applications.

The environment in which space systems will be employed has changed dramatically over the past few years. Today and for the foreseeable future, the Air Force faces significant reductions in its budget and force structure. These reductions result primarily from two factors: (1) domestic budget imperatives, as the nation tries to bring the deficit under control, and (2) the startling political and social transformations in both the Soviet Union and Eastern Europe. The latter also implies a reduced strategic and conventional threat from traditional adversaries.

Indeed, as Gen George L. Butler, commander in chief of Strategic Air Command, suggested in a recent speech on the changing geopolitical environment, multipolar relations and emerging nation-states that are asserting their independence from the boundaries of World War II may well lead to increased factionalism and a higher potential for low-intensity conflict.[2] This is already occurring in Iraq, in the Baltic states' press for independence, and in the secession movements within Yugoslavia. Though the imminent threat of global nuclear war has diminished, the geopolitical transformations in the Soviet Union and Eastern Europe do not necessarily promise a reduction in the conventional threat to US interests throughout the world. The 1990s are likely to be characterized by the military growth of nonaligned countries—the military multipolarity which Dr Robert L. Pfaltzgraff, Jr., described so well in his essay elsewhere in this book. The decade will also likely be characterized by continued economic dislocation and regional political instability.

What this means for the Air Force was captured by Secretary of the Air Force Donald B. Rice in his white paper *The Air Force and U.S. National Security: Global Reach—Global Power*. In this paper, the secretary stressed the strengths of the Air Force—its inherent characteristics of speed, range, flexibility, precision, and lethality—to meet national objectives. One of his stated objectives for the Air Force is to support US defense strategy by controlling the high ground through space, as well as command, control, and communications systems.[3] The secretary's vision that space is the ultimate high ground certainly underscores that it will undoubtedly play a more prominent role in the future of the Air Force and in our national security strategy.

As the Air Force gradually contracts and reduces its presence in Europe and in the Pacific, it will also draw down the forward-deployed, terrestrial support systems which it has counted on over the years. Many communications sites, navigational aids, weather stations, and collection activities will be disbanded. Inevitably, as the United States projects forces to future trouble spots, many of these essential support functions will be replaced by space systems.

Many people speak of air power projection and the speed with which air power responded to the events in Southwest Asia. Space power plays an important power-projection role as well: at the instant that Iraq invaded Kuwait, space systems were the first forces on the scene. This fact is very significant when one considers that the next conflict may be a come-as-you-are war. Air Force communications satellites will provide secure, reliable command and control of our forces anywhere on the globe. Space-based navigation will be readily available to provide unprecedented accuracy worldwide to soldiers, sailors, and airmen. In addition to providing high-resolution global weather data for forecasting and environmental monitoring, data from weather satellites will be directly integrated into mission planning and the selection and allocation of weapon systems.

Space will be the primary source of warning of impending attack and will characterize that attack. Highly capable satellites will also continue to monitor arms control agreements and to assess the world situation to avoid surprises. In Secretary Rice's words, "Collectively, these capabilities add up to global knowledge and situational awareness."[4] The accuracy of his comments about space would be graphically illustrated a few months later in Operation Desert Storm.

Combat Operations

Although space systems were used in operations Urgent Fury (Grenada), El Dorado Canyon (Libya), and Just Cause (Panama), the employment was incomplete and often ad hoc. That is, only a subset of the full range of space systems was used. Moreover, the individual commander's knowledge of space often determined the employment of space capabilities. For example, Gen Carl Steiner—joint task force commander in Panama—was very familiar with the tactical utility of space, having spent time with XVIII Airborne Corps at Fort Bragg, North Carolina. Consequently, when reviewing the lessons of the brief conflict in Panama, General Steiner stated that "'space doesn't just help. . . . I cannot go to war without space systems'."[5]

Despite some of their shortcomings, the operations in Grenada, Libya, and Panama were key milestones for space operations and contributed to our knowledge of the employment of space capabilities. The real test, however, was Operation Desert Storm. Air Force Chief of Staff Gen Merrill A. McPeak has described Desert Storm as "the first space war."[6] This war was a watershed event in military space applications because for the first time, space systems were both integral to the conduct of terrestrial conflict and crucial to the outcome of the war. During the five-month period of Operation Desert Shield, while the terrestrial logistic tail was being established to support the coming Desert Storm operation, the space infrastructure was also being created in-theater. A robust mix of user sets, mobile terminals, and portable receivers for receiving and disseminating space-based surveillance, weather, communications, and navigational data was deployed. Other major commands also began considering space solutions to improve their mission effectiveness. Once hostilities began, space systems were ready and made vital contributions.

Desert Storm

The global positioning system came of age in the desert of the Arabian Peninsula. The setting—miles and miles of sand dunes with few distinguishable landmarks—was perfect. GPS provided real-time, passive navigation updates to virtually every weapon system in-theater. Planes, helicopters, tanks, ships, cruise missiles—even trucks used to deliver food to the front—relied on GPS receivers to precisely establish their position, speed, and altitude (for aircraft).

During the early days of our buildup in Saudi Arabia, only a few hundred GPS receivers were in-theater. The demand—particularly by the US Army—outstripped normal production and even resulted in soldiers writing contractors directly for the small GPS lightweight receiver. The industrial base turned to, and by war's end 4,500 receivers were in use. That scenario has to be the ultimate in operational pull.

Air Force special operations forces employed GPS in all their aircraft to ensure the silent and very accurate navigation that is so essential to their survival. Special Pave Low helicopters used GPS receivers to fly nap-of-the-earth missions both day and night with equal confidence. GPS provided Air Force F-16s passive navigation to the initial point on their bomb runs. British Puma helicopters were outfitted with GPS, and, according to Squadron Leader Alexander Smyth, commander of the 33d Air Rescue Squadron, "[GPS is] essential now, especially for night flying in the desert. I am sure with GPS we will lose fewer helicopters."[7] In all cases, the system performed magnificently—well beyond expectations.

Communications capacity and channel availability have historically been shortfalls in conflict. The need to communicate easily and securely is critical to prosecuting military operations. As demand grew during Desert Storm, we moved a DSCS satellite from Pacific Ocean coverage to Indian Ocean coverage to augment our communications capacity. This was the first time a DOD satellite had been repositioned to support US combat operations, illustrating the inherent flexibility of our sophisticated geosynchronous satellites.

With three DSCS satellites, we were able to allocate sufficient channels and bandwidth to support 128 tactical terminals for the duration of the conflict. This network was so effective that Gen Colin L. Powell, chairman of the Joint Chiefs of Staff, remarked that "satellites were the single most important factor that enabled us to build the command, control, and communications network for Desert Shield."[8] The key point is that space systems for the first time were the primary means for 85 percent of intratheater as well as intertheater communications.

As for weather information, DMSP provided an unprecedented volume of meteorological data to our forces. DMSP transportable vans distributed weather data directly to the Air Force component command, to aircraft carriers, and to Marine aviation units. Because our DMSP vans are large, they are airlift-intensive. Therefore, late in the war we introduced two prototype portable satellite-receive terminals that were small enough to be carried in the back of the Army's high-mobility multipurpose wheeled vehicle.

Coalition air forces routinely planned and flew aircraft sorties based upon satellite-derived weather information. Indeed, the selection of weapons was based upon the weather conditions over the target. Accurate weather forecasting was critical in deciding whether to employ precision guided munitions, because target visibility was essential for laser designation. Further, by doing channel comparison of DMSP's microwave imagery, analysts were able to determine the moisture content of soil and thus identify routes which would support the weight of armored forces that would conduct Gen Norman Schwarzkopf's brilliant "left hook" into Iraq in late February 1991.

In addition, space-based, multispectral imagery (MSI) products provided by land satellite (LANDSAT) proved useful to all the military services. This imagery was used to identify beach landing zones in coastal areas, to update maps, and to prepare route plans and weapons-delivery plans. All phases of the preparation and execution of air, land, and sea attack were carried out more effectively due to the availability and accuracy of this multispectral environmental data.

The importance of Operation Desert Storm as a catalyst for accelerating the future development of tactical space applications cannot be overstated. However, this conflict also underscored certain shortcomings in our use of space. Operational planning for the use of space systems was not well developed when Iraq invaded Kuwait in August 1990. Military planners took advantage of the five months preceding Desert Storm to get ground- and space-based assets into the theater and to school the users in how to better employ space products. In addition, because some of the equipment used to receive signals was not standardized and not supportable by blue suiters, it ultimately had to be maintained by contractors. Last, although the Air Force demonstrated the flexibility of space systems by repositioning a satellite to support the communications demands of the Southwest Asia conflict, this feat nevertheless highlighted our need to be able to more rapidly augment our on-orbit capabilities.

The Future

What can we anticipate for the Air Force in terms of its role in space in the 1990s and beyond? First and foremost, there is no question that the flying commands of the Air Force will become much more deeply committed to integrating space systems into their force structure and operational planning.

Global Positioning System

We can anticipate that the demand for GPS receivers will increase dramatically. The Air Force has a long-range plan to install GPS capabilities into the cockpits of our first-line aircraft. Due to budget considerations, the integration plan will proceed very gradually. But the performance of GPS during Desert Storm may accelerate that process. As Air Force pilots become more familiar and comfortable with GPS, they will discover new and unanticipated applications to enhance combat capabilities. The important fact is that the user—the crew member—rather than the engineer or space operator, will develop these new applications. GPS will ultimately be like air-conditioning—people will wonder how they did without it.

Launch

The Air Force must improve its launch capacity if it wishes to maintain control of the space theater. Derived from ICBM systems, our current launch vehicles and the associated processes do not provide the responsiveness needed to rapidly replace or augment on-orbit assets.

Our space launchers have served us well, but the space community is launching the equivalent of the F-4 series fighter into space. Space launchers need the same relative modernization that our modern-day fighters have had. The Air Force and the National Aeronautics and Space Administration are currently cooperating on a National Launch System to meet a variety of civil, commercial, and military launch requirements. The military requirements for this system are affordability, responsiveness, flexibility, and maintainability. This system will mark the transition from the 1950s-based space-launch equipage to a more sustainable launch system for the twenty-first century. The United States must pursue this course if it is to remain the world's premier space power and space-faring nation.

Missile Defense

Desert Storm also gave the concept of strategic defense a substantial shot in the arm. The success of the Patriot missile against Scud missiles should win public approval—and thus congressional support—for a missile-defense system. The Patriot, which is basically a 1970s design, has shown that with today's technology it is possible to develop a system to counter far more sophisticated threats than the relatively primitive Scud. By the turn of the century, at least 20 countries will possess the capability to launch ballistic missiles of some type. If numerous countries obtain sophisticated missile inventories—combined with chemical, biological, or nuclear warheads—the US Air Force will have to respond with more advanced space-based warning sensors to track, discriminate, and target them. Ultimately, the United States will rely on space-based interceptors to negate threatening missiles, and the Air Force will continue to need a responsive surveillance-and-warning capability to deal with this multifaceted threat.

Multispectral Imagery

The military utility of multispectral imagery was also shown in Southwest Asia. MSI was the only source of wide-area coverage available, and it played an important role in trafficability and terrain analyses, as well as invasion planning. LANDSAT provided the majority of this data.

Composite Wing

Organizationally, the Air Force is taking direct steps to integrate and operationalize space. It may be able to go further by studying the possibility of establishing wings with the full spectrum of combat capabilities—deep strike, interdiction, electronic warfare, and refueling—organic to the unit. If the Air Force moves in that direction, these composite wings must also include people trained in space operations, as well as the requisite terminal and receive equipment. This would be the ultimate integration of space within the Air Force and would assuredly enhance the utility of space to our combatant units.

Onboard Processing

The Air Force also needs space systems designed to provide user-friendly data streams. One approach is to employ satellite onboard processing. Satellites on orbit collect information, do the requisite data processing and reduction on board, and then downlink the finished product directly to the combatant in the field or in the air.

This capability would have been a powerful tool in the Scud-hunting operations of Desert Storm. Currently, this capability is very expensive to incorporate on our satellites. But great technological strides in microminiaturization are being made so that in the foreseeable future, military space systems will no longer need the terrestrial ground-processing infrastructure associated with today's satellites.

Advancements are also needed in developing techniques and equipment to fuze satellite bit-streams of data together. In the past, architectures for individual space systems were developed in relative isolation or in a stovepipe fashion. Modern computer advances could enable Air Force planners and operators to have the flexibility to receive and centrally exploit fuzed bit-streams of weather, warning, navigation, surveillance, and communications.

Antisatellite Systems

It is also quite reasonable to expect that as the world evolves into a more multipolar environment, space capabilities will mirror that expansion. Simply put, space technology for the range of military functions will become available to many nations.

The successful conclusion of hostilities in Southwest Asia necessarily requires a look at what could have changed the tempo of the campaign. The ability of the United States to maintain the initiative and to sustain surprise by masking its military actions would have been much more difficult if Saddam Hussein—or a future adversary—had his own space-reconnaissance assets.

This prospect argues for an ASAT system to assure that, just as US forces achieved control of the air and the battlefield, we can control space as well (i.e., achieve space superiority). Such a proposal speaks to the idea of an indivisible regime between air and space that Gen Thomas D. White, former Air Force chief of staff, captured over 30 years ago in coining the term *aerospace*.[9] Dr Pfaltzgraff and Dr Edward N. Luttwak also refer to this in their essays elsewhere in this book as a "seamless" regime between air power and space power projection. Just as it would be unthinkable in a future conflict to permit an adversary to use an aircraft to reconnoiter our battle lines for intelligence and targeting, so is it equally unacceptable to allow enemy reconnaissance satellites free and unhindered flight over US military positions. An operational ASAT capability designed to eliminate an adversary's space capabilities must be considered an integral part of this country's force structure.

Space-Based Weapons

One final observation concerns the need to fully explore the concept of space-based force application. This subject has many political overtones, but the Air Force should—consistent with treaty obligations—conduct the research and planning necessary to assess the feasibility of such systems and the national security implications.

Conclusion

Looking ahead a few years, one can speculate that advocates of both air power and space power will likely be talking about similar issues. It is equally reasonable to expect the leadership from Strategic Air Command, Tactical Air Command, Military Airlift Command, Air Force Special Operations Command, and other commands to espouse the value of space-based sensors that provide real-time communications, weather, navigation, early-warning, and surveillance inputs directly into both the aircraft and their weapons loads. They would also be relying on satellites that designate targets, silently guide aircraft toward the objective, and identify enemy defenses as part of mission execution.

Finally, the commander of Air Force Space Command may well address the advances in defensive and offensive space-based force-application systems. The Air Force is fully committed to meet the twenty-first century by fulfilling the 1988 space policy tenet to ensure "the evolution of space power from combat support to the full spectrum of military capabilities."[10]

Notes

1. Memorandum, Secretary of the Air Force Edward C. Aldridge, Jr., and Air Force Chief of Staff Gen Larry D. Welch, to all Air Force major commands and special operating agencies, subject: Air Force Space Policy, 2 December 1988.

2. Gen George L. Butler, commander in chief, Strategic Air Command, speech to the Center for Defense Journalism, National Press Club, Washington, D.C., 29 September 1990.

3. Secretary of the Air Force Donald B. Rice, *The Air Force and U.S. National Security: Global Reach—Global Power* (Washington, D.C.: Department of the Air Force, June 1990), 12.

4. Ibid.

5. Quoted in *The United States Air Force Report to the 102nd Congress of the United States of America, Fiscal Year 1992/93* (Washington, D.C.: Government Printing Office, 1991), 25.

6. Briefing, Gen Merrill A. McPeak, Air Force chief of staff, National War College, subject: Desert Shield/Desert Storm, 6 March 1991.

7. Capt Mark Brown, "British Totally Sold on GPS," *Space Trace: The Air Force Space Command Magazine*, April 1991, 7.

8. Gen Colin L. Powell, chairman of the Joint Chiefs of Staff, speech to the Armed Forces Communications Electronics Association, Washington, D.C., December 1990.

9. House, *Testimony of General Thomas D. White before the House Committee on Science and Astronautics*, 86th Cong., 1st sess., February 1959.

10. Memorandum, Aldridge and Welch.

PART V

Factors Affecting Force Structure and Missions

Introduction

The force structure and missions of the US Air Force, as well as those of its sister services, are subject to a number of constraints imposed by diverse influences, including American public opinion, congressional oversight and budget authority, and the arms control process. As we see in this section, each of these forces has its own logic and agenda that push and pull the entire US military—and the Air Force in particular—in several directions. Such constraints on Air Force and other national security planners are related to an important abstraction—national consensus—that should not be ignored by the military.

Rep Bud Shuster provides an overview of the role of Congress in the formation and conduct of American national security policy. In particular, he focuses on the nation's intelligence requirements and derives some lessons from the Gulf war. He points to the importance of a strong intelligence capability in preserving our national security. In the Gulf war, we had "some extraordinary intelligence breakthroughs and capabilities . . . involving our satellites, aircraft, and communications systems." Particularly crucial was the role of intelligence, which allowed for more accurate bombing missions, the interdiction of strategic shipments to Iraq, the prediction of Iraqi military tactics, and the tracking of terrorists worldwide.

Congressman Shuster sees a major lesson for America in the Gulf conflict: that we still live in a very dangerous world, that military force is still part of international relations, and that America must play a major role in guaranteeing international security. To his chagrin, he notes that many of his colleagues have failed to understand this fact. As Shuster observes, "Some congressmen say that the cold war is over and that the defense budget should be cut by as much as 50 percent over the first half of the 1990s." There is also a movement in Congress toward neoisolationism, a sentiment that harks back to the old America firsters and even to the nineteenth century. One prominent senator has even called for abolishing the Central

Intelligence Agency. Congressman Shuster asks whether Congress wants to be part of the problem or part of the solution to American foreign policy challenges. With regard to America's role in the world, he believes that we must be "prepared to engage, not disengage, in the new world order." As for using force, the US has to be "willing to use [it]—not in many places and certainly not as a first resort, but as a last resort."

The budget process is closely related to congressional opinion. Brig Gen Lawrence P. Farrell, Jr., outlines how the force structure of the Air Force will be dictated increasingly by fiscal constraints; thus, the Air Force must choose "even more wisely than before, balancing the proper mix of quality and quantity." The US has historically committed a smaller percentage of its resources to the military, with support "spik[ing] during major conflicts [e.g., the cold war] and in response to the development of the Soviet Union as a major nuclear power." According to General Farrell, the force structure decline in the current Air Force program is not unlike the demobilization that followed the Vietnam War. For the first half of the 1990s, the Air Force will reduce active military and civilian strength by nearly 20 percent and increase reliance on the reserve component to the maximum extent possible. In addition, the Air Force is planning to cut its intercontinental ballistic missile (ICBM), bomber, and fighter force structure.

On a general level, the Department of Defense budget is projected to shrink 3 percent per year through fiscal year 1996, "at which time defense spending as a percentage of [gross national product] will reach 3.6 percent—its lowest point since World War II." Since 1985, the Air Force's buying power has decreased by 40–45 percent.

Such major budgetary constraints and force downsizing, according to General Farrell, may result in the Air Force's returning to a mobilization-based strategy

> that does not sacrifice its capability to react quickly and decisively. This requires that we develop military capabilities that are highly mobile and highly survivable against increasingly potent adversaries other than the Soviet Union.

The arms control process is another arena with important implications for USAF force structure and planning. Dr Edward L. Warner III makes the point that bilateral and multilateral arms control agreements concluded by the US to date have had little impact on the structure of forces deployed by the Air Force, the sole exception being the abolition of ground launched cruise missiles required by the Intermediate-range Nuclear Forces treaty. Neither of the Strategic Arms Limitation Talks (SALT I or SALT II) "produced limits that required the Air Force to alter its existing force deployment plans."

While arms control agreements of the past have failed to transform force structure, the potential for radical cuts in the strategic forces is great, according to Warner. The Strategic Arms Reduction Talks (START) agreement should "almost certainly produce a substantial reduction in the US silo-based ICBM force by the end of its seven-year implementation period." This will feature a limit of 4,900 reentry vehicles carried by sea-launched ballistic missiles and ICBMs. In addition, 100 or more B-52s currently configured to carry air launched cruise missiles (ALCM) would have to be changed to non-ALCM status if the Air Force is to stay within the aggregate ceiling of 6,000 "accountable" weapons.

The Conventional Forces in Europe (CFE) treaty would place limits on NATO's aggregate holdings of main battle tanks, artillery, armored combat vehicles, armed helicopters, and combat aircraft. Although the ceiling of 6,800 aircraft will not require any reductions in NATO's holdings, it is clear to Warner that "the much diminished Soviet threat and congressional pressures for reductions in defense spending" will cause the US "to cut back greatly its military presence in Europe in the post–cold war era." If the parties agree on the START and CFE treaties, the Air Force will be involved in a constellation of inspection projects related to implementation of the highly intensive verification regimes. Warner believes that the arms control agreements may be a prelude to even farther-reaching arms reduction initiatives. He warns that the Air Force should look ahead and prepare itself for greater cuts in the future.

Ross Gelbspan offers a journalist's perspective in discussing the interplay between the military, the press, and the public. In the recent Gulf conflict, he points out that

> the imperative of information-control policy has become a practical priority of military planning, translating itself into an extensive set of arrangements which are every bit as important as deployment and logistics.

The air campaign during the early stage of the Gulf conflict allowed for a major public relations victory, as long-range photography and nose-cone camera shots "created an impression of a very sanitary destruction—of a war almost without human consequences." It was this kind of film footage, Gelbspan maintains, that gave the public the illusion of having a front-row seat and "effectively isolated the press, cut it off from public support, and managed to carry the day with very little adverse public reaction."

Mr Gelbspan sees several potential problems in the press/public realm for both the government and the military. He warns against using disinformation, issuing overly optimistic reports of damage to the enemy, and making efforts to manipulate public opinion, any of which might resurrect allegations of a "credibility gap," as in the Vietnam War. He feels that in the future, the military should adhere "to a policy . . . of candor and a minimization of unnecessary secrecy" and that political leaders must make crystal clear the "goals, objectives, and anticipated costs of any future campaign."

Congress and National Security

Hon Bud Shuster

In a broad sense, the national security of the United States entails such areas as our economic well-being, our health, and our educational facilities. But for purposes of this essay, I will refer to national security in terms of our national defense and—most particularly—in terms of our intelligence capabilities.

The American people sometimes forget that from the very beginning, their country was born out of the pangs of people who were defending themselves and fighting for freedom. Furthermore, from the very beginning, intelligence played a critical role in that struggle. In fact, the first master spy in the history of our nation was George Washington. He ran his own spy rings, his own double-agent and counterintelligence activities, his own covert operations, and his own disinformation and propaganda operations. After sending John Hunniman across the Delaware River to Trenton, New Jersey, to scout out the situation, he used Hunniman's intelligence report as the basis for deciding to cross the river on that dark Christmas night in 1776, attack at Trenton, and help save the day. Consequently, our forces were able to continue their struggle against the British. Abraham Lincoln had his own agents as well, some of whom were hanged by the Confederacy. In World War II, the British scored an intelligence coup by breaking the cipher produced by the Germans' Enigma machine, allowing Britain to win the submarine war in the North Atlantic. Similarly, because Americans managed to break the Japanese cipher, the United States was able to win the Battle of the Coral Sea. During the cold war, Italy and Greece were preserved from communism as a result of the efforts of the Central Intelligence Agency (CIA) and its forerunner. And Poland is free today, not only because of the tremendous courage of the Polish people and the involvement of the Catholic church, but also because of a decade-long

US commitment to their cause. Indeed, much of what is happening in Eastern Europe is due to US commitments.

Most recently, some extraordinary intelligence breakthroughs and capabilities emerged during Operation Desert Storm involving our satellites, aircraft, and communications systems. We were able to track every military move of the enemy; locate targets and, largely through human intelligence, tell the Air Force exactly where "smart" bombs should be dropped; stop many critical strategic shipments to Iraq; predict, through our study of Soviet military tactics, Iraqi military tactics; and track terrorists worldwide.

Nevertheless, some naysayers complain about intelligence in the Persian Gulf. We did in fact have one significant intelligence failure: our inability to accurately predict Saddam Hussein's intentions. However, King Fahd of Saudi Arabia totally misunderstood Saddam's intentions, as did President Hosni Mubarak of Egypt, and even Israel's Mossad—perhaps the best intelligence service in the world—had no idea of what was going to happen. So it is easy for the naysayers to say that we did not know Saddam's intentions. (But one can make the case that it is unrealistic to expect us to know everything.) Once we were in the Gulf, his intentions became clear. Saddam Hussein did not intend simply to take over Kuwait. His objective was the entire Persian Gulf: Saudi Arabia and on to the United Arab Emirates and Oman. Had we let this happen, Iraq would have been on the way to becoming the world's new superpower. This is not the estimate just of our intelligence capabilities, but of virtually every intelligence operation in the Middle East.

So where does this leave us today? We find ourselves in the position of being able to contribute to President Bush's vision of a new world order—one that many of us embrace. But when we talk about Desert Storm, it is also important to see it in the larger context of what is happening around the world.

The Soviet Union is disintegrating. As bad as the political situation is there, the economic problems are even worse. Until they are addressed, there is little chance of solving the Soviets' very complex political problems. Indeed, we have taken the extraordinary step of cooperating with the KGB to be sure that that agency retains control of Soviet nuclear weapons. We are deeply concerned that some Soviet "cowboys" might sell them to somebody like Muammar Qadhafi in Libya. This is a significant intelligence issue—one that we are working closely.

In Eastern Europe, fledgling democracies are struggling. Forty years of decay make the prospects for success in Poland, Hungary, or Czechoslovakia rather tenuous.

Marxist third-world countries are virtually naked today because the Soviet Union, by and large, can no longer afford to export revolution and support them economically. Civil war might easily erupt in Cuba, and we might see a new boat exodus—not from Cuba to the US, but from Miami to Cuba, transporting people to fight in that war. Although we are thankful for Violeta Chamorro in Nicaragua, the Sandinistas still control the guns, and Nicaragua's economy is a basket case. Furthermore, the evidence is overwhelming that the Sandinistas continue to send weapons into El Salvador. Despite all the problems the Soviets have, they are sending hundreds of millions of dollars to support Mohammad Najibullah and the regime in Kabul, Afghanistan. Some members of Congress say we should stop supporting the Mujaheddin even though we have a 10-year investment in them. In Angola we have supported Jonas Savimbi and hope to see peace there, but we can't afford to hold our breath.

So what are the lessons we should learn from this world situation—in many respects a chaotic world in which the US, as the only superpower, has demonstrated its tremendous military and diplomatic capability. The fundamental lesson is that we live in a very dangerous world. In this century, almost 108 million people have been killed in some 227 wars—more war-related deaths than in all of history combined prior to the twentieth century.[1] In 1990 alone, 32 armed conflicts were being waged around the world.

The world is not only dangerous, it is largely unfree. Freedom House, an organization which monitors human rights and political freedom worldwide, reports that of the more than 5 billion people on this planet, 3.2 billion of them are not free. Unfortunately, the majority of the people on the earth today do not possess the freedoms that Americans enjoy. Those who are lucky enough to be free must never forget that freedom must be carefully guarded. Indeed, historians Will and Ariel Durant observed that man's nature has not changed and that "the first biological lesson of history is that life is competition."[2] We must not forget that, either. If we do, it will be at our peril—not only in the realm of economic competition, but also in terms of other dangerous challenges that face us around the world.

One lesson that we have certainly learned from Operation Desert Storm is that the Goldwater-Nichols Act worked, even though many people opposed it at the time. In fact, the idea of a unified command created the opportunity for success by permitting a workable structure: a single air operations plan rather than the several plans that existed in previous conflicts, and the prepositioning by the US Air Force of over a $100 billion in equipment in Saudi Arabia before the conflict began. Management expert Peter Drucker said that if habits and behavior are to be changed, then the system of recognition and rewards must also change. He went on to point out that one of the differences between the success of Desert Storm and that of previous conflicts was that under the concept of a unified command, an officer's cooperation with other services became one of the criteria for promotion.[3]

Americans should also ask themselves the question, What if? What if President Bush had not had the courage and the wisdom to take the position that he took? What if the Congress, on that cold night in January 1991, had not voted to give the president the authority to use force against Iraq? The answer, as previously mentioned, is that Saddam Hussein would control the entire Persian Gulf and 65 percent of the world's oil supplies. He would have an economic stranglehold on our energy jugular and would be well on the way to making Iraq a superpower. From a congressional point of view, therefore, we must be very careful that we learn the right lessons.

Some congressmen say that the cold war is over and that the defense budget should be cut by as much as 50 percent over the first half of the 1990s. Even some of my conservative colleagues are becoming neoisolationists—America firsters—as if this were the nineteenth rather than the twentieth century. Further, there are all too many people in Congress who want to micromanage our defense and national security policy. Secretary of Defense Dick Cheney explains this attitude by saying it's the "never-again" syndrome. That is, because Congress had problems with the Iran-Contra affair, it wants to pass laws now that say we will never again give the president the freedom to make decisions. Sen Daniel Patrick Moynihan, for whom I have great respect, introduced legislation to abolish the CIA, his reason being that it isn't needed since the cold war is over.

But we in the Congress must be prepared to engage, not disengage, in the new world order. We must be prepared to support the president and be willing to use force—not in many places and certainly not as a first resort, but as a last resort. We must help the president set new priorities for our national defense, especially in terms of rethinking our doctrine and strategy to accommodate low-intensity conflict now that the Soviet Union is no longer the target.

Personally, my work on the House Select Committee on Intelligence allows me to focus on the drug war. The intelligence field has achieved some extraordinary successes in fighting the drug war in South America. The drug lords there should be deeply concerned about US intelligence resources, which are now committed to rooting them out. Indeed, some drug lords are no longer walking around because of US intelligence and our cooperation with the South American governments.

I believe that we in Congress have indeed learned some of the lessons produced by Desert Storm and the changing world. We recognize our obligations. We are prepared to reorder national security priorities and fund the necessary programs. We are ready to heed the words of Winston Churchill, who said at the close of the Second World War that the hope of the world lies in "the strength and resolve of the United States to play a leading part in world affairs."[4] Those words are truer today than they have ever been. So let us together fight the battles that lie before us for a robust national security in America and lead this country that we love into the twenty-first century, secure and confident, a force for freedom and prosperity around the world.

Notes

1. Ruth Leger Sivard, *World Military and Social Expenditures, 1991*, 14th ed. (Washington, D.C.: World Priorities, 1991), 20.
2. Will and Ariel Durant, *The Lessons of History* (New York: Simon and Schuster, 1968), 19.
3. *Wall Street Journal*, 1991.
4. Winston Churchill, *Winston Churchill on America and Britain*, ed. Kay Halle (New York: Walker and Co., 1970), 53.

Balancing Budgetary and Force Constraints

Brig Gen Lawrence P. Farrell, Jr., USAF

As the role of the Air Force in future American military strategies evolves, we often find that the required tasks grow both larger and more complex. Operation Desert Storm clearly demonstrated that, when used properly, air power significantly affects the course of a war. For the future, force structure and fiscal constraints dictate that we choose even more wisely than before, balancing the proper mix of quality and quantity. As demonstrated in Desert Storm, if quality is chosen correctly, it has a quantity all its own.

Historical Perspective

Balancing fiscal constraints against mission requirements is not something new to the Air Force or the Department of Defense (DOD) as a whole. Our democratic process dictates that the military compete for federal funding along with the other needs of the nation. In comparison, the dictatorship in Iraq spent 33 percent of that country's gross national product (GNP) on the military in the 1980s, while the United States reached a peak of only 6.3 percent (fig. 1).

The percentage of GNP that the United States dedicates to defense has been historically low and has spiked during major conflicts and in response to the development of the Soviet Union as a major nuclear power. We can expect this trend to continue in the future. Even so, the US Air Force is a large "corporation." For fiscal year 1992, our projected "revenues" (i.e., total obligation authority—TOA) are almost $87 billion. We would rank third, just behind Ford Motor Company and General Motors Corporation, if we were a *Fortune* 500 company.

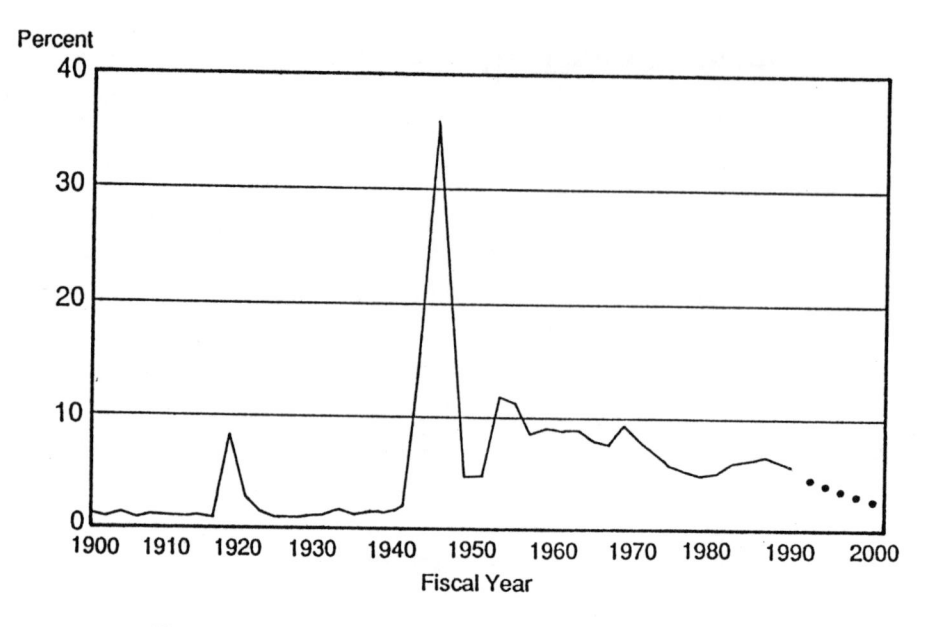

Figure 1. US Defense Spending as a Percent of GNP

Figure 2 shows the roller-coaster DOD budget topline over a 40-year span. Some definite periods are easily discernible. The FY 1953 peak was from the Korean conflict, with the drawdown complete by FY 1955. Some increases are apparent after Sputnik I in 1957, but the major buildup waited until the missile gap of the early 1960s and a strategy shift from massive retaliation to flexible response. In fact, much of the hardware that we operate today—such as the B-52, Minuteman, and C-141—was purchased in the 1960s. The large hump during FY 1967 through FY 1969 was due to Vietnam, with a large downturn lasting through the 1970s—the "decade of neglect." The DOD budget took a turn upward during the first half of the Reagan years but then took a considerable downturn beginning in fiscal year 1986. The significance of this rise and fall is discussed later.

Not surprisingly, the rise and fall of the Air Force budget has historically paralleled the fluctuations of the DOD budget (fig. 3). Throughout the 1970s, DOD investment reached an all-time low. By the 1980s we found major problems permeating the entire military.

BUDGETARY AND FORCE CONSTRAINTS

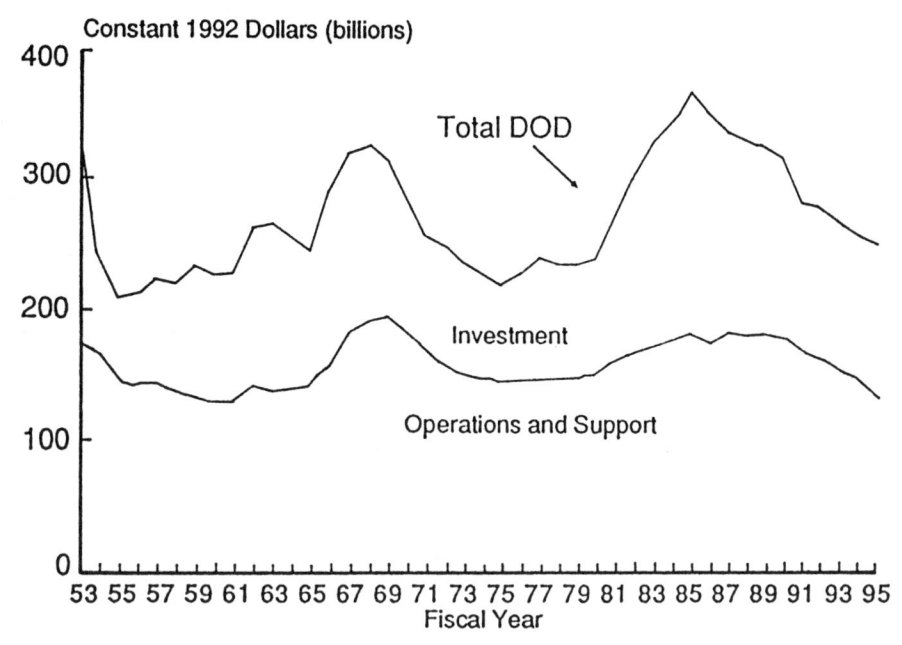

Figure 2. DOD-Military Budget Trend (Budget Authority in Constant 1992 Dollars)

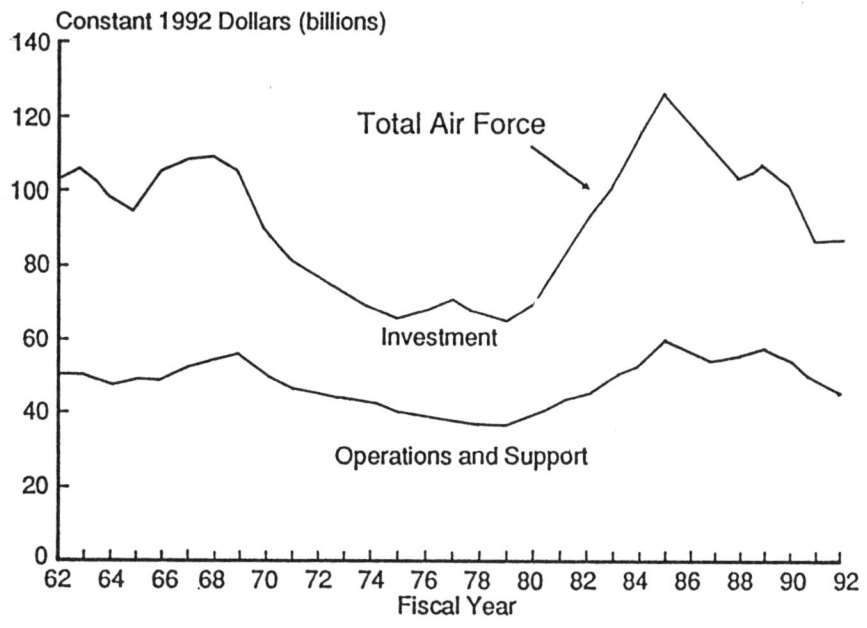

Figure 3. Air Force-Military Budget Trend (Budget Authority in Constant 1992 Dollars)

Due to a lack of investment in spares, we had a hollow force. Our training was at an all-time low, and the mission-capable rates of our forces were extremely low. Our ability to sustain a conflict of moderate intensity or duration had become questionable at best.

Budget constraints had also forced us to delay maintenance and repair of our facilities. Our backlog was rapidly increasing as our facilities began to deteriorate. Further, our military and civilian personnel were losing buying power each year due to high inflation and low pay increases. Pilot retention fell to alarmingly low levels.

The 1970s also ended on a poor note, from a strategic nuclear standpoint. The Soviet buildup during this decade had resulted in a strategic imbalance in favor of the USSR. In addition, connectivity studies revealed serious gaps in our ability to retaliate after a Soviet nuclear strike, since our ability to transmit a presidential decision to the retaliating forces was in doubt.

We ended the 1970s and began the 1980s with much to correct—a hollow force, a strategic imbalance, a connectivity issue, a large backlog of maintenance and repair, and a military compensation gap. As we saw in figure 2, the large buildup in military spending lasted only the first half of the 1980s. Fortunately, we addressed our key problems immediately. We brought programs which were ready for procurement into the force structure; replaced older equipment with modern equipment; increased research, development, test and evaluation (RDT&E) to address the imbalances that resulted from having no mature "ready-to-procure" systems; and, very importantly, sought high technology to provide leverage and cause block obsolescence in enemy force investments.

The strategy was sound. We had determined what was necessary to meet the Soviet threat. Forces were being modernized, and readiness was increasing. Spare parts were becoming available for a sustained conflict, and the military compensation issue was addressed. We very quietly took advantage of an early version of stealth technology by deploying the F-117 and operated it in secrecy for some time. We sought to deploy 40 tactical fighter wing equivalents (TFWE) to meet the conventional threat. We had plans to deploy the advanced-

BUDGETARY AND FORCE CONSTRAINTS

technology fighter for air superiority and an advanced tactical aircraft for longer-range interdiction. At the same time, we pursued a fleet of 350 heavy long-range bombers, including 132 B-2s, as well as 200 Peacekeeper missiles to meet the strategic threat. In the airlift arena, we strove to satisfy the need to deliver 66 million ton miles per day by acquiring 210 C-17s. Finally, RDT&E was maturing on the high-technology weapons. Our goal of near-zero circular error probability (CEP) was coming to fruition, as were high-probability-of-kill munitions, both for hardened and wide-area targets.

As we built the Program Objective Memorandum (POM) for FY 1986 through FY 1990, the large RDT&E efforts of the first half of the decade were coming to fruition, and we planned to deploy the new systems in the late 1980s. But the sentiment of Congress and the mood of the public for defense spending changed, and the balancing of budgetary and force constraints began in earnest.

The FY 1986 president's budget (PB) submitted in January 1985 contained a request of $143 billion in TOA for the Air Force for FY 1990 (fig. 4). The actual congressional appropriation was $94 billion.

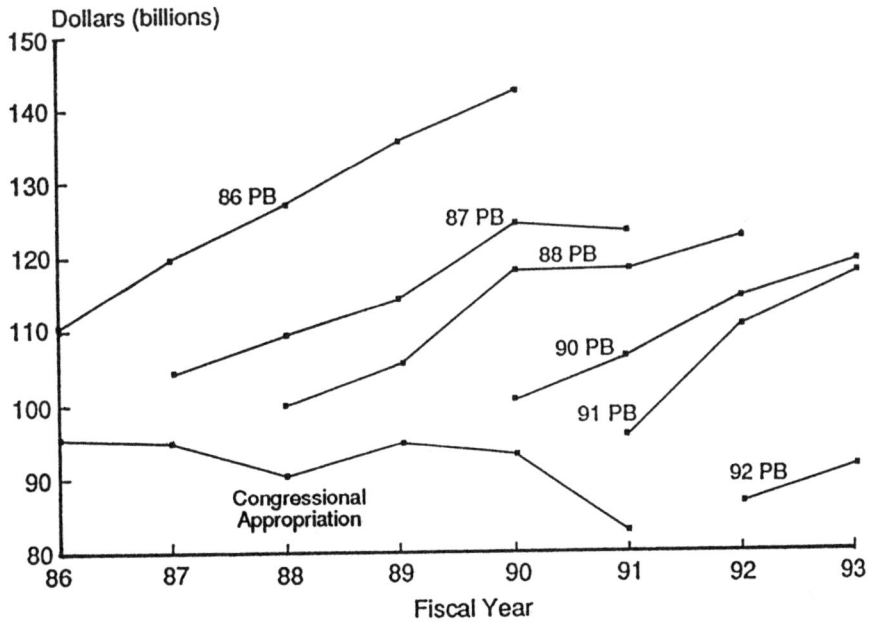

Figure 4. Air Force Five-Year Defense Plan Track

In fact, the total difference from the PB request for fiscal year 1986 and the resulting congressional appropriation was $167 billion over the five-year span—the equivalent of about three B-2 programs.

We came off a wave of rising expectations to a fiscally constrained force in the second half of the 1980s with some difficulty. Although hard choices were made, we still tended to push programs to the right. The maturing RDT&E on some of our high-technology programs created the inevitable bow wave that has been characteristic of DOD budgets since their inception. This practice served us well at times, attested to by the roller-coaster effect of the budget. When the money became available, we were prepared to spend it wisely because we had run each program through the entire Planning, Programming and Budgeting System (PPBS).

Through the PPBS, the Air Force develops its programs to achieve the defense objectives established by the president and the secretary of defense. The process begins when Air Force commanders translate those objectives into operational plans designed to safeguard our national security interests. At the same time, these senior officers identify the resources that are needed to execute their plans now and for the next six years. The military judgment of these commanders constitutes the foundation upon which the Air Force builds the POM.

The Air Force integrates operational requirements with the fiscal guidance and end-strength limits levied by the Office of the Secretary of Defense (OSD). This integration involves balancing near-term readiness and sustainability requirements with modernization programs and research and development initiatives to ensure total program balance.

After developing the POM, the Air Force submits it to OSD for formal program review and budget costing. The final result becomes part of the president's budget, which is submitted to Congress for review and approval.

Since Congress appropriates funds for the federal government on a year-by-year basis, it reviews the Air Force's proposed six-year budget each congressional year as though the budget were a new product. This process often results in drastic changes to DOD programs on a yearly basis and fails to provide the stability that is needed to get the best price on many defense programs. The result of the process is a program with little or no credibility after the first year.

The 1990 budget summit agreement may have changed this problem by looking far into the future and agreeing on a TOA allocation for DOD through 1996. This budget agreement had a major impact on the Air Force program, as it did on those of all the military services. Because the agreement goes so far into the future, it effectively eliminates the proverbial bow wave, since we can no longer push the hard decisions to the next year. More importantly, if the agreement is kept, it could provide the stability that is needed for DOD programs.

In accomplishing the Air Force program for FY 1992 through FY 1997, we had to cut over $180 billion from the baseline to comply with the budget agreement and resulting OSD fiscal guidance. In contrast, while we may have lost $167 billion from the PB for fiscal year 1986, it occurred over a period of five years, and much of it was done by the Congress in the actual budget year.

The $180-billion reduction drill was accomplished in two stages: the first $120 billion was cut in six months and the remaining $60 billion in the last few weeks of the budget exercise. This process can only be likened to carefully building the Air Force program with a micrometer in tens of weeks and adjusting it with a sledgehammer in tens of hours. The result is a very flat Air Force topline that is quite close to the shape of the congressional appropriations track (fig. 4). Cuts of these magnitudes required tough choices. No longer were the options "how to slow force-structure growth" or "how to slow modernization" but "which force structure to phase out" and "which modernization to cease." The force-structure decline in the current Air Force program is not unlike the demobilization we experienced after the Vietnam War.

The dramatic reductions in manpower are illustrated in figure 5. The Air Force is reducing active military and civilian end strength in the first half of the 1990s by nearly 20 percent and is increasing reliance on the Air Reserve component to the maximum extent

End Strength (thousands)

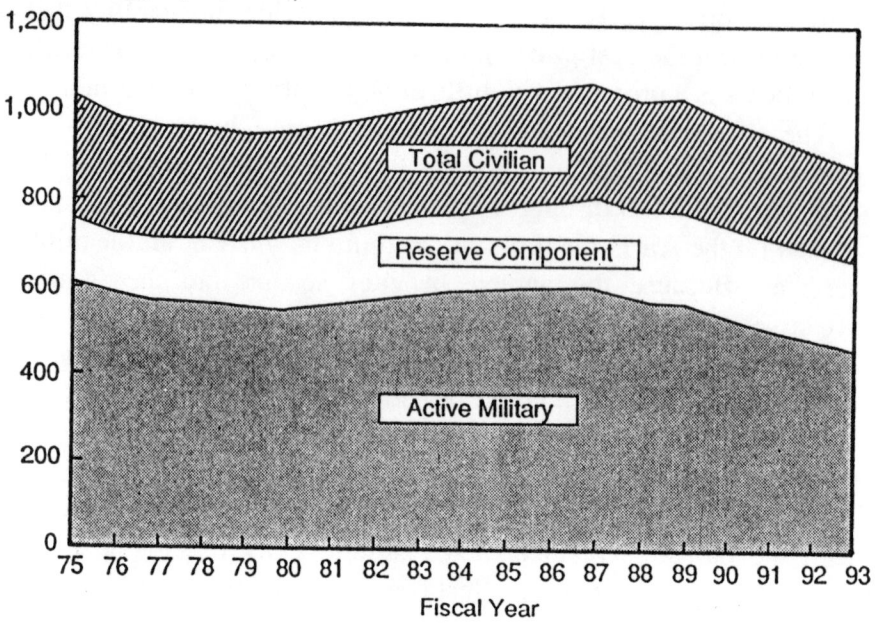

Figure 5. Total-Force Manpower (Military and Civilian)

possible. We are also planning to cut substantially our bomber, intercontinental ballistic missile (ICBM), and fighter force structure. One perspective would be to look at the decade from the peak year for military spending in FY 1985 to the FY 1995 plan. In this decade, our strategic bomber and ICBM forces decline about 40 percent each, while the number of tactical fighter wings declines 32 percent.

The Next Decade

From a historical perspective, we have made some hard choices in balancing budgetary and force constraints. Nevertheless, much remains to be done. Evaluating and reevaluating the perceived tasks of the Air Force and the forces available to accomplish those tasks is a continual process. The following data puts the situation into perspective. The entire DOD budget declined by 11.3 percent from FY 1990 to FY 1991. This budget is projected to shrink by approximately 3 percent per year through fiscal year 1996, at which time defense spending as a percentage of GNP will reach 3.6 percent—its lowest point since World War II. Since 1985, DOD has lost one-third of its buying power, while the Air Force's has decreased by 40–45 percent.

The world has changed dramatically in the last several years. The Berlin Wall has come down, and the Warsaw Pact has dissolved as a military alliance. Regionalism and a resurgence of nationalism is growing in areas previously dominated by a bipolar world. Strategies that have served us well for over 45 years are being examined carefully, both politically and militarily. The Air Force must stay abreast of these rapid changes to be sure that it does not develop a strategy/force mismatch or atrophy as an organization.

One way of viewing the Air Force program is to divide it into current and future force structures (fig. 6). A significant portion of the Air Force TOA is required to operate and maintain the current force structure, keep it ready, and make sure it can be sustained in case of a conflict. The ability to successfully prosecute a war today is the primary concern of the commanders in chief (CINC) in their

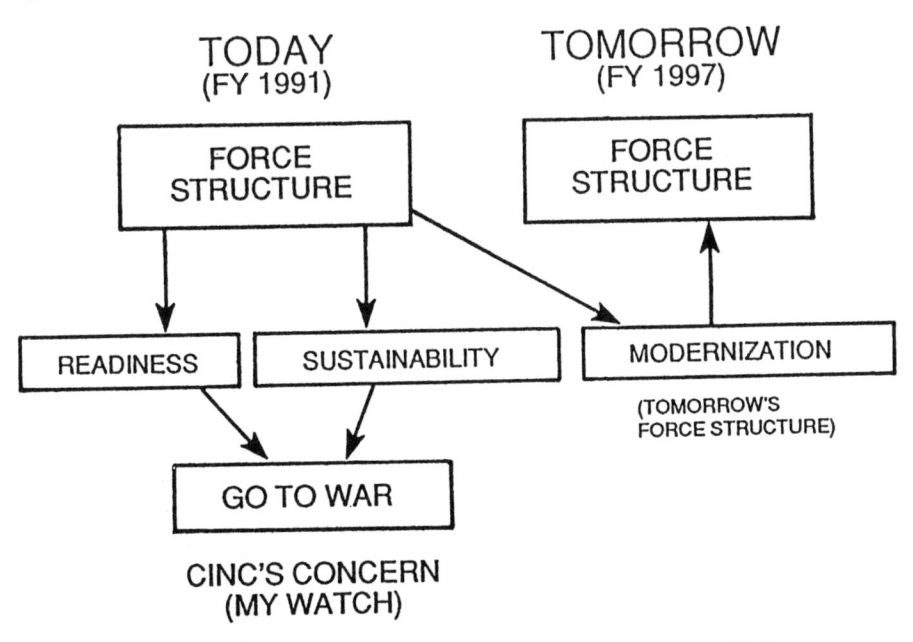

Figure 6. Current and Future Force Structures of the Air Force

respective areas of responsibility. But we must maintain this capability as tomorrow becomes today. From this perspective, we view modernization as tomorrow's force structure—the future force structure we will have to fight with as the future becomes the present. Therefore, as we look at the entire Air Force program, we must not only make sure that we choose the proper forces for tomorrow's war, but also we must balance this with today's need for deterrence and war-fighting capability.

In terms of Soviet *intentions*, any imminent threat from the USSR has eroded, but we must still be concerned about Soviet nuclear *capabilities*. The Soviet Union remains the one nation in the world with the capability to literally destroy the United States. This situation is not expected to change. Although the hostile intentions of the Soviets are not as apparent as they were just five years ago, Soviet capability has not been mitigated, and there are still many uncertainties about developments inside the USSR. Intentions can be changed with the stroke of a pen, but retaliatory capabilities and deterrent forces take decades to build. Consequently, we must maintain a modernization program and remain vigilant in the nuclear-deterrent role.

The age-old question of How much is enough? will surely continue to permeate the nuclear-deterrence equations, clouded by the perception of hostile intentions rather than extant capability. In the mission area of nuclear deterrence, we have an opportunity to field high-technology weapons which will cause block obsolescence in the Soviet attempt to thwart nuclear retaliation. Nevertheless, we will continue to evaluate all the options as our systems mature and as the results of operational test and evaluation become known.

Although Soviet capability in the strategic nuclear field is undiminished, the threat—as well as the capability—of a Soviet invasion of NATO has diminished. Since the end of World War II, when Soviet intentions of communist expansionism became well known, the United States pursued a policy of containment. Today, we are much more concerned about having to deal with a collapsing Soviet empire. Thus, DOD and the Air Force must deal with a situation radically different from the one they faced for the past 45 years.

The most significant change to affect the Air Force and its strategy will be the complete withdrawal of Soviet troops from Eastern Europe. In fact, the Soviet Union's ability to project power beyond its borders should continue to decline in the conventional forces arena, particularly as an imminent threat. We are no longer standing eyeball-to-eyeball with the Soviet Union on two sides of a divided Germany. Therefore, the need to keep a large, active Air Force in Europe should concomitantly diminish as the threat of an imminent war diminishes, causing us to look carefully at our current force-structure needs for the active forces as well as the mix of active and reserve forces. Having said that, however, prudence demands that as we reshape our force posture in the region, we do not allow a situation to develop whereby an impending imbalance becomes irreversible. This means that we will be looking over our shoulder as we adjust our forces to the changing environment in the European theater—always reevaluating and always ready to reverse the course as necessary.

As the Air Force considers the nature of the changing threat, it is evaluating a return to a mobilization-based strategy—within present fiscal constraints—that does not sacrifice its capability to react quickly and decisively. This requires that we develop military capabilities that are highly mobile and highly survivable against increasingly potent adversaries other than the Soviet Union. Our forces need to be capable of influencing a potential aggressor, thereby deterring the outbreak of a conflict.

Military forces must be ready to project power, wherever and whenever they are needed. For instance, had the Iraqi invasion not stopped in Kuwait but continued into Saudi Arabia, we would have needed to destroy columns of military hardware in road-march configuration, as we did when the Iraqis fled Kuwait. Since we had no significant capability in the region at the time, we would have operated at long ranges until the proper forces and munitions arrived by airlift. Although the shooting war in the Persian Gulf was quick and decisive, the logistical buildup took place over a six-month period—ample time to move large stocks to the theater, call up the reserve forces, and assemble a winning team. If future wars in third-world countries are of the "come as you are" variety—even from a conventional perspective—the Air Force will need power projection, which requires that USAF aircraft have sufficient range, payload, and volume.

As we look at the cost of modernization, high technology has an attractive lure. We need forces with high survivability, long range, and devastating firepower. The weapons must be precise and achieve a high probability of kill, whether in air-to-air or air-to-ground combat. High technology, however, must pass a cost-effectiveness test. At some point in the development of a weapon system, the additional cost of increased capability will far outweigh the gain. We must know what capabilities are really required and shun the whistles and bells, since—in the world of fiscal constraints—it does not behoove us to develop systems we cannot afford to field in sufficient numbers to achieve our objectives. On the other side of the coin, however, an aircraft sortie is very expensive. We must, therefore, weigh the additional sorties and the risk of survivability when we decide how far to extend technology, since the true cost of a less expensive, less capable weapon may be much higher from a mission-capability perspective.

We must also consider that not all future conflicts will be against the most advanced military equipment or the best-trained forces. Large quantities of less expensive, low-technology weapons may be sufficient against such adversaries. These are the types of hard decisions we will need to make—and make wisely—in the 1990s.

Summary and Conclusions

The events in the Persian Gulf during Operation Desert Storm demonstrated the importance of air power in modern conflict. Our forces drew upon more than 10 years of program investments to provide the nation with the responsive and flexible capabilities that were needed to underwrite US national security. Their combat effectiveness was the result of a combination of training, sustainability, and modern equipment.

Our high-technology weapon systems showed not only that air power can be decisive in war, but also that it can limit casualties to a number far smaller than previously thought possible. The initial deployments were rapid and certainly weighed on Iraq's decision not to invade Saudi Arabia. This was of key importance in containing the threat and allowing time for mobilization of our forces.

The 1990s have begun as a decade of transition. Even though our fundamental national security objective—preserving the United States as a free and independent nation—remains the same, we are reexamining the force structure that is required to achieve that objective. We must continue to deter a Soviet nuclear attack, yet our conventional focus is no longer on the canonical US-USSR battle in the central European theater. As the geopolitical map in Eastern Europe changes, this focus is shifting to regional contingencies. Many of these contingencies are in areas which require us to improve our capabilities if we are to rapidly project power there in order to deter or defeat the adversary.

As the nature of the threat changes, the need to continue a modernization program increases rather than decreases. In response to what we see on the horizon for the 1990s and beyond, the Air Force will increasingly emphasize rapid, mobile, and lethal long-range capabilities. Since our future capabilities will depend upon choices made today, the challenges which we face—both current and future—demand that we select the proper mix of active and reserve forces, as well as allocate appropriate resources to readiness, sustainability, force structure, and modernization.

The Impact of Arms Control on the US Air Force

Dr Edward L. Warner III

Over the past three decades, arms control has become a central aspect of East-West relations and an essential element of US national security policy. Force-structure arms control—that is, limits on the number, deployment patterns, and often the testing of selected weapons systems—has been applied to long- and intermediate-range nuclear offensive arms, ballistic missile defenses, chemical and biological weapons, nuclear weapons development, and conventional arms in Europe. These limits or prohibitions on selected weapons systems and their development are designed to (1) enhance stability by containing or reducing the attack potential of rival states or coalitions, (2) impede the production and use of particularly heinous weapons, and (3) contain the arms race and make it more predictable.

The superpowers and the states of Europe have also concluded a series of operational arms control agreements. These agreements include arrangements to help prevent or manage international crises as well as confidence and security building measures (CSBM) designed to place constraints on, provide advance notification of, and often facilitate observation of the peacetime activities of existing military forces. Crisis avoidance and crisis management measures have included the creation and various upgrades to the US-Soviet direct hot-line communications link, the pioneering US-Soviet incidents-at-sea agreement and several similar agreements between the Soviet Union and other Western nations, the establishment of nuclear-risk reduction centers in Moscow and Washington, and—most recently—the US-Soviet agreement on avoiding dangerous military incidents. Several CSBMs have also been concluded among the states with military forces posted in Europe under the so-called Helsinki process. These agreements have been focused on the operations of conventional land forces between the

Atlantic and the Urals. They are designed to make military operations of all participants more predictable and transparent to others, thus making a successful surprise attack difficult to achieve.

The international agreements containing these force limitations and operational constraints have had various impacts on US armed forces in general and on the Air Force in particular. Up to this point, they have only modestly shaped the air and missile forces fielded by the Air Force. The arms control process has involved Air Force personnel in drafting and negotiating such agreements and in monitoring treaty compliance by the Soviet Union and other treaty participants. Further, Air Force personnel have hosted inspections of US military bases, weapons production facilities, and "exhibitions" of US strategic offensive systems to help develop verification techniques for the Strategic Arms Reduction Talks (START). A brief review of both the role of Air Force personnel in concluding and implementing arms control agreements and the effects of past agreements on the Air Force can assist in anticipating the potential impacts of future agreements on the Air Force.

Military Participation in the Conclusion and Implementation of Arms Control Agreements

Air Force personnel and their compatriots from the other services, serving in a variety of assignments, have long participated in the development of US bargaining positions and in the negotiation of arms control agreements. The military services participate corporately in the hammering out of US negotiating approaches within the Washington-based interagency arms control process through the Joint Chiefs of Staff (JCS). The Air Force chief of staff leads the USAF effort in this regard as a member of the JCS. He is directly supported by various elements of the Air Staff, with the leading role played by the Arms Control and International Negotiations Division of the Directorate of Plans. This division also coordinates arms control compliance activities throughout the Air Force.

Many other Air Force personnel outside the Air Staff work on the formulation of US arms control policy while posted in the Joint Staff, the Office of the Secretary of Defense, the Department of State, the Arms Control and Disarmament Agency, the Department of Energy, and the National Security Council Staff. Other USAF officers serve on the delegations that seek to reach agreements in several bilateral or multilateral negotiating forums. Once an agreement is signed, the Air Force chief of staff—acting as a member of the joint chiefs—and other senior Air Force generals—serving as commanders in chief of major commands affected by a particular agreement—are generally called upon to present their views on the merits of the agreement during ratification hearings conducted by the Senate.

Quite naturally, the military services—including the Air Force—are deeply involved as well in the implementation of arms control agreements to which the US is a party. If an agreement places limits on or reduces arms or restricts the testing of selected weapons, the military must adjust its force structure and weapons testing practices accordingly. This adjustment involves keeping close track of the design and operation of weapons systems constrained by agreements and the careful phasing of arms in and out of the operational inventory in order to stay within agreed limits. Military personnel also take an active part in collecting and assessing intelligence data, often with the use of US national technical means (i.e., imaging reconnaissance satellites orbiting overhead), to monitor treaty compliance by other signatory nations. They have also assisted in the development of sophisticated technical devices to perform monitoring functions and have participated on inspection teams operating under the auspices of the On-Site Inspection Agency (OSIA).

With the emergence of the widespread use of on-site inspections in recent years, Air Force personnel are also being called upon increasingly to host inspections of USAF bases and other facilities by visiting teams of inspectors. Many of these inspections are being carried out by personnel from "hostile states," in particular from the Soviet Union. Consequently, detailed preparations by the USAF host installations are needed to help fulfill US treaty obligations without inadvertently compromising information, technology, and operational capabilities not directly related to treaty compliance.

Impact of Past Agreements

Bilateral and multilateral arms control agreements that were concluded and implemented by the United States through the middle of 1991 have had little impact on the structure of the forces deployed and operated by the US Air Force. The sole exception to this rather modest effect has been the requirement to completely scrap our ground launched cruise missiles (GLCM), the majority of which were deployed in Europe in the middle of the 1980s. This rapid retirement and destruction of the GLCMs, along with the new Pershing II theater ballistic missiles, resulted from the ban on such missiles agreed to in the Intermediate-range Nuclear Forces (INF) treaty signed by the United States and the Soviet Union in December 1987. One should note, of course, that this treaty compelled the Soviets to destroy more than twice as many land-based ballistic and cruise missiles with ranges between 500 and 5,500 kilometers, including the mobile SS-20 intermediate range ballistic missiles, the SSC-X-4 GLCMs, and the SS-23 tactical ballistic missiles.

Neither the first nor the second agreements limiting offensive arms, which were concluded during the Strategic Arms Limitation Talks (SALT I in 1972 and SALT II in 1979), produced limits that required the Air Force to alter its existing force deployment plans significantly. The US-Soviet Interim Agreement on Strategic Offensive Arms, signed in 1972, remained in effect by mutual agreement well into the 1980s following its formal expiration in 1977. This agreement prevented the United States from constructing additional fixed launchers beyond the 1,054 hardened Minuteman and Titan II silos that existed in 1972.

The US-Soviet SALT II agreement limited both parties to no more than 1,200 intercontinental ballistic missile (ICBM) and sea-launched ballistic missile (SLBM) launchers carrying multiple independently targeted reentry vehicles (MIRV) and to no more than 1,320 MIRVed ballistic missiles and heavy bombers equipped to carry nuclear-armed, long-range air launched cruise missiles (ALCM). Although this treaty was never ratified, both sides largely complied with it throughout most of the 1980s in accordance with traditional international legal practices. Consequently, the US carefully managed its ballistic missile and bomber force posture to stay within the limit of 1,320 missiles until 1988, when the Reagan administration chose to discontinue SALT II compliance. During that period of informal, reciprocal SALT II compliance, the US had to balance the deployment of new MIRVed ICBMs and SLBMs and ALCM-equipped bombers with the deactivation of older MIRVed SLBMs.

During the early to mid-1980s as B-52 bombers were equipped to carry ALCMs, they had to be modified with the addition of "functionally related observable differences," to comply with SALT II. Such structurally distinctive features would allow the Soviets to distinguish ALCM-equipped bombers from non-ALCM penetrating bombers through the use of national technical means of verification. These observable differences took the form of large "strakelets" located at the junction of the wings and the fuselage on the B-52 ALCM carriers.

Agreements limiting nuclear testing have had more substantial impacts on the Air Force. Since its signing in 1963, the ban on nuclear testing in space, in the atmosphere, and under water has prevented atmospheric or high-altitude tests to explore the impact of electromagnetic pulse and other nuclear effects. Vigorous efforts to develop new and safer weapons have nevertheless continued through the extensive use of underground testing. The threshold test ban of 1974 that limits underground nuclear tests to no more than 150 kilotons of explosive yield has prevented full-yield testing of a few of the newest US nuclear warheads. These include the Mark 20, which is carried on the Peacekeeper ICBM. Despite this constraint, the US has been able to modernize its nuclear weapons, investigate a variety of weapons designs, and check out the reliability of its nuclear weapons.

Although the landmark Conventional Forces in Europe (CFE) treaty was signed by the member states of NATO and the now defunct

Warsaw Pact in Paris in November 1990, no treaty limiting US conventional forces has yet gone into effect as of June 1991. Thus, USAF tactical aviation has not yet been affected by structural arms control. The series of CSBM agreements growing out of the original Helsinki Conference on Security and Cooperation in Europe during the mid-1970s and the various negotiations it has spawned have largely focused on advance notification and observation of major land-force exercises in Europe. They have had little impact on NATO's air activities beyond those directly connected to major land-force exercises.

Air Force involvement to date in special activities to verify compliance with various arms control agreements that were concluded over the past 30 years has also been relatively modest. The Air Force Technical Applications Center, created to monitor Soviet nuclear testing in the early 1950s, has been active in monitoring the various nuclear test ban treaties. In addition, Air Force personnel have hosted Soviet on-site inspection teams at GLCM bases in Europe in accordance with the provisions of the INF treaty. Since the conclusion of that treaty in 1987, Air Force personnel have joined other US military personnel working under the aegis of OSIA in directly inspecting Soviet intermediate-range missile bases, as well as destruction facilities for missiles and transporter-erector-launchers. They also have participated in the permanent portal monitoring of the Soviet ballistic missile production facility at Votkinsk. Further, the Air Force has helped set up the Soviet portal monitoring presence at the Hercules solid rocket motor plant in Magna, Utah.

Likely Impact of Anticipated New Agreements

The Air Force and the nation appear to be on the brink of a substantial upsurge in activity related to arms control. Both the US-Soviet START treaty and the multilateral CFE treaty are likely to go into effect late in 1991 or early in 1992.

The implementation of the long-awaited START agreement will almost certainly produce a substantial reduction in the US silo-based

ICBM force by the end of its seven-year implementation period. This amount of time will be required to reduce the current US strategic missile force, with its roughly 8,000 nuclear weapons carried in ballistic missile reentry vehicles (RV), to reach the START II limit of no more than 4,900 RVs on SLBMs and ICBMs. At this point, the US apparently plans to field a strategic ballistic missile force under START that retains the current emphasis on SLBM weapons carried aboard large, "quiet" nuclear-powered submarines.

Current US plans point toward a START-compliant US ballistic missile force by the late 1990s that includes 18 Trident submarines, each carrying 24 C-4 or D-5 SLBMs, which, in turn, are loaded with eight RVs apiece. This fleet ballistic missile submarine (SSBN)/SLBM force will account for 3,454 ballistic missile RVs under the START ceiling of 4,900 RVs. Consequently, the US ICBM force will be limited to no more than 1,444 RVs once the START force-reduction period is completed seven years after the treaty goes into effect—that is, by 1999, if START is ratified during 1992.

Current Department of Defense plans look toward an ICBM "base force" that consists of 50 silo-based Peacekeeper missiles, each carrying 10 RVs, and 500 silo-based Minuteman missiles, with some portion of the latter "downloaded" from the current three-RV Minuteman III to a single-RV "Minuteman IV" configuration. All of the older 450 single-RV Minuteman IIs are to be retired over the next several years. The downloading of the Minuteman III to create the single-RV Minuteman IV will provide the needed flexibility to fit within the ceiling of 1,444 RVs.

Some people have argued for retention of as many US silos as possible in order to continue to confront the Soviets with a sizable number of silo targets if they were ever to try to carry out a disarming first strike. A US ICBM force that includes 550 silos cannot restore ICBM survivability in the face of an anticipated Soviet ballistic missile force of perhaps 2,000 or more highly accurate ballistic missile RVs. Nevertheless, such a force could continue to extract a sizable price for an attack, particularly if the Soviets felt compelled to target two RVs against each US silo-based ICBM due to concerns about the reliability of their ICBMs.

After more than a decade of protracted debate about mobile ICBM basing and in light of strong concerns about the substantial costs of many of these options, the United States government remains unable to select and deploy a mobile basing mode for ICBMs that would improve their survivability. Consequently, Air Force plans are confined to conducting two development programs over the next few years in order to provide options for the mobile deployment of ICBMs in the latter part of the 1990s. In accordance with congressional direction, the Air Force intends to complete the tests needed to validate the rail-garrison approach for basing the Peacekeeper missiles that are currently deployed in silos and then mothball this approach for possible future use. The Bush administration also proposes to complete development work on the various elements needed to deploy the small ICBM, often called the Midgetman, in a road-mobile configuration. Current plans look toward a possible deployment decision in 1993–94 that could lead to an initial operational deployment of the Midgetman in 1998.

There are no plans at this time to produce and deploy the Midgetman on a hardened mobile launcher, in silos (a proposed "interim" option), or in some combination of these two basing modes. Nevertheless, both mobile ICBM basing options will be available in the late 1990s and could be implemented if deemed necessary, due either to a resurgence of US-Soviet hostility or to the emergence of a domestic American consensus in favor of spending the necessary funds to acquire added survivability for the ICBM force through mobility. Both mobile systems could be deployed under START, which permits each superpower to deploy up to 1,100 RVs on mobile ICBMs.

Implementation of the START agreement will also compel some adjustments in the US bomber force. The START counting rules are very permissive for penetrating bombers—that is, bombers that are not configured to carry long-range, nuclear-armed ALCMs. Each non-ALCM bomber is counted as only one accountable weapon against the aggregate ceiling of 6,000 weapons, despite the fact that modern heavy bombers like the American B-1B or B-2 and the Soviet Blackjack can carry roughly 16 gravity bombs or short range attack missiles. Consequently, the US will have the opportunity to deploy as large a force of these bombers as the domestic political scene will permit, within the 1,100 accountable weapons available after one subtracts the 4,900 RVs associated with the ICBM and SLBM forces from the overall ceiling of 6,000 accountable weapons.

Current Bush administration plans call for retaining all 97 B-1Bs and producing 75 B-2s as non-ALCM bombers. There is, of course, great controversy in the Congress regarding production of the expensive B-2 stealth bomber. The favorable counting rules under START make sizable B-2 deployments attractive if one desires to maximize the number of weapons deployed within treaty provisions. Nevertheless, the ultimate number of B-2s that are approved by Congress appears likely to have little to do with START limits or, for that matter, with the B-2's role as a strategic nuclear delivery system. Rather, it will likely hinge on judgments about costs and the contributions that the versatile B-2 could make in regional conflicts as a stealthy bomber able to rapidly deliver a heavy payload of modern conventional weapons over great distances.

START will have a direct impact on the number of US bombers that are configured to carry long-range, nuclear-armed ALCMs. Roughly 200 B-52Gs and Hs were converted for this role during the 1980s. Under START, up to 150 ALCM-capable B-52s will be counted as 10 accountable weapons each against the ceiling of 6,000 weapons, although the treaty stipulates that these bombers can be equipped with up to 20 ALCMs—the maximum ALCM loading for the B-52. Any ALCM-equipped B-52 beyond the 150 would be counted as 20 accountable weapons. If the US opts to fill its entire quota of 4,900 ballistic missile RVs and to field 97 B-1s and 75 B-2s as penetrating bombers, there will be room under START for 92 ALCM-equipped B-52s, which will count as 920 accountable weapons. The majority of these B-52s will probably carry the stealthy advanced cruise missile.

START will also permit the US to retain up to 75 heavy bombers that are designated and equipped solely for the delivery of conventional weapons. The US will almost certainly avail itself of this opportunity to retain a sizable number of B-52s for such missions.

The START treaty calls for extensive and highly intrusive verification measures, including 12 different types of on-site inspections. For example, the agreed approach for verifying the number of RVs carried on US ICBMs will involve a quota of short-notice, on-site inspections in which randomly selected missiles are pulled from their silo launchers, the protective shroud covering the RVs mounted on the post boost vehicle (PBV) is removed, and the RVs—"draped" with a special cover to hide the exact details of US warhead design and PBV technology—are individually counted by a visiting team of Soviet inspectors. Similarly intrusive on-site scrutiny of US bombers is also included. Consequently, it is clear that US Air Force personnel who are posted at bomber and missile bases throughout the Strategic Air Command (SAC) will be deeply involved in preparing for and hosting these inspections. Other USAF personnel, many on temporary duty assignments, will serve on the OSIA teams that will conduct similar inspections at Soviet missile and bomber bases.

There is already talk of a possible follow-on START agreement that would produce much deeper cuts than those mandated by START I. Many people have also suggested that under START II the superpowers should seek to reduce the number of weapons carried on individual missile launchers, particularly if these launchers are fixed silos that are highly vulnerable to attack with high-accuracy ICBMs and SLBMs of substantial yield. Some critics have taken this point to its logical extreme and have called for banning the deployment of highly MIRVed ICBMs in silos. A ban of this type would necessitate either completely eliminating the 50 silo-based Peacekeeper ICBMs or, much less likely, coming up with the funds to deploy the Peacekeeper missiles in a rail-garrison configuration.

The much lower ceilings for START II, perhaps permitting deployment of only 3,000–4,000 actual weapons (rather than a US force with roughly 9,000 actual weapons under START I), would compel the US to make heavy cuts in its ICBMs, SLBMs, and bombers. Such an agreement might be negotiated using the basic framework and verification regime from START I. Were this to occur, the US ICBM force might have to fit under a limit of, say, 2,000–2,400 ballistic missile RVs. Thus, the ICBM force could be reduced to only 400–600 RVs carried on road-mobile, single-RV Midgetman and/or Midgetman or single-RV Minuteman IV missiles deployed in silos.

Substantial reductions in the US bomber force would likely be required as well under a deep-cut START II agreement. If START I counting rules were retained, the number of ALCM carriers—whether B-52s or B-1Bs—might be reduced to 30–50, while the non-ALCM bombers—B-2s and possibly B-1Bs—might be capped at 50–75. Thus, it is clear that a deep-cut follow-on START agreement could lead to much more radical changes in the strategic nuclear forces fielded by the US Air Force.

Likely to be ratified in the fall of 1991, the CFE treaty places limits on the collective holdings of main battle tanks, artillery, armored combat vehicles, armed helicopters, and combat aircraft that are held by the member states of both NATO and the now-defunct Warsaw Pact within the Atlantic-to-the-Urals region. The agreed ceilings are pegged, in most cases, at only 5–10 percent below existing NATO levels in 1990. The ceiling of 6,800 combat aircraft is actually higher than NATO's total holdings of such aircraft within the reductions area. Thus, CFE will require no reduction in USAF tactical aircraft based in Europe.

Nevertheless, major withdrawals of US military equipment, including combat aircraft, will certainly occur over the next few years. Responding to the much diminished Soviet threat and congressional pressures for reductions in defense spending, the US plans to cut back greatly its military presence in Europe in the post–cold war era. By the mid-1990s, these unilateral US withdrawals will likely leave roughly four tactical fighter wing equivalents stationed at four or five main operating bases in England, Germany, and possibly Italy, as compared to the 11 USAF fighter units located at 11 bases that were present in Europe in the late 1980s.

The CFE treaty also contains complex verification provisions and information exchange measures that will affect the US Air Force. Data on USAF aircraft stationed in Europe were already provided for the initial data exchange at the time the treaty was signed in November 1990 and will have to be revised and resubmitted on an annual basis. Verification measures under CFE will include a variety of inspections carried out at "declared sites" where equipment subject to treaty limits has been declared to be present by the possessing state. These measures will also include challenge inspections at specified areas. In both cases, the treaty's protocol on inspection lays out in immense detail the procedures to be followed in conducting inspections, the rights of the inspection team, and the obligations of the host country and its escort team. US Air Force commanders and their staffs will have to master these details in order to be able to host such inspections effectively at USAF air bases in Europe.

The new CSBM agreement—negotiated during the late 1980s between 34 nations that maintained forces in Europe and signed in Vienna in November 1990—will not have great impact on US Air Force activities in Europe in the years ahead. Throughout these negotiations, the US and its NATO allies repeatedly turned aside Soviet proposals to include provisions that would have placed restrictions on the conduct of independent air exercises in Europe or provided for prior notification or observation of such exercises.

Elements of the Vienna document that impinge upon USAF activities include the following requirements: to provide data on the normal peacetime location, organization, manpower, and major weapons and equipment of US air units stationed in Europe during the annual exchanges of military information; to provide information annually on any plans to deploy major new weapons systems with these same USAF units based in Europe; and to arrange at least one visit within a five-year period to a USAF air base in Europe to which representatives from all signatories of the Vienna document will be invited. Visits of the latter type are scheduled to last for a minimum of 24 hours and will involve a briefing on the purpose and function of the air base and current activities at the base, as well as opportunities for discussions with commanders and other personnel assigned at the base and arrangements for viewing all types of aircraft located there.

The Vienna CSBM agreement also mandates that USAF air bases in Europe that are included in the annual information exchange will be subject to short-notice evaluation visits. These sojourns, which can last up to 12 hours on a single working day, must be conducted within five days after a request has been received and accepted by the United States. In addition to hosting the various types of air base visits, USAF personnel will take part in visits to the air bases of other participating states.

The short-term prospects are not particularly good for the conclusion of additional arms control agreements regarding conventional forces in Europe beyond the CFE treaty and the Vienna document on CSBMs. The so-called CFE-1A talks got off to a rocky start in the winter and spring of 1991 due to the controversy over Soviet compliance with the CFE agreement, which was not resolved until June 1991. Even if CFE-1A eventually bears fruit, the national manpower ceiling it might produce for US forces stationed in Europe will likely be higher than the ceiling imposed by the US Congress. Conclusion of an aerial inspection monitoring regime for CFE, also being sought under CFE-1A, would be more consequential since it would establish the ground rules for such inspections. The implementation of aerial inspections would certainly involve USAF personnel as airborne inspectors and possibly as aircrew members. Such flights might also involve the use of USAF aircraft and onboard reconnaissance sensors.

Although the Conference on Security and Cooperation in Europe to be held in Helsinki in the spring of 1992 will almost certainly renew the mandates for additional negotiations on further reductions in conventional forces and additional CSBMs for Europe, there is little reason to expect rapid progress in either area. With the breakup of the

Warsaw Pact, the CFE follow-on negotiations can no longer be organized in terms of collective ceilings on selected armaments held by the member states of the opposing alliances in Europe. At this point, there is no consensus on a new approach for a next round of force reductions and little pressure to do so, as the Soviets are likely to remain absorbed with their troop withdrawal from Eastern Europe, the multiple internal crises they face, and the likely implementation of the CFE agreement.

Since the West achieved the vast majority of its objectives in the Vienna document and the US, at least, remains adamantly opposed to naval arms control, there is modest enthusiasm for pressing ahead to conclude a new set of CSBMs. Nevertheless, continued CSBM talks for Europe appear inevitable, and this next round could readily produce the first agreement that requires advance notification and possibly observation of independent air exercises beyond a given size and duration. If such is the case, it should not be beyond the skill of NATO military planners and negotiators to come up with well-crafted provisions that provide for notification and, in some cases, observation of large-scale air exercises. At the same time, these provisions should protect NATO's future training options and allow timely USAF reinforcement of Europe, should circumstances require it.

For the past several years, the US has taken part in multilateral US-sponsored negotiations in Geneva, seeking to conclude a chemical weapons convention that would ban the production and storage of chemical weapons on a global basis. In 1990 the United States and the Soviet Union concluded a bilateral agreement committing both superpowers to destroy the vast majority of their existing chemical weapons stocks by the year 2002, with an eye toward eliminating the remaining weapons altogether once the worldwide ban on chemical weapons is successfully concluded. The US-Soviet agreement alone will lead to substantial demilitarization of existing USAF chemical munitions over the next decade. Moreover, in the wake of the US-Soviet agreement, President George Bush announced that the

United States would unilaterally halt its production of new binary chemical munitions, including the Bigeye bomb.

The monitoring activities undertaken by the Air Force and the other services due to the implementation of the new START and CFE treaties, examples of which were briefly discussed above, will be very significant. Both treaties contain extensive and highly intrusive verification regimes, including a wide range of on-site inspections. Consequently, the Air Force has already developed detailed compliance plans and procedures for implementing and verifying each treaty. These preparations include several specially developed computerized data-management systems to track the status of USAF forces covered under the START, INF, and CFE treaties. The data bases that these systems help generate will also serve as a basis for regular status reports which must be made available to the other parties to the agreements.

Elaborate compliance plans drafted by the Air Staff set forth standard operating procedures for the conduct of the various on-site inspections. The Air Force has also developed a detailed training program that includes mock "red team" on-site inspections that will be carried out prior to actual visits by other nations in order to prepare American tactical air bases in Europe, SAC bomber and missile bases in the United States, and other USAF installations for the rigors of highly intrusive inspections by "hostile" personnel. In addition, the Air Force is working with industry to arrange for permanent portal monitoring by Soviet inspectors of additional US missile production facilities. Air Force personnel will undoubtedly be deeply involved in carrying out similar inspections at military bases and facilities in the Soviet Union and throughout Eastern Europe.

Conclusion

Over the past few decades the Air Force has gained substantial experience in the negotiation and, to a lesser extent, the implementation of a wide range of arms control measures. Much of the activity has focused on US-Soviet efforts to strengthen deterrence, enhance stability, and limit competition in the testing and deployment of strategic nuclear arms. More recently, this activity has been supplemented by multilateral negotiations involving the members of NATO, the Warsaw Pact, and other nations of Europe that seek to reduce conventional arms on that continent, as well as conclude confidence and security building measures as a means to lower tensions and make surprise attack more difficult.

At this point, it appears that in the latter part of 1991 and the first part of 1992, the long-awaited US-Soviet START agreement will likely be ratified and that the CFE agreement will go into effect following ratification by its 22 signatory states. The entry into force of these landmark agreements will trigger an unprecedented level of Air Force involvement in treaty implementation and monitoring. For example, in order to reach the START limits by the late 1990s, the Air Force will have to reduce its ICBM force by retiring several hundred Minuteman II ICBMs and destroying their silo launchers, and by reducing the number of weapons carried on several hundred Minuteman IIIs. The Air Force will also be required to cut its ALCM-equipped B-52 force roughly in half. Although the terms of the CFE treaty will not require any destruction of USAF aircraft deployed in Europe, the much improved East-West political atmosphere that CFE fosters and reflects will result in substantial withdrawals of USAF units from Western Europe over the next several years.

The most significant effects of these agreements, however, will not be on US Air Force strategic or tactical force posture. Rather, due to the verification regimes included in these treaties, a host of Air Force bases in the United States and in Europe will become subject to short-notice, highly intrusive, on-site inspections carried out by representatives from the Soviet Union and other states. Consequently, a much wider cross section of the Air Force must become knowledgeable about the specifics of these agreements and will be directly involved in their continuing implementation.

The anticipated execution of the START and CFE agreements will not, of course, mark the end of arms control. Negotiations on chemical weapons, nuclear testing, and other matters—as well as follow-on talks about US-Soviet strategic arms and conventional forces in Europe—will certainly take place. Thus, the Air Force and the nation are fated to remain deeply involved in arms control matters for the foreseeable future.

The Sky's the Limit: The Pentagon's Victory over the Press, the Public, and the Peaceniks

Ross Gelbspan

Using the Gulf conflict as a case study for examining the topic of domestic constraints on the use of force in the post–cold war period, one finds that there appear to be precious few constraints involving public opinion and the media. However, there are some lessons to be learned and some observations reinforced during the recent experience.

To a lay spectator with virtually no knowledge of military history, Operation Desert Storm was very impressive. One is impressed, first of all, by the ability of the commanders to achieve the functional integration of significant numbers of forces from more than two dozen countries. Most obviously, the technological achievements behind the Tomahawk cruise missiles and Patriot antimissile missiles—as well as our planes, Apache helicopters, and Abrams tanks—were mind-boggling. Few displays of technological performance in the field were more impressive. Equally impressive to the untutored mind was the ground strategy of outflanking the Iraqi artillery forces in the final days of the war, surrounding them, cutting off their avenues of withdrawal, and putting them in a situation of total, dead-end loss. More germane to the theme of this book was the extraordinary effectiveness of US air power. In retrospect, it is clear that the Iraqi high command did not have a clue as to the potential effect of the prolonged bombardment on their forces and their strategies. When the long-anticipated mother of battles finally came to pass, it was clear that the bombing campaign had reduced a potentially formidable ground foe to a splintered, disoriented force capable of mounting only a few highly isolated and localized battles of resistance. In short, regardless of one's feelings about the wisdom of the war, the performance of the Air Force, the Marine Corps, the Navy, and the Army was extremely impressive.

In moving from the area of military accomplishments to the specific focus of this essay—the constraints of public opinion and the media—one finds that the accomplishments of military planners were also quite effective. It is apparent that the imperative of information-control policy has become a practical priority of military planning, translating itself into an extensive set of arrangements which are every bit as important as deployment and logistics. In this case, the Pentagon's accomplishments are remarkable.

The initial and prolonged use of air power in this instance effectively prevented the press from covering the ugliest aspects of warfare—those most likely to turn public opinion against the campaign. An air war, by its very nature, is extremely difficult to cover. Even if all military censorship and restrictions on reporters were lifted, it is difficult to see how the press could have covered the bombing of targets and reported its effects in any kind of comprehensive way. In short, long-range aerial warfare is every bit as effective in maintaining public support as in disabling an enemy force. The images that were made available in place of reportage, involving long-range photography or nose-cone camera shots, created an impression of a very sanitary destruction—of a war almost without human consequences. Add to that the apparent accuracy of the precision bombing of Baghdad during the first month of the war, and you have a major public-relations victory. Saddam Hussein's claims of mass destruction of civilian lives have found little acceptance in the media or the public. The extraordinary measures taken to avoid indiscriminate bombing of civilian areas were well worth the risk to pilots, compared to the long-range benefit in the eyes of the public. Those relatively surgical bombing raids, moreover, stood in sharp contrast to the indiscriminate Scud attacks on Israeli apartment buildings and Saudi neighborhoods.

Moving from the specific area of air combat to the military's overall control of information flow, one congratulates the Pentagon on yet another aspect of the operation. While Gens Thomas Kelly,

Richard Neal, and Norman Schwarzkopf all came in for some fairly antagonistic treatment at the hands of reporters on the scene, they outflanked the complaints of the press by going over their heads to the public—the large majority of whom were far more sympathetic to the generals than to the reporters. Many of the latter were angered and frustrated by the lack of operational details, the failure of the briefers to provide damage assessments and Iraqi casualty figures, and the apparently arbitrary delays in providing some types of information that—to the reporters' minds—had precious little military sensitivity. Reporters claimed that, without such information, they were unable to provide the public with the information it needed to assess the progress of the war. In the absence of such assessment, the ability of the public to make judgments about the effort was effectively curtailed. Nevertheless, the fact remains that by providing spectacular footage of Star Wars in the desert, of Patriot intercepts, and of Tomahawk hits, the Pentagon was able to give the public the illusion of having a front-row seat, of sharing prized military information, and of knowing enough to draw its own conclusions. As a result of that strategy, the Pentagon effectively isolated the press, cut it off from public support, and managed to carry the day with very little adverse public reaction.

Inherent in such information-control policies are dangers that need to be heeded, for they cut to the heart of the Pentagon's credibility, which, in the past, has been a major Achilles' heel in the battle for public support. Obviously, the first concern about any information monopoly is reliability. Unduly optimistic estimates can become serious problems down the line. For instance, early briefing reports indicated that initial bombardments had destroyed something like 30 of 36 fixed Scud launchers and the lion's share of mobile launchers. The subsequent succession of Scud attacks raised serious questions of credibility, which evoked implicit retractions in later briefings. Imagine the scrambling in the Pentagon if those Scuds had extracted serious civilian damage. Although the damage was reasonably contained, it should sound a caution.

Again, we were told—within four or five days of the outbreak of the war—that coalition air power had disabled large numbers of Iraqi planes, only to be told shortly thereafter that many of these planes were protected in hardened bunkers. Later, we were told that they were sequestered in Tehran. Further, we were alerted early on to the imminent defection of large numbers of Iraqi deserters about to cross the border, rifles pointed downward. That too turned out to be prematurely optimistic. In a similar vein, William Safire of the *New York Times* recently took the Pentagon to task for its overly pessimistic assessments of Iraqi ground power when he wrote,

> Military briefers painted a dire picture of defenses: half a million mines, ditches filled with burning oil, battle-hardened troops, etc. That was said to prepare public opinion for the worst; in truth, most experts said privately that the air war had made resistance along the front line unlikely.[1]

The point here is that, given a situation of domination of information, there are strong temptations to bend the truth to manipulate public opinion. But that temptation should be indulged, if at all, most cautiously and sparingly. If the Pentagon's credibility comes into serious jeopardy, it will be very difficult to pacify a jilted press. Once the press feels it has been taken to the cleaners, it will fight very hard to impart that view to the public.

There is a second, less obvious but probably more tempting, pitfall here. That is the use of the media as a conduit for disinformation aimed at the enemy. Clearly, information is a weapon, and in a time of war it can be a very potent one. But the use of the media for disinformation cuts both ways. Recall the outcry in 1982 when the Reagan administration leaked a report to the *Wall Street Journal* that it was launching a covert operation to take out Muammar Qadhafi, when in fact no such operation existed. It would have been interesting to have been a fly on the wall in the editor's office when the next White House tidbit was leaked to the *Journal*.

In the case of the Gulf war, one is reminded of reports at the beginning of the ground war that allied forces had occupied Failaka Island off the coast of Kuwait. It seems clear in retrospect that that piece of disinformation was designed to keep Saddam Hussein off balance by implying the imminence of an amphibious landing from the Gulf. The tactic was successful in diverting Iraqi forces from the western stretches of the Iraqi border, but—in terms of public opinion—it is a step down a slippery slope and could lead to a serious credibility problem.

More to the point is the question surrounding the military's persisting reports of Iraqi strength. When the dust cleared, that strength vanished like a mirage. But the uncomfortable question remains: Was the Pentagon's overestimation of Iraqi capability part of an information strategy designed to lull Saddam Hussein into overconfidence, to make our forces appear more heroic to the American public, and to cover the Pentagon in the event of battlefield setbacks? Or was it a significant miscalculation of our military intelligence? The question is all the more unsettling because of a layering of secrecy which drives home how little we really know.

The issue of trust suggests itself at this point. The residual mistrust between the press and the military is, on one level, a product of the institutional imperatives on both sides. While surprise and secrecy are critical elements of war, truthfulness and accuracy are critical elements of the public's ability to judge something as costly and controversial as a military campaign.

A digression on the care and feeding of reporters is in order here. Many reporters pride themselves on what they think of as their finely tuned bullshit detectors. They assume that the stuff is all around them. Experience teaches them that the walls of institutions are painted with it and the floors carpeted in it.

If one begins with that kind of professional skepticism, then the imposition of secrecy serves only to heighten the alerts. My own experience as an investigative reporter tells me that, nine out of 10 times, the purpose of secrecy is to cover up mistakes, incompetence, or fraud. It catapults me deeply into stories I might have otherwise ignored.

Unfortunately, not all reporters share my personal priorities. I was, for instance, disappointed that the press acquiesced in the pool arrangements and other restrictions. Personally, I believe they should have opposed them vigorously from the beginning. It is all very well in retrospect for Walter Cronkite to announce that "this was the most rigid control in modern times" and for Harrison Salisbury to compare the press restrictions to those imposed by the Soviets during World War II.[2] In real time, however, the press as protector of the public's right to know was nowhere in sight.

Things might have been different in the face of a protracted ground war. In that case, reporters might well have broken ranks to cover the stories without the guidance of military censors. The confrontation could have forced an interesting crisis.

For many reporters assigned to the Gulf, the experience must have troubled their professional souls—pretending to cover a war when, in truth, they did not know a damned thing other than what they were told by people with decided personal and professional interests. While the public clearly disapproved of reporters' thorny—and at times disrespectful—questioning, that reaction is irrelevant to reporters. They are not in the business of winning popularity contests. Their first responsibility is, after all, to the most truth they can get their hands on.

Although the Pentagon has justified its censorship rules on the ground of protecting militarily sensitive operational details, there are many examples of information suppression that seem ludicrous. For instance, some reporters probably had a very hard time being told that the Iraqis had flooded the Gulf with millions of gallons of oil—and then having to wait six days before being permitted to witness the oil slick. Was that restriction designed to cover the fact that the oil slick turned out, by some accounts, to be far smaller than was initially advertised?

Again, if I were told that 12 Marines had been killed at the time of the Iraqi engagement at Khafji, Saudi Arabia, it would have been important to view the scene and record the hit that was absorbed by their armored personnel carrier. In fact, I was troubled that evening (especially so, since I had to perform the dreadful assignment of interviewing the families of the victims) to see the television networks feature rather routine footage of planes hitting an Iraqi bridge when the real story of the day was the fact that we suffered our first ground-combat casualties. I do not believe that information was withheld to conceal the fact that the Marines had been killed by friendly fire. But reporters are quick to assert that kind of interpretation in an atmosphere of what they perceive as excessive and unwarranted secrecy.

Reporters' suspicions are not entirely unwarranted. There are ample precedents in the recent history of the Republic. Witness, for example, the legacy of the Tonkin Gulf, the revelations of the Pentagon Papers, the sordid components that collectively comprised what we call Watergate, and a legacy of covert and amoral abuses that culminated most recently in the Iran-Contra affair. From a more strictly military viewpoint, there are today lingering and unanswered questions about manipulation of the number of fatalities in the 1989 invasion of Panama.

The point of all this is that while the Pentagon has done an admirable job of engineering the control and content of information, it should not forget the importance of peaceful coexistence with the press. The public image of the military's basic credibility depends to a large extent on the success of that coexistence.

Having digressed, let me now turn to the obvious question of what makes war acceptable to the citizenry. The first task of the military and its political sponsors is to persuade the public that a war is, first of all, morally acceptable; that it is, moreover, warranted by some acceptable proportion of goals and costs; and, finally, that war is the only remaining means of achieving those goals.

One element of public acceptability is a credible enemy. Ho Chi Minh, that follower of Abraham Lincoln, didn't quite make it; neither did Maurice Bishop. Manuel Noriega represented a distinct improvement, but even he couldn't hold a candle to Saddam Hussein, a man who came to be portrayed as someone not even his mother could love. In this *People*-magazine age of highly personalized news coverage, a major ally in disguise is an enemy who is so humanly loathsome that public revulsion alone is enough to overcome other questions or ambiguities involving political goals or international morality.

A second element, whose importance lies, perhaps, in inverse proportion to the demonic persona of the enemy, is a persuasive geopolitical rationale for war—a clear, demonstrable threat to national security and an equally clear and compelling proof that no means short of armed force will succeed in eliminating that threat. The main criticism of President George Bush's decision in August 1990 to mount a military response to Iraq was the lack of clarity of his rationale for using force. Whereas the president cited the need to resist "naked aggression," the liberal columnists and peace activists cited the nation's insatiable hunger for cheap oil. Whereas the president expressed concerns about the destabilization of the Middle East by Iraq's occupation of Kuwait and its threat to Saudi Arabia, his critics expressed concerns about the destabilization of the Middle East by a protracted US presence in the region.

It is worth recalling that, in August 1990 when the president announced his decision to send a purely defensive force to protect the Saudi border, the nation was almost equally divided over that proposal. At the time, most polls had the country pretty well split over the continued use of sanctions versus the use of force, with such respected military figures as Adm William Crowe, former chairman of the Joint Chiefs of Staff, counseling against the initiation of war. It was not until the president made the decision to commit nearly half a million service personnel and announced in December 1990 his intention to use offensive force if Iraq did not withdraw by the deadline of 15 January 1991 that the public closed ranks in support of their president and their sons and daughters in the Gulf.

This approach is only partially meant to be flippant, for in the post–cold war era I can imagine very few scenarios in which a call to arms will automatically evoke universal support. The world has become too ambiguous, our national interests too diffuse and ill-defined, and our potential enemies too frequently the past recipients of our foreign aid.

Thus, the issue of casualties becomes all the more problematic. Certainly, numbers of casualties—especially American—pose a major threat to public support. More specifically, the appearance of casualties, which the Pentagon went to great lengths to place off-limits to cameras, obviously enhances disapproval of the war.

But casualties are not the entire story. The degree to which they are acceptable is a function of the overall persuasiveness of the goals of the war. In the case of Vietnam, it became clear that the domino theory did not justify tens of thousands of casualties in the public mind. On the other hand, close to a million casualties were acceptable when citizens, fighting for the right to be free of the oppression of a large, alien, centralized government, engaged counterparts willing to die for the very survival of the Union. The principles of the Civil War were worth dying for and worth absorbing casualties for.

Unfortunately, no formula tells us what number of casualties is acceptable relative to the degree of acceptance of the goals of a war. This matter of casualties—either prospective or real, small or large—is a gateway into the next topic for consideration: the peace movement.

From a military perspective, the peace movement is a latent virus embedded in the body politic. Although a virtual nonfactor in the Gulf war, the peace movement—if properly read—may provide a telling barometer as to what is and is not acceptable to the public at large. Left alone, without any triggering events, the antiwar movement is a weak and negligible force. It is only when conditions conspire to make the large population susceptible that the movement can grow in size and influence.

The peace movement is generally thought to have sprouted and flourished during the Vietnam War and to have persisted in the nearly two decades since. But a reading of American history indicates that the peace sentiment—or at least a deep public reluctance to engage in foreign wars—long predates Vietnam. One recalls the tremendous public opposition to the commitment of US troops in World War I by President Woodrow Wilson, as well as the formidable resistance to

President Franklin D. Roosevelt's ability to mobilize public support for our intervention in World War II.

My assessment of the current peace movement—admittedly impressionistic and in no way scientific—is that antiwar proponents represent at the very maximum perhaps 20 percent—more likely 15 percent—of the electorate in normal times. Of that 20 percent, about one-tenth is basically pacifist. These are people who are philosophically opposed to any form of organized force and for whom no amount of provocation justifies the use of violence. Again, using very impressionistic figures, one estimates that another 40 percent of the residual antiwar constituency in the country is composed of previously politicized activists, generally liberal and left-wing anti-imperialists who have become disillusioned by various aspects of postwar history and who have conditioned themselves to see the United States as the immediate villain in virtually every controversial international encounter it involves itself in. The final 50 percent or more of peace activists are traditionally citizens who have no history of either pacifism or political activism but who are spurred by events to take action to express their opposition to government policies.

The last peace movement of significance was the Central America movement of the 1980s, which had a small contingent of religious pacifists, a core of veteran antiwar activists—many of them carryovers from the Vietnam period—and a far larger number of people who were repulsed by atrocities in El Salvador and angered at what they perceived as the government's unjustifiably bellicose policies toward Nicaragua. Although that movement had no direct bearing on official military policy, it had enormous impact—through its influence in Congress—on the administration's unofficial military policy, driving the White House and National Security Council underground to pursue their support of the Nicaraguan Contras illegally and in violation of US law in one of the more disturbing scandals the country has seen—the Iran-Contra affair.

In the case of the Gulf war, however, the peace movement was doomed almost from the start. Borrowing a headline from a *New York Times* op-ed piece, one might say that this time around, it was not the generals but the protesters who were fighting the war.[3] From a tactical point of view, the peace movement was weakened when it split into two separate camps. One group, called the Coalition to End US Intervention in the Middle East and headed by Ramsey Clark, former US attorney general, alienated a large number of activists by refusing to condemn Saddam Hussein's invasion of Kuwait, by opposing the administration's use of sanctions, and by implying that what was clearly an act of Iraqi aggression was yet another episode of US imperialism. Because of the generally unacceptable approach of the Clark group, a second national group, called the National Campaign for Peace in the Middle East, came into being. That group, which attracted a large constituency and represented a more mainstream liberal coalition, did condemn the Iraqi invasion while calling for the US to forego the use of military force.

The power struggle of the two groups further crippled the movement. For one thing, both groups persisted in holding separate national rallies in Washington on separate weekends, thus diluting their impact on the national television audience and, by extension, on Congress. For another, the Clark coalition accepted into its fold a number of organizations on the extreme right, many of whom were motivated by a pre–cold war isolationism, and many of whom alienated a traditional source of strength for the movement—liberal Jewish activists—by blaming the war on Israel and invoking extensive anti-Semitic sentiments. These groups included organizations like the Liberty Lobby, the Lyndon LaRouche group, and Dr Louis Farrakhan's Nation of Islam—strange bedfellows indeed in the politically dyslexic 1990s.

Putting aside the Byzantine politics of the movement, one may conclude that the major reason for the failure of the success of antiwar groups lies in the lack of any significant feeling of fundamental moral opposition to the war. What distinguished the opposition to this war—compared to the opposition to policies in Vietnam or Central America—was the fact that the opponents of the military option based their opinion on politically tactical, rather than moral, considerations. Many people hoped that sanctions would provide a way to avoid the loss of life, especially American life. Others felt that while Saddam Hussein's threat to destabilize the region was checked by the defensive presence of half a million alliance troops, they feared that an offensive US-led military presence would trigger a different kind of destabilization by uncorking the pent-up forces of Pan-Arab nationalism and Islamic fundamentalism. But these were tactical and strategic considerations. They did not reflect any basic moral disagreement with the goals of the war. It was pretty hard to make the argument that the United States was the imperialist villain and that Saddam Hussein was the good guy in this case. So when President Bush secured the approval of the United Nations to use offensive force in Iraq and Kuwait, the public had little difficulty in closing ranks, putting tactical differences behind them, uniting in support of what was generally perceived as a worthy goal, and leaving the peace groups out in the cold.

An ironic concern heard from a number of quarters as the direction of the Gulf war became clear was that it was too easy. To paraphrase those concerns, The cowboys in the Pentagon will have no limits on the future use of force. The sky's the limit. There are no opponents anywhere in the world capable of standing up to our technological and military superiority. The military will use its might wherever and whenever a Pax Americana wants to be enforced.

Those concerns reflect somewhat the historical aversion to foreign wars mentioned earlier. But there are antidotes available. One is an adherence by the military to a policy, wherever possible, of candor and a minimization of unnecessary secrecy. Despite the acquiescence of both the press and the public this time around, it is important to remember that the American people are far more likely to forgive honest mistakes honestly admitted than to forgive deliberate lies. A second is the continued use of war technology for the most military-specific kind of targeting. This technology, which carries such potential for destruction, paradoxically also contains the potential for disabling enemy forces with a degree of precision and civilian survival never before known.

At the level of politics, our leadership must—in considering the use of force—make crystal clear the goals, objectives, and anticipated costs of any future campaign. The president's promises prior to the start of the war have apparently been kept. But they have also established a standard which may be very difficult to guarantee in future circumstances. The public may have come to expect wars without surprises, and that represents a heavy burden for considering future campaigns. One hopes, as well, that future presidents will recognize that the most difficult and intractable problems of all the ones threatening mankind domestically and globally are not susceptible to the quick fix of war.

A final hope rests on the improved technology of communications, rather than the improved technology of weapons, so that the public will continue to get the picture. As improvements in communications make the destructiveness of war increasingly immediate and vivid, the public—not only in the US but also around the world—will finally become terminally intolerant of the use of force as an instrument for solving human problems. To quote a former general of the Army who parlayed his World War II triumphs into bigger and better things, "People want peace so much that one of these days governments had better get out of the way and let them have it." [4]

Notes

1. William Safire, "Four White Lies," *New York Times*, 25 February 1991.
2. Chris Reidy, "Press Faced a Leakproof Front," *Boston Globe*, 2 March 1991.
3. Paul Berman, "Protesters Are Fighting the Lost War," *New York Times*, 31 January 1991.
4. Dwight D. Eisenhower, *Public Papers of the Presidents of the United States: Dwight D. Eisenhower, 1959* (Washington, D.C.: Government Printing Office, 1960), 625.

PART VI

Acquisition Priorities and Strategies
A View from Industry

Introduction

Parts I through V have attempted to present a diversity of views from senior Air Force commanders—both operational and managerial—civilian strategists, and academics concerned with national security affairs. The issues that they raise have touched virtually every relevant dimension of the debate on air power in a changing world order, save one key arena—private industry. The two writers in this section represent the views of a sector that will be in the vanguard of America's efforts to protect its vital interests from potential aggressors. The preceding essays have established that air power has provided a military advantage to the United States and that it will form a unique part of our future military posture, especially in view of its strong performance in the Gulf war. If we are to sustain this advantage, we must make a serious effort to understand and heed the views of private industry.

Harold K. McCard of Textron Defense Systems leads off this part with an analysis of research and development (R&D) strategies designed to provide America with the air power advantage in a future conflict. He points out, as have many others in this volume, that "the world order has changed immensely in the last few years, so new R&D strategies are in order." Following a review of these changes, Mr McCard observes that "many regions of the world will continue to be very unstable and unsafe." He also asserts that "the probability of recurring midintensity conflicts will be fairly high, and the probability of low-intensity conflicts will be quite high." If the US is to adjust to these changes, the military services and the Department of Defense (DOD) must "become more efficient, flexible, and responsive to the demands of the new world order."

Mr McCard offers a planning model that is designed to rationalize the procurement process. His central rule is that "systems are meant to perform tasks needed to support a concept of operations that underwrites particular military strategies and missions." In his model, weapon systems "flow down" from military and national security planning activities. The latter are concerned with establishing "required military response options" consistent with new or evolving "concepts of operations—as well as strategies and missions—to cope with certain threats." Mr McCard cites a Defense Science Board report that urges "senior Pentagon brass [to] issue strong statements of where the Defense Department and industry should head over the next decade 'if [the] bottom-line resource allocation' is going to be changed."

Mr McCard agrees that recent changes in the world order will continue to generate budget-driven changes in US strategies for war fighting and preparedness. He observes that "it is equally clear that coherent R&D and investment strategies must be established so these changes can be made in an orderly fashion." To achieve this goal, Mr McCard's planning model links weapon system requirements to threat characteristics and military response options by means of existing or newly developed concepts of operations and/or missions. This linkage leads the author to place greater importance on multipurpose weapon systems that are effective against a variety of threats.

His general framework—devised to rationalize corporate investment strategies—applies R&D resources to enhance the flexibility of existing weapon systems and improve the effectiveness of operations, training, and maintenance. Further, one should establish "fast-track" action plans for certain high-priority upgrades to avoid unnecessary "starts, stops, and stretch-outs." Mr McCard asserts that the Air Force budget for fiscal year 1991 does not follow this principle, in that research, development, test and evaluation (RDT&E) spending continues to be driven by three major aircraft-development programs (the B-2 stealth bomber, the F-22 advanced tactical fighter, and the C-17 airlifter) and the intercontinental ballistic missile (ICBM) modernization program.

In terms of current force structures for the Air Force, Mr McCard affirms the soundness of the triad but is not convinced that the B-2 is necessary. At any rate, he believes that the B-1 should be fixed, the B-52 upgraded, and the development of a mobile launcher included in ICBM modernization. In addition, he supports retention of the A-10 for the close-air-support mission and favors upgrading the avionics and payloads of the A-10, F-15, and F-16 aircraft for multiple roles/missions. Although replacing the C-141 with the C-17 may be indicated, such a move should be driven by required military response options and concepts of operations. Further, the Air Force should emphasize systems for command, control, communications, and intelligence—such as the joint surveillance target attack radar system (JSTARS). Such guidelines will help ensure that the Air Force "can and will remain a comprehensive air force and the best air force in the world—not just a good air force."

Dr John Blair of the Raytheon Company examines the future course of technological development and the challenges in this arena for the American defense industry. Dr Blair observes that aggressive technological innovation will continue to occur outside the United States. To meet this challenge, the US must overcome a chronic shortage of trained scientists and engineers and set aside negative images of the perceived adverse impact of technology on the environment, as well as on health and society. Dr Blair also notes how federal R&D spending has been hamstrung by expanding budget deficits.

In response to these constraints, Blair predicts that a "new breed of technology managers will emerge who not only will produce scientific discoveries but also will apply and transfer technology rapidly into implementation." The demands on these managers will be heightened by the anticipated 25 percent reduction in force structure by 1996. Dr Blair observes that by the end of 1996 only 3.6 percent of the gross national product will be allocated to defense outlays, in contrast to much higher figures approved during the height of the Reagan buildup, the Vietnam War, and the Korean War. Further, a decline in federal funding for R&D has prompted a widespread realization of the importance of strengthening the scientific and technological base.

Although DOD budget appropriations have dropped, Dr Blair notes that the RDT&E account represents a larger share of the overall DOD allotment: "The increase from $34.6 billion for FY 1991 to $39.9

billion for FY 1992 represents a 15 percent increase in RDT&E funding." Significantly, the Air Force's portion of the RDT&E request shows sizable expansion, reflecting the high priority which the Air Force has placed on technological superiority.

If the US is to facilitate the process of technology development, Dr Blair maintains that the adversarial relationship between government and industry must be transformed into government/industry partnerships. Additionally, industries must forge ties among themselves and with universities to strengthen the resource base of technology R&D in the future. Funds for independent research and development (IR&D) provided by the government to the industrial sector will aid in this effort to maintain a competitive position on the leading edge of technology. However, Dr Blair comments that "although the application of these funds is largely within the discretionary power of a defense contractor, both DOD and Congress imposed a number of controls and limitations on such application."

As for congressional action, Dr Blair notes that the House Armed Services Committee has written measures into the defense authorization bill to protect the technology base and reinforce its earlier recommendations to authorize a real growth rate of 2 percent per year in RDT&E. Further, the committee report called for more liberal standards to be applied to IR&D—specifically, the removal of both arbitrary ceilings and unnecessary DOD reviews. The Senate's position on the change in status for IR&D, however, is still unclear.

In closing, Dr Blair points out that the weapons used in Operation Desert Storm embodied technology choices made at least two decades ago. The decisions that mandated these choices, though controversial at the time, have been vindicated by the Gulf war. Blair asserts that

> the performance of currently deployed systems was exceedingly impressive, but future systems originating from the current technology base will be even more precise and effective. Moreover, they will require less manpower and be less costly to deploy.

Research and Development Strategies

Harold K. McCard

In many ways, research and development (R&D) planning in the past was rather straightforward. The United States–Soviet Union and NATO–Warsaw Pact bipolar world was stable, and evolutionary changes in threats allowed the US to identify and take a suitable technology-driven course of action. However, the world order has changed immensely in the last few years, so new R&D strategies are in order.

Major Changes in World Order

Unprecedented changes have occurred since 1988. The major ones that pertain to this discussion include the following:

- 1988—The Iran/Iraq war ends, and Soviet troops withdraw from Afghanistan in accordance with an agreement mediated by the United Nations (UN).
- 1989—Socioeconomic crises in Eastern-bloc countries cause disintegration of the Warsaw Pact threat.
- 1990—NATO and Warsaw Pact allies declare that they are no longer adversaries; optimism over the Strategic Arms Reduction Talks (START) and the Conventional Forces Europe (CFE) treaty grows; demands for a "peace dividend" cause drastic reductions in the defense budget. Meanwhile, Iraq invades Kuwait, and a massive, US-led, UN-mandated, multinational coalition of military forces is deployed within five months to that region.
- 1991—Economic sanctions and diplomacy fail, and war starts in the Middle East. The world observes in real time as Cable News Network not only dramatizes but also influences the course of events. A five-week air campaign of unprecedented intensity achieves

unimagined air superiority and inflicts massive damage throughout Iraq's command, control, and communications (C^3); war-fighting capacity; and supply systems. Subsequently, an equally unprecedented airland campaign leads to the liberation of Kuwait and the end of offensive military operations within four days with incredibly few allied casualties.

Postwar Euphoria versus Reality

As in prior wars, postwar euphoria will be evident after the Gulf war. The most widely held perceptions will likely include the following:

- We have won the cold war, and Saddam Hussein is back in his cage.
- We can be sure that technological superiority and economic strength were key factors.
- We can withdraw, dismantle, disarm, and reduce defense budgets now.
- We can continue with some R&D, but we should put it on the shelf.

Many regions of the world will continue to be very unstable and unsafe. The probability of a high-intensity conflict will remain very low. However, the probability of recurring midintensity conflicts will be fairly high, and the probability of low-intensity conflicts will be quite high. These subjective estimates may be—and hopefully are—too pessimistic. However, the fact remains that the sole purpose of the Department of Defense (DOD), the military services, and the defense industry is to deter and, if necessary, to defeat those enemies who threaten the sovereignty and peace of the United States and her allies. Therefore, it is clear to most people that each element of our defense structure must become more efficient, flexible, and responsive to the demands of the new world order. For example, Gen Merrill A. McPeak, Air Force chief of staff, has stated that the Air Force and defense industry are likely to get much smaller. . . . The Air Force will be roughly 25 percent smaller by 1995. . . . We must research less, develop less, and purchase less [but] we simply must provide the complete range of aerospace capabilities. We must be a comprehensive Air Force, not just a good Air Force.[1]

Planning Model

Planners have their preferred models, and mine is shown in table 1. It reflects the view that systems are meant to perform tasks needed to support a concept of operations that underwrites particular military

TABLE 1
DEFENSE PLANNING MODEL

Source: Textron Defense Systems (51–0254), 1991.

strategies and missions. In my model, therefore, weapon system requirements "flow down" from the closed-loop planning activities that seek to establish required military response options consistent with existing or developing concepts of operations—as well as strategies and missions—to cope with certain threats in accordance with national security policy directives. Weapon systems requirements include all characteristics of the prime items' support systems, together with related logistics functions pertaining to operations, training, and maintenance. The model also reflects the view that technology must be applied across the full spectrum of requirements for new weapon systems and, more importantly, for upgrades to existing weapon systems to satisfy future national needs.

Alternative Futures
An Approach to Strategic Planning

The Defense Science Board says that the current DOD investment strategies

> "do not establish linkage between future [threat] scenarios, future military capabilities, future technology goals and future investments. . . ." Senior Pentagon brass must issue strong statements of where the Defense Department and industry should head over the next decade "if [the] bottom-line resource allocation" is going to be changed.[2]

A brief description of the approach to strategic planning used by Textron Defense Systems may be useful to DOD and military strategic planners who are responsible for resource allocation. Textron's strategic planning approach includes a process called alternative futures, outlined in tables 2–5. This planning approach is straightforward:

1. Define what is needed, where, and when. Choose a time horizon that will permit major changes in strategic direction.

2. Define some number of possible futures that are likely to bound the possible range (Textron chose four).

TABLE 2
ALTERNATIVE FUTURES:
AN INPUT TO THE STRATEGIC PLANNING PROCESS

- Alternative futures is a means to develop an unbiased view of potential external environments.

- The concept acknowledges two fundamental truths.

    — Predicting the future accurately is almost impossible.

    — Hindsight is superior to foresight.

- It provides both a means of ensuring that the full range of possible outcomes has been considered and the likelihood of understanding the implications of current events.

Source: Textron Defense Systems (51–0255), 1991.

TABLE 3
PROCESS OF ALTERNATIVE FUTURES

- Define period of interest: Textron picked 1990–2000.

- Define some number of possible futures: Textron settled on four.

    — Do not be concerned with probabilities of any particular "future."

    — Try to bound the possible range.

- Develop a "reasonable sequence of events" that might lead from "now" to each "then."

- Interpret implications for your strategic plan.

    — Identify common features or other factors that would influence decisions and actions.

    — Over time, use the "reasonable sequence of events" to help interpret real-world events to identify the path the world is following.

Source: Textron Defense Systems (51–0256), 1991.

TABLE 4
TEXTRON DEFENSE SYSTEMS' IMPLEMENTATION OF THE CONCEPT

- Textron enlisted two independent groups representing different backgrounds and expertise.
  - Institute for Foreign Policy Analysis (IFPA) provided political perspectives.
  - Burdeshaw Associates Ltd. (BAL) provided military perspectives.
- IFPA defined the alternative futures for year 2000.
  - IFPA determined potential national security policy.
  - IFPA developed rational series of events leading to each "future."
- BAL took IFPA output and developed likely military response.
- Textron's role was to provide guidance and funding.

Source: Textron Defense Systems (51–0257), 1991.

TABLE 5
ALTERNATIVE FUTURES—2000: A PROCESS

PURPOSE: TO DEFINE THE PROCESS OF LINKING ALTERNATIVE FUTURES FOR THE YEAR 2000+ AND ASSOCIATED NATIONAL POLICIES WITH OPERATIONAL SCENARIOS AND SYSTEM BUSINESS OPPORTUNITIES.

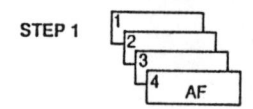

STEP 1 — DEVELOP A SET OF FOUR CANDIDATE ALTERNATIVE FUTURES (AF).
- ANOTHER ICE AGE
- RISE OF NEW SUPERPOWERS
- REGIONAL MAELSTROMS
- ONWARD TO DEEP PEACE

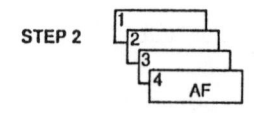

STEP 2 — DEVELOP RELATED NATIONAL POLICIES, CONFLICT SITUATIONS, AND US NATIONAL POLICY DIRECTIVES RELATED TO EACH AF.

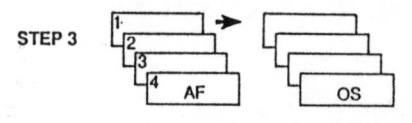

STEP 3 — DEVELOP AN OPERATIONAL SCENARIO (OS) FOR EACH CONFLICT SITUATION (E.G., IRAN RESURGENT AS LEADER OF MOSLEM WORLD).

STEP 4 — SELECT TACTICAL SCENARIOS THAT SATISFY OPERATIONAL SCENARIOS AND DRIVE WEAPON SYSTEM DEPLOYMENT IN AREAS OF INTEREST.

STEP 5 — CONDUCT FUNCTIONAL AND SYSTEM ANALYSIS OF TACTICAL SCENARIOS LEADING TO IDENTIFICATION OF SYSTEM REQUIREMENTS AND SHORTFALLS.

TACTICAL SCENARIOS (E.G., SUPPRESSION OF ENEMY AIR DEFENSES TACTICAL SCENARIO)

Source: Textron Defense Systems (51–0258), 1991.

3. Develop a reasonable sequence of events for each future.
4. Identify common features or other factors that would influence strategic decisions and actions.

Further, this approach allows construction of a map and a course of action that link goals and decisions (e.g., technology and investment pertaining to R&D strategies) to drive weapon system development in areas of interest. This approach would also be useful to DOD and military strategic planners.

Although this discussion has stressed the importance of required options consistent with concepts of operations, many people in industry pay too little attention to—or may not understand—the relevancy of pertinent aspects of concepts of operations. One might extend this statement to include military and DOD system developers. It is true that a so-called statement of operational need and similar documents are supposed to cover this imperative. However, our attention is primarily focused on threat characteristics and weapon systems requirements, and few of us truly understand or are able to articulate the relationships between these factors and concepts of operations.

Global Reach—Global Power
The Air Force's Strategic Planning Framework

During a congressional briefing on the subject of "Global Reach—Global Power: Sustaining the Vision," General McPeak outlined the Air Force's strategic planning approach, objectives, and guiding principles used in developing the Air Force budget. The major objectives were as follows:

- Sustain deterrence (nuclear forces). Maintain the nuclear triad, and sustain military sufficiency, flexibility, and stability in the post-START force.
- Provide a versatile combat force (theater operations and power projection). Enhance capability to project power; increase lethality and freedom of action.

- Supply rapid global mobility (airlifters and tankers). Enhance rapid response and service interoperability capabilities.
- Control the high ground (space and command, control, communications, and intelligence [C^3I] systems). Balance funding to meet a range of critical requirements.
- Build US influence (strengthen security partners and relationships).

General McPeak explained that the B-2 was needed to form the backbone of the future bomber force and sustain strategic deterrence but that the intercontinental ballistic missile (ICBM) force could be "adjusted to the new realities." He also noted that

> Our Desert Storm forces drew upon 20 years of investment as regards responsiveness and flexibility; combat effectiveness resulting from training, readiness, and modern equipment; and the roles of B-52s, F-117s, precision guided munitions, and standoff weapons. We will study the lessons of this war to prepare for the next conflict. So will our potential adversaries. We need to learn from this war, not repeat it.[3]

Some Thoughts on R&D Strategies

Clearly, the recent changes in world order have set in motion major budget-driven changes in the war-fighting and preparedness strategies of DOD and the military services. Therefore, it is equally clear that coherent R&D and investment strategies must be established so these changes can be made in an orderly fashion.

As previously noted (and shown in table 1), my planning model links weapon system requirements to threat characteristics to military response options by means of existing or newly developed concepts of operations and/or missions. This leads me to place greater importance on weapon systems that can satisfy multirole/multimission requirements against a variety of threats and forms. The framework for my R&D and investment strategies, simply stated, is as follows: Apply R&D and investment resources to adapt existing weapon systems to broaden response flexibility while improving effectiveness and efficiency as regards operations, training, and maintenance. Then (1) apply remaining resources to new weapon systems to fill shortfalls and (2) pursue a limited set of "breakthrough" technologies that have the potential of revolutionizing military capabilities.

It is much easier to describe a planning framework than to apply it. Nonetheless, the Air Force research, development, test and evaluation (RDT&E) budget decreased from an FY 1990 level of $13.6 billion to $11.7 billion in FY 1991, and it will probably continue to decrease to perhaps $8–9 billion (in FY 1991 dollars) by FY 2000. Therefore, new strategies are in order.

Table 6 contains a breakdown of the Air Force RDT&E budget for fiscal year 1991 by budget activity and research category. Within budget activity, nearly 60 percent ($6,856 million) of the budget is allocated to strategic programs and tactical programs, whereas only 12.6 percent ($1,473 million) is allocated to technology base and advanced technology. Further breakdown of the strategic program budget would show that the largest allocation is 50 percent ($1,735 million) to the B-2 bomber, followed by 16 percent ($565 million) to ICBM modernization; the remainder ($1,205 million) is allocated to 35 other programs. Similarly, further breakdown of the tactical program budget shows 29 percent ($958 million) allocated to the advanced tactical fighter (ATF) program, 16 percent ($536 million) to the C-17 program, and the remainder ($1,857 million) to 85 other programs. Seventeen percent ($1,989 million) of the budget is allocated to intelligence and communications; further breakdown of that element shows that 92 percent ($1,821 million) is designated "special activities."

The breakdown by research category in table 6 shows 62.5 percent ($7,308 million) of the budget allocated to the R&D category and 37.5 percent ($4,388 million) to operational systems development. Within the R&D subcategory, 39 percent ($757 million) of the advanced development budget is allocated to the ATF. Likewise, within the engineering development subcategory, 43 percent ($1,735 million) is allocated to the B-2 bomber program, 14 percent ($565 million) to the ICBM modernization program, 13 percent ($536

TABLE 6
AIR FORCE RDT&E BUDGET ($11.7 BILLION)
FISCAL YEAR 1991

By Budget Activity	$ Million	Percent
Technology Base	782	6.7
Advanced Technology	691	5.9
Strategic Programs	3,505	30.0
Tactical Programs	3,351	28.6
Intelligence and Communications	1,989	17.0
Defensewide Mission Support	1,378	11.8

By Research Category	$ Million	Percent
R&D	7,308	62.5
Research	203	1.7
Exploratory Development	579	4.9
Advanced Development	1,949	16.7
Engineering Development	4,015	34.4
Management and Support	562	4.8
Operational Systems	4,388	37.5

Source: *RDT&E Programs (R-1), Department of Defense Budget for Fiscal Years 1992 and 1993* (Washington, D.C.: Government Printing Office, 4 February 1991), F-1. (Unclassified)

million) to the C-17 program, and 5 percent ($201 million) to the ATF program.

The above discussion highlights the fact that the Air Force RDT&E budget for fiscal year 1991 continues to be driven by three major aircraft development programs (B-2, ATF, and C-17) and the ICBM modernization program, which consume 52 percent ($3,794 million) of the R&D budget and 32 percent of the total RDT&E budget, compared to 37.5 percent for operational systems development. The Air Force must select a strategy that gives higher priority to upgrading existing weapon systems and related operations, training, and maintenance activities rather than continuing to allocate increasingly scarce R&D funds to the simultaneous development of several new major weapon systems. Perhaps 20 percent of the

RDT&E budget should be allocated to the development of new major weapon systems and 50 percent to upgrading existing systems.

Such a shift to an evolutionary strategy will require major changes in roles and missions of development, as well as in operational organizational structures, in order to map and take new courses of action. Current DOD acquisition policy—as set forth in DOD Directive 5000.1, *Major and Non-Major Defense Acquisition Programs*, and DOD Directive 5000.2, *Defense Acquisition Program Procedures*—does not recognize such a strategy and should be changed.

Furthermore, "fast track" action plans should be established for certain high-priority upgrades to include (1) prototype development, (2) operational suitability testing and evaluation, and (3) achievement of initial operational capability, in a streamlined acquisition approach that allocates funds up front and avoids unnecessary starts, stops, and stretch-outs that have become so common.

No simple set of new priorities readily offers itself to Air Force strategic planners. However, within the context of General McPeak's congressional briefing, mentioned above, the following thoughts may be useful:

1. Sustain deterrence (nuclear forces). Maintain the nuclear triad. Whether or not the B-2 is necessary, it should be justified—as is any other weapon system program—within the planning framework (i.e., one should provide an essential military response option to cope with certain threats in accordance with national security policy directives if existing systems do not provide such an option). Fix the B-1. Upgrade the B-52 (reengine it if necessary). Maintain competent cruise missile payloads. Continue ICBM modernization, including development of mobile launchers, until sufficient confidence in US-USSR relations exists. Reexamine theater and regional nuclear deterrence strategies (nonnuclear response options might suffice).

2. Provide a versatile combat force (theater operations and power projection). Certainly the Desert Shield and Desert Storm operations will provide valuable insights into military operations, as well as weapon system capabilities and limitations. Had the B-2 been

operational, it might have made a difference in the Desert Storm air campaign since it is more productive than the B-52. However, the B-2 may not be needed to cope with low- and midintensity conventional conflicts. Perhaps the F-117 will provide enough stealth. Furthermore, the B-52s appear to have been quite effective. The A-10 Warthogs should be retained for the close-air-support mission, but the avionics and payloads of the A-10, F-15, and F-16 should be upgraded to leverage electrotechnologies in multiple roles/missions. This strategy has the potential of not only increasing the effectiveness and productivity of the existing platforms, but also enhancing related changes and payoff in operations, training, and maintenance support systems and activities.

Although Saddam Hussein's military strategy is unclear, the Iraqi air force certainly did not tax the allied air forces. If Iraq had adopted a more aggressive defense strategy, the time and cost to gain air superiority might have been different. But the outcome probably would have been the same, and allied losses would have been moderate. Again, for this reason, existing F-15 and F-16 platforms should be upgraded and extended to multiple roles/missions.

The ATF may be needed someday—perhaps after the year 2010. More than likely, however, it will not be needed for low- and midintensity conflicts before then, and it is doubtful that the ATF provides much deterrence value related to high-intensity conflicts, which are less probable.

3. Supply rapid global mobility (airlifters and tankers). Desert Shield/Desert Storm clearly validated the role/mission and the utility of airlifters and "filling stations in the sky." The C-17 would have made the job easier and would have accomplished it faster, but the job was done without it. The C-17 may be needed as a replacement for the C-141, but the timing should be driven by required military response options and concepts of operations. Although recent comparisons of the potential utility of the C-17 as regards Desert Shield/Desert Storm are compelling, no one else has made much of a case for less intense conflicts. Furthermore, if the strategy of upgrading avionics and payloads for existing platforms significantly

improves force effectiveness and productivity, lift requirements should decrease.

4. Control the high ground (space and C^3I systems). Surveillance—especially target-location information—is absolutely essential to national security needs and military operations. Finding relocatable targets underscores that need. The capabilities and limitations of existing space and airborne assets are probably well understood. For example, the joint surveillance target attack radar system (JSTARS) appears to be a winner. New systems as well as upgrades to existing systems may be necessary.

5. Build US influence (strengthen security partners and relationships). The coalition of allied forces that shaped and brought about the outcome of the Gulf war was underwritten by the US Air Force.

We should have every confidence that our Air Force can and will remain a comprehensive air force and the best air force in the world—not just a good air force—even though R&D funds will be scarce. However, military and industry planners need to develop strategies that they can adapt to the new world order, as well as some alternative futures.

Notes

1. Gen Merrill A. McPeak, Air Force chief of staff, address to the Air Force Acquisition Conference, Washington, D.C., 15 January 1991.
2. Richard McCormack, "Defense Science Board Develops an R&D Strategy for the 1990s," *Defense Week* 12, no. 10 (25 February 1991): 2.
3. House, *Global Reach—Global Power: Sustaining the Vision: Hearings before the House Armed Services Committee*, 102d Cong., 1st sess., 26 February 1991.

Advanced Technology Challenges in the Defense Industry

Dr John Blair

The changing structure of the global economy and the increasingly rapid global diffusion of technology present unprecedented challenges to American industry.[1] The growing technological and manufacturing sophistication of Japan and the newly industrializing countries on the Pacific Rim is shifting the previously undisputed position of industrial leadership away from Western countries. The changing distribution of global economic power is resulting in a geographically diverse investment in technology, from basic research to the development of new products. In addition to these forces, events affecting the US defense industrial base are causing increasing concern. Forces that affect the general industrial posture will also change the research and development (R&D) climate, much as they have significantly changed it already during the past decade.[2]

Technological development will continue to occur aggressively outside the United States. As a result, successful corporations will have to view intellectual property and technology as strategic resources. R&D organizations will be required to manage their activities against quantifiable goals and objectives and shift away from the laissez-faire outlook characteristic of the not-too-distant past. Pressures for short-term results will continue to exist and are likely to increase. Furthermore, staffing of the R&D effort is going to be more difficult. There will be fewer vigorously trained scientists and engineers to perform the innovative tasks required to move technology forward. This projected shortfall is due to demographic shifts in the high school population and to the decreasing interest in mathematics and sciences among young people.

Pressures for the expansion of technology will continue to increase in spite of the fact that technology will have to overcome certain negative perceptions. These perceptions will continue to be due in part to media treatment of perceived adverse effects of technology on the environment, our health, and social structure. Technology must overcome this image if it is to maintain a vigorous, healthy stance. Moreover, federal budget deficits that should—hopefully—be gradually reversed will continue to limit the growth of federal R&D spending in any major way. Issues of quality, environment, health, and safety will provide new impetus for R&D activities and will place new demands on resources, not only in terms of R&D investment but also in terms of capital outlays. Because of all these pressures, increasing emphasis on the management of technology will continue. A new breed of technology managers will emerge who not only will produce scientific discoveries but also will apply and transfer technology rapidly into implementation. Pressure on protecting intellectual property within our own country against the incursion of foreign interests will also continue.

The defense industry will experience considerable pressure during the next decade. Secretary of Defense Dick Cheney has stressed a decline during the five-year outlook, anticipating a 25 percent reduction in the force structure by 1996.[3] This translates into the reduction of the active duty roster by 521,000 personnel from the present strength level of 2.1 million. Such a reduction is approximately equal to the number of US troops deployed during Operation Desert Storm. By 1996 only 18 percent of the federal budget will be spent on defense, in contrast to 57 percent during the Korean War and 43 percent during the height of the Vietnam War. By the end of this period, 3.6 percent of the gross national product (GNP) will be allocated to defense outlays, in contrast to much higher figures approved during the height of the Reagan buildup, the Vietnam War, and the Korean War—namely, 6, 9, and 12 percent, respectively.

In view of these pressures and their attendant challenges, it is instructive to examine R&D spending trends during a three-decade period beginning with 1960 (fig. 1). During the early years, federal spending dominated the national R&D scene, and the Department of Defense (DOD) was the single major force of technological

ADVANCED TECHNOLOGY CHALLENGES

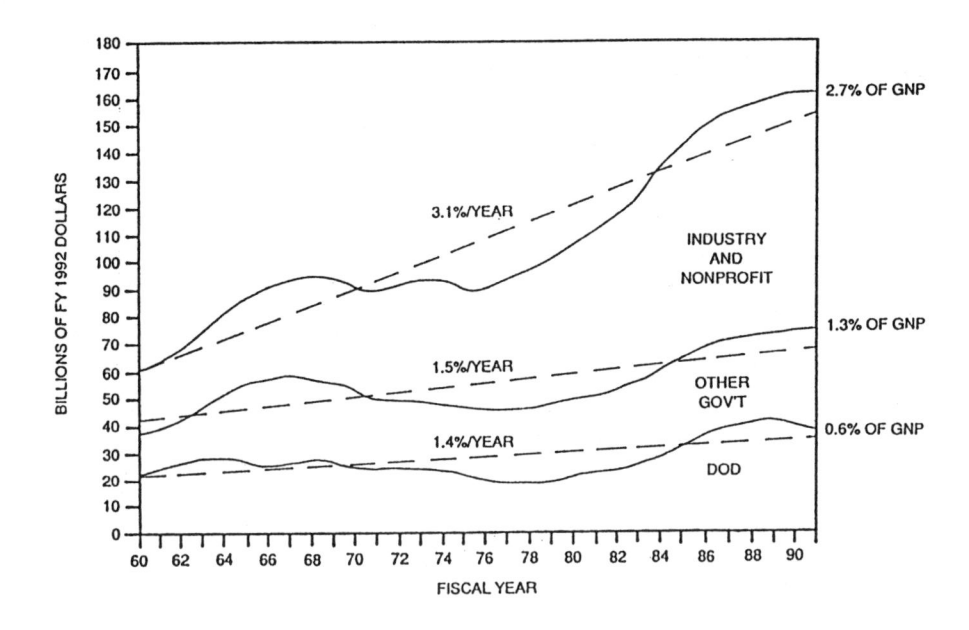

Figure 1. US R&D Trends (from Electronic Industries Association viewgraph, March 1991)

investment. During the 30-year period, government spending grew at a rate of about 1.5 percent a year, whereas the overall R&D outlay increased at more than twice that rate (3.1 percent per year). By 1990, therefore, DOD and government outlays were surpassed by those from the private sector. In addition, one should note that federal spending—particularly within DOD—leveled off and began to decline during the past few years. During this period of declining federal R&D investment, a broadly based realization of the importance of strengthening the scientific and technology base began to emerge. The sections that follow demonstrate that this realization is indeed resulting in aggressive action taken by President George Bush to ensure a competitive level of federal R&D investment. As of this writing, the president's 1992 budget calls for an 18 percent increase in federal R&D outlays. The following section examines the nature of this increase with regard to DOD.

Research and Development Trends in DOD

As stated above, DOD budgets plan for a 3 percent decline per year in real dollars during the next five-year period. Figure 2 shows the apportionment of the DOD budget by appropriations accounts as estimated for 1991 and as requested by the president for 1992 and 1993. Then-year dollars increase by 2 percent from $273 billion in 1991 to $278.3 billion in 1992. In view of a projected inflation rate of 5 percent, this change translates to a 3 percent decline in buying power. Examination of the elements of appropriations accounts in figure 2 shows an increase in research, development, test and evaluation's (RDT&E) share of the overall DOD budget. Figure 3 shows the distribution of RDT&E dollars among the various DOD constituents. The increase from $34.6 billion for FY 1991 to $39.9 billion for FY 1992 represents a 15 percent increase in RDT&E

FY 1991 ESTIMATE

- OTHER (3.4%)
- PROCUREMENT (23.5%)
- OPERATIONS AND MAINTENANCE (31.5%)
- RDT&E (11.6%)
- MILITARY AND CIVILIAN PAY (28.9%)
- SDI (1.1%)

$273 BILLION
(THEN-YEAR DOLLARS)

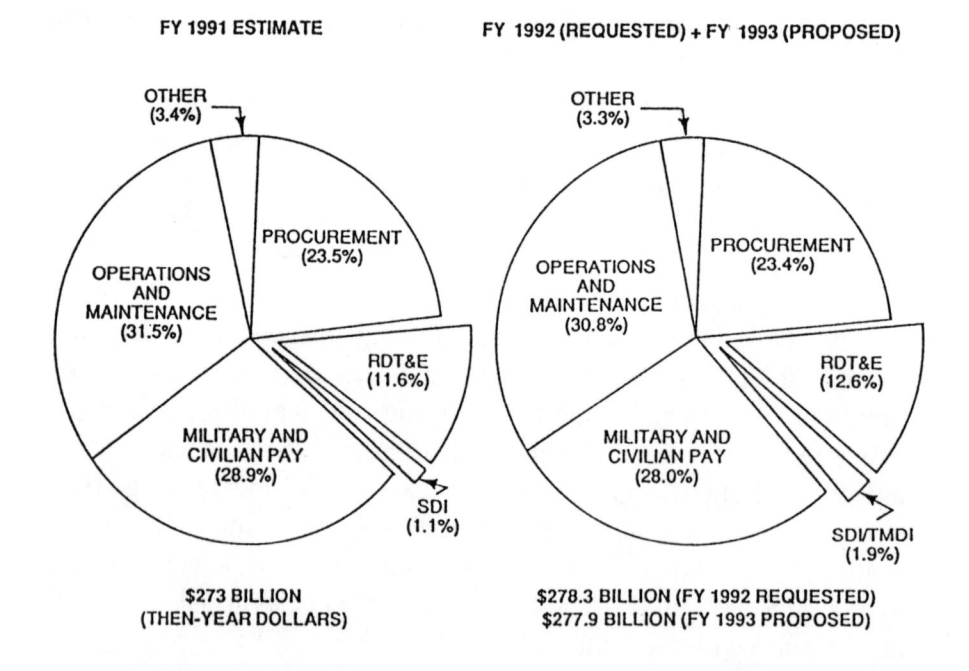

FY 1992 (REQUESTED) + FY 1993 (PROPOSED)

- OTHER (3.3%)
- PROCUREMENT (23.4%)
- OPERATIONS AND MAINTENANCE (30.8%)
- RDT&E (12.6%)
- MILITARY AND CIVILIAN PAY (28.0%)
- SDI/TMDI (1.9%)

$278.3 BILLION (FY 1992 REQUESTED)
$277.9 BILLION (FY 1993 PROPOSED)

Figure 2. DOD by Appropriations Account (from Electronic Industries Asssociation viewgraph, March 1991)

ADVANCED TECHNOLOGY CHALLENGES

FY 1991 ESTIMATE

- ARMY (15.5%)
- AGENCIES (18.2%)
- STRATEGIC DEFENSE INITIATIVE ORGANIZATION (SDIO) (8.3%)
- NAVY (24.1%)
- AIR FORCE (33.9%)

$34.6 BILLION (THEN-YEAR DOLLARS)

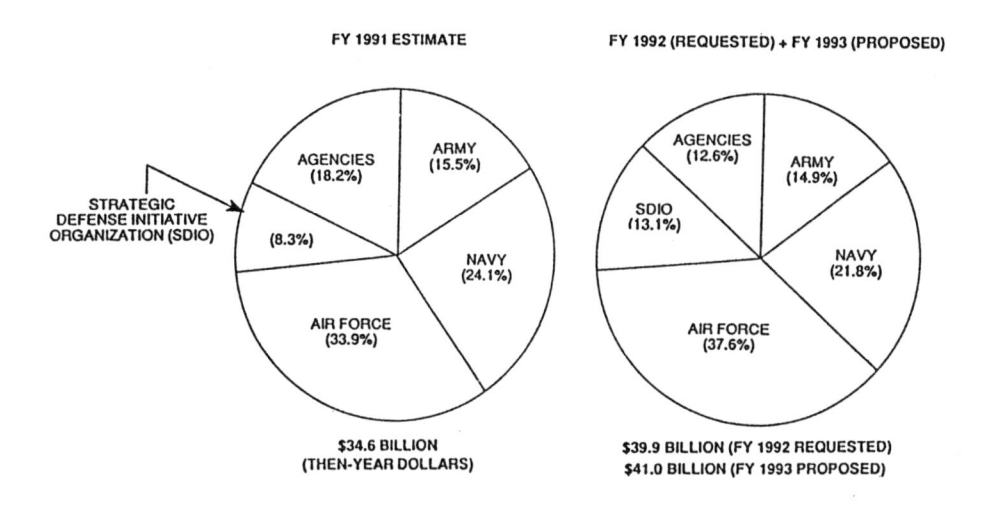

FY 1992 (REQUESTED) + FY 1993 (PROPOSED)

- AGENCIES (12.6%)
- ARMY (14.9%)
- SDIO (13.1%)
- NAVY (21.8%)
- AIR FORCE (37.6%)

$39.9 BILLION (FY 1992 REQUESTED)
$41.0 BILLION (FY 1993 PROPOSED)

Figure 3. RDT&E by Service (from Electronic Industries Association viewgraph, March 1991)

funding. Funding for the Strategic Defense Initiative (SDI) as well as the Tactical Missile Defense Initiative (TMDI—added as a result of our experience in Desert Storm) shows growth. Very significantly, the Air Force's portion of the RDT&E request shows aggressive expansion. Table 1 summarizes the funding changes by DOD element.

TABLE 1

Requested DOD Budget Changes, 1991/1992

Segment	% Change
DOD Overall	2
DOD Procurement	1.5
Independent Research and Development	4
RDT&E Overall	15
Navy	4
Army	11
Air Force	28
Strategic Defense Initiative Organization	83

The 28 percent increase for Air Force RDT&E supports an investment strategy which includes the following priorities:

- Maximize readiness
- Maintain technological superiority
- Modernize existing forces
- Develop new systems

Note that technological superiority is second in importance only to readiness. In support of this strategy, the presidential budget request reverses the declining RDT&E trend shown in figure 4 and places the Air Force in a leadership position as the technology driver among the three services. (The Defense Advanced Research Projects Agency, not shown in these illustrations, also enjoys vigorous support.)

During the congressional markup process yet to come, the budgetary figures are likely to be modified. However, support for science and technology faces a favorable climate in both houses of Congress. Thus, it appears that in budget year 1992, science and technology will receive support both from the legislative and executive branches of government.

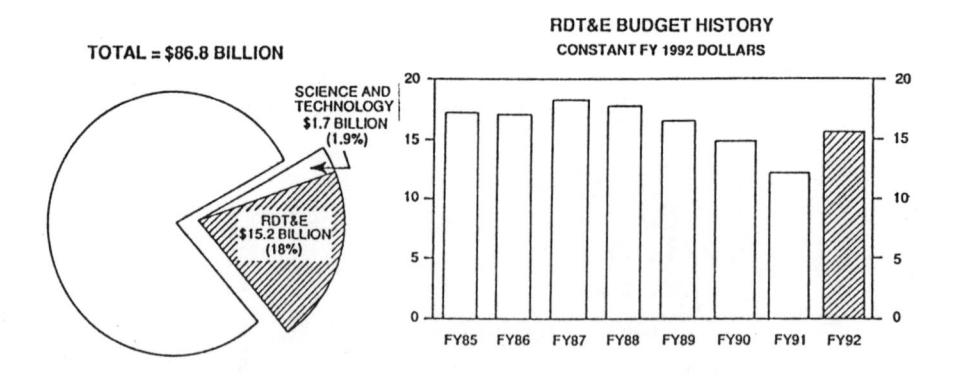

Figure 4. USAF RDT&E Request for FY 1992 (from Electronic Industries Association viewgraph, March 1991)

Critical Technologies Activities

Because of a perceived encroachment on this country's technological superiority, an examination of critical technologies that are needed to reverse this trend has proceeded on a broad front. Indeed, the first such study—the Air Force's Project Forecast—has now been conducted the second time. This broadly based technology plan clearly enunciates the technology needs of each Air Force mission area. In keeping with the spirit of this study and as a result of a congressional request, DOD identified 22 technologies critical to maintaining a viable national defense program (table 2). Following suit, the Army, Navy, and the Air Force separately identified technologies from the DOD listing that they deemed critical to the fulfillment of their respective missions. Further, they often augmented the DOD list with their own vision of specialized technology needs.

In the defense industrial base, the Aerospace Industries Association (AIA) defined its own critical technology needs as the culmination of a broadly based industry-wide planning exercise. To focus attention on these needs and to help further implementation, AIA established the National Center for Advanced Technologies with support derived from the association.

During this period, there were a number of parallel studies in this broadly based activity. In addition to those already mentioned, the White House Office of Science and Technology Policy (OSTP) conducted its own technology planning from a national perspective and published a list of critical technologies. The list of emerging technologies from the Department of Commerce is another important addition. Finally, a list of sensitive technologies has been used for a long time for the purpose of export control (see table 3 for a summary of all such lists).

TABLE 2
DOD Critical Technologies

Critical Technology	Objective	Raytheon
1. Microelectronics Circuits and Their Fabrication	The Production of Ultra-Small Integrated Electronic Devices for High-Speed Computers, Sensitive Receivers, Automatic Control, Etc.	√
2. Preparation of Gallium Arsenide (GaAs) and Other Compound Semiconductors	The Preparation of High Purity GaAs and Other Compound Semiconductor Substrates and Thin Films for Microelectronic Substrates	√
3. Software Producibility	The Generation of Affordable and Reliable Software in Timely Fashion	√
4. Parallel Computer Architectures	Ultra-High-Speed Computing by Simultaneous Use of All Processing Capabilities in the Next Generation of Computers	√
5. Machine Intelligence/Robotics	Incorporation of Human "Intelligence" and Actions into Mechanical Devices	√
6. Simulation and Modeling	Testing of Concepts and Designs without Building Physical Replicas	√
7. Integrated Optics	Optical Memories and Optical Signal and Data Processing	√
8. Fiber Optics	Ultra-Low-Loss Fibers and Optical Components such as Switches, Couplers, and Multiplexers for Communications, Navigation, Etc.	√
9. Sensitive Radars	Radar Sensors Capable of Detecting Low-Observable Targets and/or Capable of Noncooperative Target Classification, Recognition, and/or Identification	√
10. Passive Sensors	Sensors Not Needing to Emit Signals (Hence Passive) to Detect Targets, Monitor the Environment, or Determine the Status or Condition of Equipment	√
11. Automatic Target Recognition	Combination of Computer Architecture, Algorithms, and Signal Processing for Near Real-Time Automation of Detection, Classification, and Tracking of Targets	√
12. Phased Arrays	Formation of Spatial Beams by Controlling the Phase and Amplitude of Radio Frequency Signals at Individual Sensor Elements Distributed along an Array (Radar, Underwater Acoustic, or Other)	√
13. Data Fusion	The Machine Integration and/or Interpretation of Data and Its Presentation in Convenient Form to the Human Operator	√

ADVANCED TECHNOLOGY CHALLENGES

TABLE 2—continued

Critical Technology	Objective	Raytheon
14. Signature Control	The Ability to Control the Target Signature (Radar, Optical, Acoustic, or Other) and Thereby Enhance the Survivability of Vehicles and Weapon Systems	√
15. Computational Fluid Dynamics	The Modeling of Complex Fluid Flow to Make Dependable Predictions by Computing, Thus Saving Time and Money Previously Required for Expensive Facilities and Experiments	√
16. Air-Breathing Propulsion	Lightweight, Fuel-Efficient Engines Using Atmospheric Oxygen to Support Combustion	
17. High-Power Microwaves	Microwave Radiation at High-Power Levels for Weapon Applications to Temporarily or Permanently Disable Sensors or to Do Structural Damage	
18. Pulsed Power	The Generation of Power in the Field with Relatively Lightweight, Low-Volume Devices	
19. Hypervelocity Projectiles	The Generation and Use of Hypervelocity Projectiles to (1) Penetrate Hardened Targets and (2) Increase the Weapon's Effective Range	
20. High-Temperature/High-Strength/ Lightweight Composite Materials	Materials Possessing High Strength, Low Weight, and/or Able to Withstand High Temperatures for Aerospace and Other Applications	√
21. Superconductivity	The Fabrication and Exploitation of Superconducting Materials	√
22. Biotechnology Materials and Processing	The Systematic Application of Biology for an End Use in Military Engineering or Medicine	√

Source: US Department of Defense, *Critical Technologies Plan* (Washington, D.C., 15 March 1990, 1 May 1991)

TABLE 3

Critical Technologies Activities

- Project Forecast
- DOD Critical Technologies
- Air Force/Army/Navy Key Technologies
- Aerospace Industries Association Key Technologies (National Center for Advanced Technologies)
- White House Office of Science and Technology Policy Critical Technologies
- Department of Commerce Emerging Technologies
- Sensitive Technologies for Export Control

Now that the critical technologies studies of three federal agencies have been made public, one can correlate OSTP's list of national critical technologies with the Department of Commerce's list of emerging technologies and DOD's list of critical technologies (table 4). Very significantly, strong overlap and important correlation exist among the areas of the separate studies.

TABLE 4

Comparison of National Critical technologies with Department of Commerce Emerging Technologies and DOD Critical Technologies

National Critical Technologies	Commerce Emerging Technologies[a]	Defense Critical Technologies[b]
MATERIALS • Materials synthesis and processing • Electronic and photonic materials • Ceramics • Composites • High-performance metals and alloys	• Advanced materials • Advanced semiconductor devices • Superconductors • Advanced materials	• Composite materials • Semiconductor materials and microelectronic circuits • Superconductors • Composite materials
MANUFACTURING • Flexible computer-integrated manufacturing • Intelligent processing equipment • Micro- and nanofabrication • Systems management technologies	• Flexible computer-integrated manufacturing • Artificial intelligence	• Machine intelligence and robotics
INFORMATION AND COMMUNICATIONS • Software • Microelectronics and optoelectronics • High-performance computing and networking • High-definition imaging and displays • Sensors and signal processing	• High-performance computing • Advanced semiconductor devices • Optoelectronics • High-performance computing • Digital imaging • Sensor technology	• Software producibility • Semiconductor materials and microelectronic circuits • Photonics • Parallel computer architectures • Data fusion • Data fusion • Signal processing

[a] US Department of Commerce, *Emerging Technologies: A Survey of Technical and Economic Opportunities* (Washington, D.C., Spring 1990).
[b] US Department of Defense, *Critical Technologies Plan* (Washington, D.C., 15 March 1990, 1 May 1991).

TABLE 4—continued

INFORMATION AND COMMUNICATIONS (cont.) • Data storage and peripherals • Computer simulation and modeling	• High-density data storage • High-performance computing	• Passive sensors • Sensitive radars • Machine intelligence and robotics • Photonics • Simulation and modeling • Computational fluid dynamics
BIOTECHNOLOGY AND LIFE SCIENCES • Applied molecular biology • Medical technology	• Biotechnology • Medical devices and diagnostics	• Biotechnology materials and processes
AERONAUTICS AND SURFACE TRANSPORTATION • Aeronautics • Surface transportation technologies		• Air-breathing propulsion
ENERGY AND ENVIRONMENT • Energy technologies • Pollution minimization, remediation, and waste management		
		• No national critical technologies counterpart: high-energy density materials, hypervelocity projectiles, pulsed power, signature control, weapons system environment

Source: *Federal Contracts Report*, vol. 55 (Washington, D.C.: Bureau of National Affairs, Inc., 29 April 1991), 604.

A formidable challenge lies in supporting the findings of these various planning activities and focusing funding and management resources on the development and application of broadly critical technologies. In an era of limited resources, moving forward efficiently can occur only if one attempts to break down existing barriers.

The mistrust and sometimes adversarial relationship between government and industry must be transformed into government/industry partnerships. Industry must reaffirm its belief in the importance of the educational system and help stimulate interest in science and mathematics education of the first quality in primary and secondary schools. As for higher education, industry/university partnerships must reinforce and focus our universities' research base and must strengthen the quality and quantity of scientific and technical graduates. Last, industries must form partnerships among themselves to move precompetitive technologies into the realm of applications.

Independent Research and Development

In every industrial operation, R&D activities and the resources available to support them are an important part of maintaining a position on the leading edge of competition. In the defense industrial base, this is known as independent research and development (IR&D). Although the application of these funds is largely within the discretionary power of a defense contractor, both DOD and Congress have imposed a number of controls and limitations on such application. These controls are in contrast to the application of R&D resources in the commercial sector, where competitive forces alone determine the extent and specificity of such funding. In its guidelines to industry on IR&D, DOD states that

[it] recognizes that contractor Independent Research and Development . . . programs are a necessary part of doing business in a high-technology environment. The DOD objectives in support of IR&D are:
- To encourage research and development of innovative concepts
- To develop technical competence in two or more contractors to increase competition and promote a strong technical base. . . .

- To recognize the necessity for contractors to independently select technical projects to develop their business
- To promote better communication between DOD and defense related industry

DOD recognizes that each contractor must retain the freedom to choose the IR&D efforts that will best enhance its competence and competitive position.[4]

Nevertheless, a number of limitations were imposed on the application of these funds. In particular, a congressionally established cap limited the extent to which contractors were allowed to apply IR&D funds for the furtherance of their technologically competitive position. Upper limits on each contractor's ability to apply IR&D funds were determined through advance-agreement negotiations. Thus, the congressional cap imposed on DOD was passed on to the industrial base by means of this negotiation mechanism. By 1991, however, congressional concern about the health of the defense industrial base loosened the controls over the expenditure of IR&D and removed the congressional cap on expenditures.

Specifically, section 824 (which addresses IR&D) of the Defense Authorization Act for fiscal year 1991 requires advance agreements to include the maximum IR&D/bid and proposal (B&P) costs that DOD will pay in the current fiscal year. However, it broadens provisions that allowable costs must be for work of potential interest to DOD or for R&D activities that (1) strengthen the US defense industrial and technology base, (2) enhance US industrial competitiveness, (3) promote development of DOD critical technologies, (4) develop dual-use technologies for private and public sectors, and (5) develop technologies benefiting the environment. Section 824 also directs DOD to prescribe regulations governing IR&D/B&P costs and repeals section 203 of Public Law 91-441, thus removing the cap on IR&D expenditures.[5]

Congressional Update

At the time of this writing, the House defense authorization bill—which contains provisions prepared by the Committee on

Armed Services that deal with RDT&E and the science and technology base—has been voted in. The bill also moves IR&D more in the direction of the commercial practices of the competitive world.[6] The committee report recognizes the increasing pressures exerted by worldwide participation in technology development and by aggressive Pacific Rim countries, particularly Japan. The report further recognizes pressures brought about by the scaling down of the defense budget as enunciated earlier by Secretary Cheney. The committee moved to protect the US technology base and reinforce its earlier recommendations to authorize a real growth rate of 2 percent per year over a five-year period. This action was designed to set in motion a growth plan which will strengthen our technology infrastructure, meet the international challenges to our leadership, and help ensure our national security.

As a result of this posture, the committee strengthened the RDT&E budget and recommended growth in basic research, applied research, and advanced development. Further, it strengthened the Defense Advanced Research Projects Agency, recommended programs in the arena of precompetitive technologies, and proposed the strengthening of IR&D by simplifying its structure and eliminating cumbersome DOD oversight.

The most sweeping change came with the committee's view on IR&D. The committee report recognized that when a company does research for the commercial purpose of improving its products or improving technology to attract customers, the cost of such research is recovered in the price of the company's products. With this statement, the committee moved IR&D in the direction of commercial practice by removing arbitrary ceilings and dispensing with unnecessary DOD reviews. Furthermore, the report recommended the allowance of full IR&D costs as recoverable items in the price of products and services sold by the contractors to all its customers, including DOD. In providing for full recovery of all reasonable IR&D costs, the committee directed that regulations to implement these new statutory provisions be issued by DOD no later than 1 February 1992.

ADVANCED TECHNOLOGY CHALLENGES

These provisions were voted in as part of the House National Defense Authorization Act for FY 1992 and FY 1993.

The Senate's position on these provisions, particularly those concerning IR&D, is still unclear. Through its general counsel, the Office of the Secretary of Defense expressed concern to the Senate Armed Services Committee that liberalization of IR&D to the extent approved by the House of Representatives would unduly increase the costs to DOD. Reportedly for the purpose of allowing time for more study, the Senate report contains no language pertaining to IR&D, and—in all likelihood—the Senate version of the authorization act is going to be mute on the subject. The final outcome, therefore, will depend on a resolution to be reached in conference. Starting October 1992, companies will get 105 percent of the 1992 budget as a ceiling for IR&D plus an inflation factor each year, arrived in conference as the congressional compromise (as of October 1991).

Desert Storm Experience

The Desert Storm conflict was a severe and significant test of the high-technology capabilities built into our weapons systems. It is important to note that the technology choices embodied in these weapons were made at least two decades ago. Thus, the technology base supporting full-scale engineering development, manufacturing, and operational deployment provided a snapshot of our technological capabilities over a relatively narrow window of past time. We have made great progress since these early decisions. Granted, the performance of currently deployed systems was exceedingly impressive, but future systems originating from the current technology base will be even more precise and effective. Moreover, they will require less manpower and be less costly to deploy. (See table 5 for a selection of the systems recently deployed in the Persian Gulf conflict, together with their underlying technologies.)

The lesson learned from this experience should be that public attitudes as well as congressional and administration actions—while singularly important in determining rate and direction of

343

TABLE 5
Examples of Technology Choices (Operation Desert Storm)

Weapons System	Technology
Abrams Tank	Long Wavelength Infrared (LWIR) Night Sight Laser Range Finder Armor/Antiarmor Propulsion
Maverick	LWIR Imaging Infrared Domes
Patriot	Phased Array Radar Warhead Fuze Signal/Data Processing Guidance Algorithms
ALQ-184	Multibeam Antenna Digital Radio Frequency Memory Improved Traveling Wave Tubes
F-16 and Payload	Aerodynamics Propulsion Materials Radar LWIR Imaging Ordnance
Airborne Warning and Control System (AWACS)	Antennas Radar Displays Signal/Data Processing Communications

progress—can be implemented only with the participation of properly trained and dedicated individuals. Thoughtful people made the choices in technology and weapons systems; in spite of turbulence and criticism, their choices have been vindicated.

With this in mind, a statement made by Gen Colin Powell, chairman of the Joint Chiefs of Staff, seems appropriate in conclusion:

[Whatever] victory takes, you come out with people. You come out with people in the GI's family. . . . You come out with people who designed and made Patriot missiles and M-1 tanks and F-16 aircraft and Aegis cruisers and Apache helicopters and light armored vehicles for our marines, and all the thousands of other pieces of equipment that gave our troops the decisive edge. . . . But ultimately, success in war belongs to those on the line, who win in a cockpit or tank or foxhole. [It belongs to all those who] put their lives on the line to win.[7]

Notes

1. See National Academy of Sciences, *Finding Common Ground: US Export Controls in a Changed Global Environment* (Washington, D.C.: National Academy Press, 1991).

2. F. Peter Boer, "R&D Planning Environment for the 90's—America and Japan," *Research-Technology Management* 34, no. 2 (March–April 1991): 12–15.

3. Secretary of Defense Dick Cheney, "America's New Defense Policy," address, George Washington University, March 1991.

4. *DoD Guidelines for Contractor Presentation of IR&D Information* (Washington, D.C.: Department of Defense, August 1990), 1.

5. House, *National Defense Authorization Act for Fiscal Year 1991, Conference Report to Accompany H.R. 4739*, 101st Cong., 2d sess., 23 October 1990, 123–25.

6. See House, *National Defense Authorization Act for Fiscal Years 1992 and 1993, Report of the Committee on Armed Services, House of Representatives, on H.R. 2100*, 102d Cong., 1st sess., 13 May 1991, Report 102-60.

7. Gen Colin Powell, chairman of the Joint Chiefs of Staff, speech to the Veterans of Foreign Wars, Washington, D.C., 4 March 1991.

CONTRIBUTORS

Maj Gen Robert M. Alexander is director of plans, Deputy Chief of Staff for Plans and Operations, Headquarters USAF, Washington, D.C. General Alexander served in Vietnam in the late 1960s with the 21st Tactical Air Support Squadron, Nha Trang Air Base, as an O-1 forward air controller. From 1982 to 1985 he was vice-commander and then commander of the 379th Bombardment Wing, Wurtsmith AFB, Michigan. In March 1985 he returned to Headquarters USAF as assistant for general officer matters, Office of the Deputy Chief of Staff, Personnel. In July 1986 he was assigned to Strategic Air Command as commander of the 19th Air Division, Carswell AFB, Texas. He again returned to Headquarters USAF in June 1988 and served as assistant chief of staff for studies and analysis, and as commander, Air Force Center for Studies and Analysis. He received a BS degree from the US Air Force Academy and an MS degree in physics from Ohio State University. General Alexander is a graduate of Squadron Officer School, Air Command and Staff College, the National Security Management Course of the Industrial College of the Armed Forces, Air War College, National War College, the Joint Flag Officer Warfighting Course, and the Harvard University Program for Senior Executives in National and International Security.

Dr John Blair is director of corporate research for the Raytheon Company. He is responsible for the advanced technology activities performed throughout the company's various divisions, including the central research laboratories. Before joining Raytheon, Dr Blair was a member of the electrical engineering faculty at the Massachusetts Institute of Technology, where he did research and taught applied physics. He has served on a number of government committees, including the President's Interagency Panel on Energy Research and Development and National Progress, the National Sea Grant Review Panel, and the National Oceanic and Atmospheric Administration of the Department of Commerce. Dr Blair currently serves on a number of university advisory boards, as well as the Industrial Executive Board, Executive Committee, Navy League of the United States. He formerly served on the Army Science Board.

Lt Gen John B. Conaway is USAF chief, National Guard Bureau, Washington, D.C. After completing basic pilot training in 1957, General Conaway attended advanced combat-crew training, graduating in 1958. In 1960 he joined the West Virginia Air National Guard (ANG) as an SA-16 pilot, flying a special forces operations mission. In 1963 he was transferred to the Kentucky ANG's 123d Tactical Reconnaissance Wing as an RB-57 pilot and in 1963 became an air technician flight-training instructor in operations, flying RF-101s. In 1968 General Conaway was called to active duty with the Kentucky ANG and served in Alaska, Panama, Japan, and Korea. He returned to the Kentucky ANG in 1969 as operations officer. In 1972 General Conaway was appointed air commander of the Kentucky ANG and in 1974 was appointed vice-commander of the 123d Tactical Reconnaissance Wing. He was recalled to active duty in 1977 and became director of the ANG in 1981. General Conaway was appointed to his present position in 1990.

Dr Jacquelyn K. Davis is executive vice president of the Institute for Foreign Policy Analysis (IFPA), Inc., Cambridge, Massachusetts, and Washington, D.C., and president of National Security Planning Associates, Inc., a subsidiary of IFPA. Dr Davis specializes in arms control, the Atlantic Alliance and NATO, the US-Soviet strategic balance, and French policy. From 1984 to 1988 she served as a member of the Defense Advisory Committee on Women in the Services (DACOWITS), where she was national chairperson (1986–88). She has written numerous articles and books, including her most recent collaborative effort, *U.S. Defense Policy in an Era of Constrained*

Resources (1990), in association with the Fletcher School of Law and Diplomacy. She also is the acting coeditor of *National Security Decisions: The Participants Speak* (1990). Over the last two years, Dr Davis has been a project coordinator of a study on strategic nuclear forces issues and arms control.

Brig Gen Lawrence P. Farrell, Jr., is deputy director of programs and evaluation, Office of the Deputy Chief of Staff, Programs and Resources, and chairman of the Program Review Committee, Headquarters USAF, Washington, D.C. General Farrell was commissioned upon graduation from the US Air Force Academy in June 1965. He completed pilot training at Reese AFB, Texas, in September 1966. He was then assigned to the 366th Tactical Fighter Wing, Da Nang Air Base, Republic of Vietnam, as a combat pilot. From 1970 to 1971 he flew F-4s with the 23d Tactical Fighter Squadron, 36th Tactical Fighter Wing, Spangdahlem Air Base, West Germany. In 1978 he was assigned to the Directorate of Plans, Headquarters USAF, as chief of the Strategy Division and later served as the chief of the Capability Assessment Division. During the 1980s, he served with Air Force Logistics Command at Hill AFB, Utah, as an F-4 and F-16 systems program manager. He later served in the 401st Tactical Fighter Wing, Torrejon Air Base, Spain, as vice-commander. In September 1988 General Farrell became the deputy chief of staff for plans and programs, Headquarters United States Air Forces in Europe, Ramstein Air Base, West Germany. He assumed his present duties in June 1990. General Farrell is a graduate of Air Command and Staff College and National War College.

Ross Gelbspan has held a number of positions in journalism since 1961. From 1969 to 1973, Mr Gelbspan wrote for the *Village Voice* in New York City. Along with his local investigative reporting, he wrote about environmental issues and spent one month interviewing Soviet dissidents and human-rights advocates in the USSR. His four-part series on members of the Soviet underground was reprinted in the

Congressional Record. In 1974 he edited a book for Scripps-Howard on the congressional Watergate hearings and also taught on an adjunct basis at Columbia University's School of Journalism. In 1979 Mr Gelbspan joined the staff of the *Boston Globe* as special-projects editor, conceiving and editing a series of articles on racial discrimination in employment that won a Pulitzer prize in 1983. In 1985 Mr Gelbspan returned to reporting, specializing in subjects related to civil liberties and national security. He is currently working for the *Boston Globe* on various local reporting projects.

Lt Gen Glenn A. Kent has been a staff member at the Rand Corporation in Washington, D.C., since 1982. At Rand he is engaged in efforts related to national security—particularly in the areas of strategies and concepts. From 1950 to 1974 General Kent (US Air Force, Retired) served in a number of positions in the Air Force and the Department of Defense, including chief of development plans, Air Force Systems Command (1966–68); assistant chief of staff for studies and analyses, Headquarters USAF (1968–72); and director of the Weapons Systems Evaluation Group, Office of the Secretary of Defense (1972–74). From 1974 to 1982 General Kent managed his own consulting firm, providing management and marketing advice and analyses to various aerospace corporations.

Maj Gen Charles D. Link is commander of Third Air Force, RAF Mildenhall, United Kingdom. After receiving his commission in 1963 and his wings in 1967, General Link served as a forward air controller in Vietnam. In the early 1970s, he was assigned to the 23d Tactical Fighter Squadron at Spangdahlem Air Base, West Germany. In 1975 he served in the Office of the Deputy Chief of Staff for Plans and Operations, Headquarters USAF, as an international political-military affairs officer. From 1980 to 1983 General Link held a number of assignments in Korea. From 1986 to 1990 he served as director of Joint Staff and National Security Council matters, Office of the Deputy Chief of Staff for Plans and Operations, and then as deputy director for political-military affairs, J-5, Organization of the Joint Chiefs of Staff. General Link was commandant of the Air War College and vice-commander of Air University, Maxwell AFB, Alabama, from 1990 to 1991.

Dr Edward N. Luttwak holds the Arleigh Burke Chair in Strategy at the Center for Strategic and International Studies, Washington, D.C. Since 1973 Dr Luttwak has served as a consultant for strategic matters to the Office of the Secretary of Defense, the under secretary of defense for policy, the National Security Council, the White House chief of staff, and the Department of State. Since 1974 he has conducted military studies on a range of topics, including the political uses of sea power; the defense of Korea; the first rapid-deployment-force concept (the basis of US Central Command); the original operational-level-of-war concept, as well as the original light-infantry concept; and, most recently, nonnuclear strategic bombardment. He was the 1987 Nimitz lecturer at the University of California at Berkeley and the 1989 Tanner lecturer at Yale University. In addition to his teaching, Dr Luttwak serves on the editorial boards of the *European Journal of International Affairs*, *Washington Quarterly*, *Journal of Strategic Studies*, *Geopolitique*, *National Interest*, and *Orbis*. He is also the author of several books, including his forthcoming *Dictionary of Modern War* (with Stuart Koehl).

Harold K. McCard is president of Textron Defense Systems. He is responsible for all divisional activities in strategic systems, tactical systems, and surveillance systems, as well as AVCO Research Laboratory. Mr McCard was also recently assigned responsibility for the Bell Aerospace Textron Division. He joined Textron Defense Systems in 1959 as a junior engineer and subsequently progressed through various engineering and managerial assignments until he was named vice president and general manager in 1982 and then president in 1985. He received BS and MS degrees in electrical engineering management from the University of Maine and Northeastern University, respectively. Mr McCard earned an MS degree in management from the Massachusetts Institute of Technology as an AVCO-Sloan Fellow.

Lt Gen Thomas S. Moorman, Jr., is commander of Air Force Space Command, Peterson AFB, Colorado. General Moorman received his commission through the Air Force Reserve Officer Training Corps in 1962. From August 1965 to 1967 he was assigned as mission planner with the newly established SR-71 unit at Beale AFB, California. He then served as operations officer, Udorn Royal Thai AFB, Thailand. From 1975 to 1979 he was executive and then deputy director of plans and programs, Office of Space Systems, Office of the Secretary of the Air Force. In 1981 he was assigned to the North American Aerospace Defense Command, Cheyenne Mountain Complex, Colorado, as director of space operations. In March 1982 he became deputy director, space defense, Office of the Deputy Chief of Staff for Plans, Peterson AFB, where he was deeply involved in planning and organizing the establishment of Air Force Space Command. In March 1985 he became director of Space Systems, Office of the Secretary of the Air Force. In 1987 he became director of Space and Strategic Defense Initiative programs, Office of the Assistant Secretary of the Air Force for Acquisition. General Moorman assumed his present position in March 1990.

Dr Williamson Murray is professor of European military history at Ohio State University. Dr Murray has taught at various universities, including Yale, Air War College, US Military Academy, and Naval War College. He served in the active US Air Force from 1964 to 1969 and holds the rank of lieutenant colonel in the Air Force Reserve. He is the author of numerous books, among them *Strategy for Defeat: The Luftwaffe, 1933–1945* (1983); *The Change in the European Balance of Power, 1938–1939: The Path to Ruin* (1984); *Luftwaffe*

(1985); and *Military Effectiveness* (three volumes, 1988). Dr Murray received BA, MA, and PhD degrees from Yale University.

Lt Gen Michael A. Nelson is deputy chief of staff for plans and operations, Headquarters USAF, Washington, D.C. General Nelson entered the Air Force in 1959 and completed his pilot training in 1960. From 1967 to 1968 he was a member of the Tactical Air Warfare Center's anti-surface-to-air missile combat-assistance team at Takhli Royal Thai AFB, Thailand. While serving in this capacity, he also flew F-105s with the 333d Tactical Fighter Squadron of the 355th Tactical Fighter Wing, completing 100 combat missions over North Vietnam. From 1969 to 1971 General Nelson was operations and plans adviser to the Korean air force at Seoul. In 1976 he was assigned to Headquarters USAF in the Directorate of Plans, first as chief of the Europe-NATO Division, and then as Air Force planner in the Deputy Directorate for Joint and National Security Matters. He was commander of the 21st Tactical Fighter Wing at Elmendorf AFB, Alaska, from 1979 to 1981; commander of the 313th Air Division, Kadena Air Base, Japan, in 1983; and commander of the Thirteenth Air Force, Pacific Air Forces, Clark Air Base, Philippines, in 1984. In 1987 he became assistant chief of staff for operations, Supreme Headquarters Allied Powers Europe. He assumed his present position in February 1991.

Dr Robert L. Pfaltzgraff, Jr., is the Shelby Cullom Davis Professor of International Security Studies at the Fletcher School of Law and Diplomacy, Tufts University. Dr Pfaltzgraff is also president of the Institute for Foreign Policy Analysis, an internationally recognized research organization committed to enhancing the dialogue on national security issues within government and the private sector. He has taught at the University of Pennsylvania, the College of Europe in Belgium, the Foreign Service Institute in Washington, D.C., and the National Defense College in Japan. He has served as a consultant to the National Security Council, Department of Defense, Department of State, and US

Information Agency. The author of many articles and books, Dr Pfaltzgraff's most recent publications include *Guerrilla Warfare and Counterinsurgency* (1989); *Contending Theories of International Relations* (with James Dougherty, 1990); *U.S. Defense Policy in an Era of Constrained Resources* (coeditor and contributor, 1990); and *The United States Army: Challenges and Missions for the 1990s* (coeditor and contributor, 1991).

Dr Donald B. Rice is the secretary of the Air Force. Formerly president and chief executive officer of the Rand Corporation from 1972 to 1989, Secretary Rice has also served as a deputy assistant secretary of defense and as assistant director in the Office of Management and Budget. A graduate of the University of Notre Dame with a BS degree in chemical engineering, he also holds a master's degree in management and a doctorate in economics from Purdue University.

Dr Richard H. Shultz, Jr., is director of the International Security Studies Program and associate professor of international politics at Tufts University. Dr Shultz frequently lectures at US military academies and war colleges. He has been a research associate at the Consortium for the Study of Intelligence and a consultant to various US government agencies concerned with national security affairs. He has been a nonresident fellow of the Hoover Institution on War, Revolution, and Peace, and a recipient of an Earhart Foundation Research Fellowship and a United States Institute of Peace Research Fellowship. Dr Shultz is the author and coeditor of several books, including *U.S. Defense Policy in an Era of Constrained Resources* (coeditor and contributor, 1990) and *The United States Army: Challenges and Missions for the 1990s* (coeditor and contributor, 1991).

Hon Bud Shuster is a Republican member of the US House of Representatives from Pennsylvania. Congressman Shuster serves as the ranking member of both the House Select Committee on

Intelligence and the Surface Transportation Subcommittee, the second-ranking member of the Public Works and Transportation Committee, and the senior member of the aviation and investigations subcommittees. He has been the principal author of much of the House's transportation legislation during the past two decades. A former infantry officer and counterintelligence agent, Congressman Shuster served as the senior transportation adviser to George Bush during his 1988 campaign for the presidency and chaired the National Transportation Policy Commission. He has served on the Budget Committee and its Defense Task Force and on the Education and Labor Committee and its Subcommittee on Higher Education, and as chairman of the Republican Policy Committee and delegate to NATO's North Atlantic Assembly. Congressman Shuster is a Phi Beta Kappa graduate of the University of Pittsburgh. He holds a master of business administration degree from Duquesne University and a PhD in management and economics from American University.

Col John A. Warden III is currently deputy director for strategy, doctrine, and plans, Directorate of Plans, Deputy Chief of Staff for Plans and Operations, Headquarters USAF, Washington, D.C. After completing pilot training at Laredo AFB, Texas, and MacDill AFB, Florida, Colonel Warden reported to the 334th Tactical Fighter Squadron at Seymour Johnson AFB, North Carolina. He later served in Vietnam as a forward air controller and in 1969 flew missions over the Ho Chi Minh trail. He was later assigned to the Pentagon as an action officer in the Middle East/Africa Division of the Directorate of Plans, Headquarters USAF, and in 1979 became the assistant executive officer for the Air Force chief of staff. He was then transferred to Eglin AFB, Florida, where he flew F-15s and served as the director of wing inspections. In 1986 he reported to Bitburg Air Base, West Germany, as vice-commander of the 36th Tactical Fighter Wing. A graduate of the US Air Force Academy, Colonel Warden earned a master's degree in political science from Texas Tech University and graduated from the National War College.

Dr Edward L. Warner III is a senior defense analyst at the Rand office in Washington, D.C. A former US Air Force officer, Dr Warner conducts studies on Soviet defense and foreign policy, East-West arms control issues, and American national security policy. His 20 years of service in the Air Force included duty as an assistant air attaché in the US Embassy in Moscow and work as special assistant to Gen Lew Allen, Jr., former Air Force chief of staff. He is an adjunct professor at George Washington University and Columbia University, where he teaches graduate seminars on Soviet defense and arms control policy. Dr Warner's recent publications include *The Defense Policy of the Soviet Union* (1989) and *Next Moves: An Arms Control Agenda for the 1990s* (coauthor with David A. Ochmanek, 1989).

Gen Larry D. Welch is president and chief executive officer of the Institute for Defense Analysis in Washington, D.C. General Welch (US Air Force, Retired) enlisted in the National Guard and then the Air Force in 1951, entering officer and pilot training in 1954. He served in Vietnam and in many other operational and staff assignments overseas before commanding a tactical fighter wing from 1974 to 1976. From 1981 to 1982 he was commander of the forerunner of Air Force Central Command and of Ninth Air Force, and from 1982 to 1984 he held the position of deputy chief of staff for programs and resources, Headquarters USAF. From 1984 to 1985 he served as Air Force vice chief of staff and from 1985 to 1986 as commander of Strategic Air Command. General Welch was the Air Force chief of staff from 1986 to 1990.

Index

A-6: 75
A-7: 229
A-10: 12–13, 186, 223, 326
A-37: 155
Abrams tank: 295, 344
AC-130: 155, 223
Advanced medium-range air-to-air missile. *See* Missiles, AMRAAM
Advanced tactical fighter (ATF): 267, 323–24, 326. *See also* F-22
Aerial ordnance: 33–35, 203
Aerospace Industries Association (AIA): 335, 337
Afghanistan: 152, 315
Africa: 146, 150, 161
Agency for International Development: 146
Airborne warning and control system (AWACS): 11, 92, 117, 134, 138, 186, 207–8, 222, 344
Aircraft development programs. *See* Advanced tactical fighter (ATF), B-2, and C-17
Air defense: 25, 27, 46, 74–75, 185, 188, 222, 230
Air Defense Command: 100, 104, 106
Air Force and U.S. National Security: Global Reach—Global Power, The: 11, 220, 228, 239
Air Force Communications Command: 229
Air force, Iraqi: 75, 326
Air Force Logistics Command: 221
Air Force Manual (AFM) 1-1, *Basic Aerospace Doctrine of the United States Air Force*: 98
Air Force Materiel Command: 221
Air Force Reserve: 220, 226, 228, 269
Air Force Space Command: 235, 237–39, 248
Air Force Special Operations Command: 248
Air Force Systems Command: 221, 238
Air Force Technical Applications Center: 282
Air interdiction (AI): 31
AirLand Battle: 96, 223
Air launched cruise missile. *See* Missiles: ALCM
Airlift: 5, 22–23, 30–31, 52, 86, 93, 124, 127, 133–34, 140, 155–56, 186, 196, 208, 220, 223, 229, 232, 267, 322, 326
Air National Guard (ANG): 214, 220, 225–33
Air refueling: 31, 155, 198, 200, 207, 222, 229, 246
Air Staff: 221, 278–79, 291

Air superiority: 5, 44, 76, 78, 96, 100, 103, 186, 206, 267, 316
Air supremacy: 128, 136
Air tasking order: 9, 187
Air University: 84
Albania: 218
Aldridge, Edward C., Jr.: 238
Alexander, Robert: 185
Allenby, Edmund H. H.: 21
Allied Command Europe (ACE): 204, 207
Alpha Jet aircraft: 204
Al Salman airfield, Iraq: 196
Alternative futures: 318–21, 327
Angola: 152, 259
Antiaircraft artillery (AAA): 27, 74–75, 77
Antisatellite. *See* Missiles: ASAT
Apache helicopter: 208, 295, 344
Appropriations accounts: 332
Arab-Israeli wars: 21, 150
Arab League: 156
Argentina: 147, 152, 174
Armenia: 61
Arms and Influence: 179–80
Arms control: 240, 255, 277–93
Arms Control and Disarmament Agency: 279
Army
    Iraqi: 3–5, 12, 19, 26, 63, 70, 73, 77–78, 80, 95, 157, 186, 202, 335
    US: 11, 98, 105, 107, 115, 118, 122, 127, 133, 152, 156, 197, 222–23, 242–43, 296, 333, 335, 337
Army Air Forces: 99
Army Space Command: 237
Art, Robert: 177
Atlantic Alliance: 128, 193
Atlantic force: 219
Aviation Classification Repair Activity Depot: 232

B-1: 15, 95, 199, 285, 287, 325
B-2: 4, 15, 30, 95, 124, 130, 135–37, 185, 267–68, 285, 287, 322–26
B-29: 95, 101–2
B-52: 11–12, 15, 35, 95, 108, 186, 221–22, 281, 285–87, 322, 325–26
Baghdad: 4, 15, 19, 24–26, 71, 73–74, 78, 182, 185, 196, 201
Ballistic missile systems: 53, 132, 151–52, 173, 182, 207, 219–20, 245, 277, 280, 283. *See also* Missiles
Basra, Iraq: 73
Battlefield air interdiction (BAI): 201–2, 207, 209

Battle of the Coral Sea: 257
Beijing: 150
Berlin: 19, 61
Berlin airlift: 117
Berlin crisis: 226
Berlin Wall: 118, 231, 271
Bigeye bomb: 291
Bipolar structure: 39, 41–42, 173, 181, 271, 315
Bishop, Maurice: 301
Blackjack aircraft: 285
Bomb damage assessment: 13, 26–29, 36–37, 297
Bombing campaign: 24, 29
Bradley, Omar: 100
Brazil: 147, 152, 174
Brussels: 232
Buccaneer aircraft: 203
Budget
    Air Force: 92, 237, 239, 263–75, 321, 323–25
    cuts in: 218, 226, 260, 270, 287, 315, 330
    DOD: 14, 218, 228, 264–65, 268, 270, 313, 330–32, 343
    president's: 267–68, 331
    summit agreement: 269
Burden sharing/shifting: 43–44, 197, 214, 232
Burdeshaw Associates Ltd.: 320
Bush, George: 9, 82, 92, 119, 121, 159, 209, 218, 230, 258, 260, 284, 291, 302, 306, 331
Butler, George Lee: 218, 239

C-17: 15, 124, 208, 219, 267, 323–24, 326–27
C-47: 107
C-119: 107
C-130: 107, 223, 233
C-141: 219, 264, 327
Cable News Network: 19, 315
Carthaginian solutions: 63
Castro, Fidel: 141
Center of gravity: 61–69, 174
Central America: 141, 305
Central Intelligence Agency (CIA): 257, 261
Chad: 195–96
Chamorro, Violeta: 259
Charters, David: 148
Chemical warfare/weapons: 25, 205, 290, 293
Cheney, Dick: 119, 213, 218, 225, 233, 261, 330, 342

Chevènement, Jean-Pierre: 195
Chile: 174
China, People's Republic of: 100, 122, 139, 148, 152
Churchill, Winston: 261
Circular error probability (CEP): 267
Clark, Ramsey: 305
Clausewitz, Carl von: 62, 83, 142
Close air support (CAS): 31, 103, 194, 201, 209–10, 223
Coalition forces: 45, 72–73, 75–80, 115, 118, 121, 130, 157, 188, 194–95, 199, 209, 327
Coalition to End US Intervention in the Middle East: 305
Coast Guard, US: 30
Coercive power: 156–57
Cohen-Nunn Amendment: 144–45
Cold war: 10, 17, 39–41, 167, 171, 173–80, 218, 260–61, 305, 316
Colombia: 147, 174
Command, control, and communications (C^3): 4, 53, 65, 140, 220, 222, 240, 243, 316
Command, control, communications, and intelligence (C^3I): 13, 53, 125, 134, 187, 221–22, 313, 322, 327
Commanders in chief (CINC): 271
Communications: 50, 54, 65, 70–71, 78–79, 120, 125, 233, 239, 242, 244, 247–48, 258, 277, 306, 324, 338–39
Compellence: 167, 171, 177, 179–80, 182–85, 188
Composite wing: 125, 185, 214, 220–23, 246
Confidence and security building measures (CSBM): 277, 282, 288–90, 292
Congress: 129, 141, 144, 147, 149, 219–20, 253–54, 257–62, 267–69, 285, 289, 304, 334, 340–43
Containment. *See* Strategy
Continental Air Command: 99
Contingency force: 213
Conventional Forces in Europe (CFE) treaty: 193, 255, 281–82, 287–89, 290–92, 315
Counterair: 194
Counterinsurgency: 208–9
Creek Party deployment program: 232
Cronkite, Walter: 300
Crowe, William: 302
Cruise missile. *See* Missiles
Cuba: 141, 150, 152, 218, 259
Cuban missile crisis: 117
Czechoslovakia: 217, 259

Decade of neglect: 264
Defense
    Advanced Research Projects Agency: 334, 342
    Authorization Act: 341
    Department of (DOD): 15, 125, 142, 145, 227–28, 232, 237, 242, 263, 269, 271–72, 283, 311, 316, 318, 321–22, 325, 330–33, 335–43
    industry: 14, 219, 316, 329–44
    Meteorological Satellite Program (DMSP): 215, 236, 243
    planning: 13–15, 28, 39, 45, 122, 127–29, 199, 218–19
    Satellite Communications System (DSCS): 215, 236, 242–43
    Science Board: 318
    spending, cuts in: 197, 253–54, 264, 266, 270–71
    Support Program: 236
Defensive counterair (DCA): 31
Department of Commerce: 335
Department of Energy: 279
Department of State: 279
Deputy Chief of Staff for Plans and Operations, USAF: 220
Desert Shield/Storm. *See* Operations
Deterrence: 15, 17, 39, 41–42, 47–48, 55, 95, 97, 124, 148, 167–68, 171, 176–78, 180, 182, 188, 219, 228, 272, 322, 325–26
Dhahran, Saudi Arabia: 121
Diego Garcia: 130, 136
Diplomacy: 6, 9
Disarmament: 118
Doctrine, military: 91, 95–96, 98–100, 103–4, 106–7, 109–10, 153, 178, 238
DOD Directive 5000.1, *Major and Non-Major Defense Acquisition Programs*: 325
DOD Directive 5000.2, *Defense Acquisition Program Procedures*: 325
Douhet, Giulio: 21–22, 85, 108, 207
Drucker, Peter: 260
Drugs, war against: 230, 232, 261
Dual-capable aircraft (DCA): 200, 204–6
Durant, Will and Ariel: 260

EA-6B: 143
Eaker, Ira C.: 207
East Asia: 103
Eastern bloc: 315
Eastern Europe: 10, 95, 109, 123, 146, 172, 176, 198, 217, 239, 258–59, 273, 275, 290–91
East-West relations: 277, 292
Economic strategies: 6, 9, 146–47
EF-111: 11, 186
Egypt: 147, 173–74, 258

XVIII Airborne Corps: 241
8th Fighter Wing: 108
82d Airborne Division: 195
Eisenhower Doctrine: 141
El Dorado Canyon. *See* Operations
Electronic warfare: 32, 196, 207, 229, 246
El Salvador: 259
Endara, Guillermo: 155
Enigma machine: 257
Euphrates River: 73, 201
Europe: 58, 122, 128, 174, 198–200, 205–8, 217, 219, 225, 231–32, 239, 273, 277, 282, 287–93

F-4: 106, 173, 245
F-14: 11, 173
F-15: 11, 13, 22, 75, 117, 131–33, 173, 186, 222, 230, 326
F-16: 133, 173, 186, 222–23, 230, 242, 326, 344
F-22: 15, 131, 185
F-100: 106
F-102: 106
F-105: 106
F-111: 13, 22, 75, 143, 186
F-117: 11, 15–16, 22, 74–75, 79, 132, 155, 185–87, 266, 322, 326
Falklands War: 174
Far East Air Forces: 102
Farrakhan, Louis: 305
First Aero Company: 226
1st Special Operations Wing: 223
1st Tactical Fighter Wing: 92, 117
Flexible response: 264
Force structure/reductions: 10, 43, 51–52, 57, 91, 197, 213, 254, 269, 271–72, 275, 277, 317, 330
Foreign military sales: 230
Fort Bragg, North Carolina: 241
Forward air control: 223
Forward looking infrared radar (FLIR): 80
487th Tactical Fighter Squadron: 108
France: 195–96, 204–6
Freedom House: 259

Geneva, Switzerland: 290
George, Alexander: 177–78
Germany: 53, 57–58, 63, 67, 76, 97, 127, 217, 273, 288

Global
  positioning system (GPS): 215, 236, 242, 244–45
  reach/power: 11, 13, 50, 129, 187, 231–32, 240, 321–22
  security: 55, 122, 124, 220
  war: 3, 219, 239
Goebbels, Joseph: 19
Goldwater-Nichols Act: 85, 260
Gordon, Charles George ("Chinese"): 116, 123
Gorman, Paul: 145
Great Britain: 53, 58–59, 68, 116, 197, 203, 205–6, 257, 288
Greece: 147, 257
Grenada: 44, 208
Gross national product (GNP): 263–64, 271, 313, 330–31
Ground forces: 17–18, 26, 42, 48, 51, 108, 140, 155, 157, 195, 201, 277, 282
Ground launched cruise missile. *See* Missiles: GLCM
Guided bombs: 33, 73, 120. *See also* Aerial ordnance

Hanoi: 143
Harold II: 68
Harrier aircraft: 208
HC-130: 223
Helsinki Conference on Security and Cooperation in Europe: 282, 289
Helsinki process: 277
High-intensity conflict: 20, 44, 48–49, 107, 127–38, 140, 143, 145, 156, 161, 174, 199, 207, 316, 326
High-mobility multipurpose wheeled vehicle: 243
High-tech weaponry: 51, 58, 151–52, 218, 231, 233, 266–68, 272, 274–75
Hitler, Adolph: 19
HMS *Sheffield*: 174
Ho Chi Minh: 301
Ho Chi Minh trail: 108
Horner, Chuck: 120
House Committee on Appropriations: 147
House Committee on Armed Services: 341–43
House National Defense Authorization Act: 342
House of Representatives: 343
House Select Committee on Intelligence: 261
Hungary: 217, 259
Hunniman, John: 257
Hurlburt Field, Florida: 223
Hussein, Saddam: 9–11, 19, 45–46, 52, 70, 73, 77, 92, 115, 118, 121–23, 126, 129, 156–58, 161, 182, 186, 188, 209, 213, 247, 258, 260, 296, 298–99, 305–6, 316, 326
hyperwar: 79, 81–82

Identification, friend or foe (IFF): 196–97
Inchon, South Korea: 101
Incirlik Air Base, Turkey: 221
Independent research and development (IR&D): 314, 340, 342
India: 152, 174
Indian Ocean: 134, 242
Indonesia: 174
Inspection, arms control: 288–89, 291–92
Institute for Foreign Policy Analysis: 320
Intelligence: 6, 50, 53, 120, 188, 196, 248, 253, 257–59, 279, 324
Intercontinental ballistic missile. *See* Missiles: ICBM
Interdiction, air: 121, 203, 208, 246, 267
Intermediate-range Nuclear Forces (INF) treaty: 280, 282, 291
International politics/relations: 172
Invasion of Kuwait, Iraq's: 3, 171–72, 182, 240, 244, 305
Investment strategies: 318, 323, 334
Iran: 129, 152, 182, 188, 320
Iran-Contra affair: 261, 301, 304
Iran-Iraq War: 173, 196, 201, 315
Iraq: 9, 11–12, 18, 20–21, 23, 25, 30, 38, 41, 50, 52, 57, 59, 63, 65, 67, 70–73, 75–76, 78–80, 95, 117, 129–31, 138, 152–53, 156–57, 173, 182, 185, 187–88, 195–96, 201, 203, 205, 207, 209, 218, 239, 243, 258, 260, 263, 275, 302, 306, 315, 340–43
Israel: 3, 11, 46, 147, 152, 173–74, 258, 305
Italy: 102, 257, 288

Jaguar bomber: 196, 203
Japan: 57, 63–64, 67, 100, 206, 329, 342
Jeremiah, David E.: 219
Johnson, Lyndon B.: 25, 105, 159
Joint Chiefs of Staff (JCS): 105, 217, 219–20, 243, 278–79, 302, 344
Joint force air component commander: 7, 86, 109, 187
Jointness: 85–86, 100
Joint surveillance target attack radar system (JSTARS): 11, 80, 130–35, 137, 186, 201, 313, 327
Just Cause. *See* Operations

Kabul, Afghanistan: 259
Kaiserslautern, Germany: 232
KC-10: 143, 222
KC-135: 221–22, 230
Kelly, Thomas: 296
Kemp, Geoffrey: 181
KGB: 259

Khafji, Saudi Arabia: 77–78, 300
King Fahd: 258
Kissinger, Henry: 12
Kitchener, Horatio H.: 116, 123
Korean War: 17, 20, 38, 40, 91, 98–104, 109, 226, 264, 330
Kurds: 70
Kuwait: 9, 12, 19–20, 25–26, 50, 52, 63, 70, 73, 76–78, 95, 118, 120, 129–30, 153, 156–57, 182, 186–88, 194–95, 258, 302, 306, 315–16
Kuwaiti theater of operations (KTO): 196, 202–3, 207

Land satellite (LANDSAT): 243, 246
Land warfare: 84
LaRouche, Lyndon: 305
Laser-guided glide bombs: 20, 22, 28
Latin America: 141, 146, 150, 174, 183
Lebanon: 117
Lessons learned: 23, 80–81, 91–92, 96–97, 100, 103, 109–10, 115, 118, 120–22, 125–26, 158–59, 183, 193, 195, 198, 201, 204, 241, 259–61, 343
Liberty Lobby: 305
Libya: 44, 173, 259
Lincoln, Abraham: 257, 301
Logistics: 25, 193, 197, 200–201, 208–9, 221, 296, 318
Low-intensity conflict (LIC): 49–50, 93, 139–47, 150–61, 174–76, 183, 209, 239, 261, 316, 326
Luftwaffe: 19

Magna, Utah: 282
Major, John: 204
Manchuria: 101–2
Maneuver: 243
Marine Corps, US: 11, 84, 98, 103, 115, 156, 195, 197, 243, 296
Marshall, George: 14
Marshall Plan: 141
Mass destruction, weapons of: 10, 173, 182, 186, 188, 205
MC-130: 223
McNamara, Robert S.: 98, 105–6, 178
McPeak, Merrill A.: 125, 168, 184–85, 221–23, 241, 316, 321–22, 325
Media: 256, 295–301
Mexico: 147, 174
Middle East: 9, 12, 21, 41–42, 46, 52, 122, 140–41, 150, 152, 158, 161, 174, 183, 196, 199, 204, 208, 258, 302, 315
Midintensity conflict: 140–42, 144–45, 151, 153, 158, 161, 207, 316, 326
MiG-15: 101–2
MiG-21: 106

MiG-23: 173
MiG-25: 173
MiG-29: 173
Military Airlift Command (MAC): 117, 186, 248
Military responsiveness: 3, 10, 38, 52, 60–61, 115, 140, 157, 232, 244, 275
Mirage aircraft: 173
Mirage F1-CR: 196–97
Missile defense alarm system (MIDAS): 236
Missiles
    air-to-air: 131
    air-to-ground: 29, 33, 204–6
    ALCM: 29, 255, 281, 284–85, 287, 292
    AMRAAM: 131
    ASAT: 237, 247–48
    cruise: 136–37, 151, 201, 280, 286, 295
    Exocet: 151, 174
    forces: 95, 187
    GLCM: 280, 282
    Hercules: 282
    ICBM: 235, 245, 254, 270, 280–81, 283–87, 292, 322–25
    Lance: 205
    Maverick: 13, 344
    Midgetman: 284, 287
    Minuteman: 280, 283, 287, 292
    nuclear: 104
    Patriot: 46–47, 132, 245, 295, 297, 344
    Peacekeeper: 281, 283–84, 286–87
    Pershing II: 280
    radiation-homing: 28, 34
    RV: 283–87
    SAM: 77, 106, 133, 207, 283–84, 286
    Scud: 3, 23, 25, 38, 72, 75, 132, 205, 245, 247, 296–97
    SLBM: 280–81, 283, 285–87
    SLCM: 29
    Stinger: 151, 174
    surface-to-surface: 131, 205
    TASM: 204–6
    Titan II: 280
    Tomahawk: 16, 34–35, 79, 295
    V-1: 38
Mitchell, William ("Billy"): 22, 108
Mitterrand, François: 195
Momyer, William: 100
Moscow: 277

Mossad: 258
Moynihan, Daniel Patrick: 261
Mubarak, Hosni: 258
Mujaheddin: 259
Multiple independently targeted reentry vehicle (MIRV): 280–81, 286
Multiple launch rocket system (MLRS): 202
Multipolarity: 41–42, 44, 46–48, 55, 173, 239, 247
Multispectral imagery (MSI): 243, 246
Mutual assured destruction (MAD): 178

Najibullah, Mohammad: 259
Namsi, North Korea: 102
Napoléon Bonaparte: 57
National Aeronautics and Space Administration: 245
National Campaign for Peace in the Middle East: 305
National Center for Advanced Technologies: 335, 337
National Guard: 209, 214, 226–27
Nationalism: 271
National Security Council: 144, 158, 279, 304
NATO: 10, 30, 41, 43, 127, 169, 193–98, 200, 204–6, 208, 217, 272, 282, 287–88, 290, 292, 315
NATO Strategy Review: 204
Naval blockade: 18
Naval Space Command: 237
Navy, US: 11, 84, 106–7, 115, 155, 195, 197, 222, 296, 333, 335, 337
NBC. *See* Weapons
Neal, Richard: 297
New world order: 9, 55, 109, 129, 138, 172, 221, 254, 258, 261, 312, 315–16, 327
New York National Guard: 226
New York Times: 298, 304
Nicaragua: 218, 259, 304
Night operations: 187
Nixon, Richard M.: 178
Noriega, Manuel: 60, 155
Norstad, Lauris: 97
North Africa: 18, 21, 30
Northeast Asia: 17, 174, 183, 199
North Korea: 60, 174, 206, 218
Nuclear
    proliferation: 167
    testing: 281–82
    triad: 219, 322, 325
    war: 96–98, 179, 239, 266
Nuclear, biological, and chemical weapons. *See* Weapons: NBC

OA-10: 223
Offensive counterair (OCA): 31
Oman: 258
On-Site Inspection Agency (OSIA): 279, 282, 286
Operational Air Command: 184
Operations
    Daguet: 195
    Desert Shield: 9, 30, 85, 87, 115, 118, 123, 125, 195, 198, 218, 222, 226–27, 241, 243, 326–27
    Desert Storm: 3–4, 9, 13, 15, 19–20, 29–30, 33–35, 40–45, 48–52, 85, 87, 115, 118–20, 123, 125, 130, 186, 193, 195–96, 198, 201–3, 207, 209, 215, 217, 221, 226–27, 235, 240–42, 244–45, 247, 258, 260–61, 263, 274, 295, 322, 326–27, 330, 333, 343
    El Dorado Canyon: 44–45, 49, 143, 151, 186, 226, 241
    Instant Thunder: 4–5, 25–26, 28
    Just Cause: 44, 60–61, 123, 143, 154–55, 160, 223, 226, 241, 301
    Linebacker: 107–8
    Proven Force: 221
    Rolling Thunder: 25, 105
    Strangle: 38, 102
    Urgent Fury: 60–61, 143, 153–55, 226, 241
Options for Change study: 197, 204
Ordnance. *See* Aerial ordnance
Ortega, Daniel: 218
Osirak nuclear reactor: 182
Ostfriesland: 80
OSTP. *See* White House Office of Science and Technology Policy

Pacific Air Forces: 104, 107
Pacific force: 213, 219
Pacific Rim: 329, 342
Pakistan: 147, 174
Panama: 44, 208, 229–30, 233
Panamanian Defense Force: 143
Paris: 282
Paris Peace Accords: 108
Pas de Calais: 38
Pave Low helicopters: 223, 242
Payload: 5, 52, 274
Peace dividend: 197, 315
Penetrability, aircraft: 5, 52–54
Pentagon: 109, 198, 296–301, 303, 306
Pentagon Papers: 301

Persian Gulf: 3, 18, 42, 52, 127–28, 132, 138, 143, 150–51, 158, 174, 183, 258, 260, 273–74, 300, 302, 343
Philippines: 174
Planning, military: 138, 196–97, 209, 311–12, 317–18
Planning, Programming and Budgeting System (PPBS): 268
Poland: 217, 257, 259
Post boost vehicle (PBV): 286
Post–cold war era: 171–73, 176, 180–81, 183, 197, 205, 218, 228, 255, 288, 295
Powell, Colin: 25, 119, 121, 213, 219–20, 243, 344
Power projection: 40, 44–45, 49, 92, 115–17, 123–25, 168–69, 185–87, 210, 219, 239, 273–75, 322
Precision guided munitions (PGM): 13, 20, 26, 52, 78, 115, 125, 143, 174, 185, 187, 201, 207, 220, 239, 306, 322
Press. *See* Media
PRIME BEEF: 229
PRIME RIBS: 229
Prisoners of war (POW), Iraqi: 12, 76
Professional military education: 84, 238
Program Objective Memorandum (POM): 267–68
Project Forecast: 335
Prussia: 62
Public opinion: 296–307
Pueblo crisis: 226
Puma helicopter: 242
Pusan, South Korea: 100–101

Qadhafi, Muammar: 259, 298
Quesada, Elwood: 99

Rail-garrison missile system: 284, 286
Rand Corporation: 10, 221
Range, aircraft: 5, 52, 115, 125, 136, 157, 200, 220, 239, 275
RC-135: 11
Reagan, Ronald: 159, 175, 178, 264, 281, 330
Reconnaissance, air: 229, 289
RED HORSE: 229
Red Sea: 132
Reentry vehicles. *See* Missiles: RV
Regionalism: 40, 42, 271–75, 285
     instability and conflict: 173–76, 181, 183, 233, 239
     security environments: 43, 48, 52, 167, 173–76
Reorganization, Air Force: 221
Republican Guard: 26, 74–75, 129, 196

Research and development (R&D): 14, 55, 214, 220, 235, 268, 315–27, 322, 329–31
Research, development, test and evaluation (RDT&E): 266–68, 311–14, 324, 332–34
Restructuring, force: 214, 218–20, 223, 225, 228
Rich, Mike: 10
Rivet Joint electronic reconnaissance system: 134
Riyadh, Saudi Arabia: 130
Rockeye cluster bombs: 203
Roosevelt, Franklin D.: 304
Rosenfeld, Stephen: 126
Ross, Andrew L.: 174
Royal Air Force (RAF): 27–28, 203
Russo-Japanese War: 80

Saddam Hussein. *See* Hussein, Saddam
Safire, William: 298
Sandinistas: 259
Sarkesian, Sam: 142
Satellites: 236, 240, 242, 246, 279
Saudi Arabia: 46, 52, 117, 130–32, 152, 156–57, 173, 186, 194, 242, 258, 260, 273, 275, 296, 302
Savimbi, Jonas: 259
Schelling, Thomas C.: 171, 179–80
Schlesinger, James R.: 178
Schriever, Bernard A.: 236
Schwarzkopf, Norman: 25, 70, 77, 82, 116, 119, 121, 243, 297
Sea-launched ballistic missile. *See* Missiles: SLBM
Sea-launched cruise missile. *See* Missiles: SLCM
Sea lift: 5, 30, 133–34
Sea lines of communications: 18
Second World War. *See* World War II
Secretary of Defense, Office of (OSD): 136, 160, 268, 279, 342
Senate: 138, 279, 342
Senate Armed Services Committee: 145, 342–43
Seventh Air Force: 108
VII Corps: 196
Single air commander: 92, 120, 159
Single integrated operational plan (SIOP): 97, 230
Smith, Frederic H.: 99
Smoke, Richard: 177–78
Smyth, Alexander: 242
Somme River: 105
Sorties, Desert Storm: 31–32

370

South Africa: 174
South America: 261
South Asia: 140, 146, 161, 183
South Korea: 174, 206
Southwest Asia: 92, 115, 121, 161, 219, 239–40, 244, 246–47
Soviet-Afghan War: 174
Soviet Union: 17, 39–41, 43, 47–48, 57, 95–96, 98, 100, 103, 109, 123, 127, 139, 141, 148, 150, 152, 172, 176, 178–79, 181, 194, 198, 205, 207, 217, 219, 237, 239, 258–59, 261, 263, 266, 272–73, 278–80, 290–92, 315, 325
Spaatz, Carl ("Tooey"): 99, 208
Space: 5, 53–54, 86, 120, 125, 213, 215, 219, 222, 233, 235, 237–38, 240–41, 322, 327
    battlefield in: 215
    first war in: 202, 241
    sensors in: 47, 132, 140, 208, 238, 240–41, 246
Space systems, Soviet: 237
Special operations forces (SOF): 140, 142–45, 151, 155, 161, 194, 209, 219, 222–23, 242
Spectrum of conflict: 5, 41, 49, 144, 161, 186
Speed, aircraft: 5, 53–54, 115, 220, 239–40
Sputnik I: 235, 264
Stealth: 6, 14–15, 27–29, 46–47, 53–54, 74, 78–81, 120, 136, 185, 187, 199, 201–2, 208, 266, 285–86. *See also* B-2, F-117
Steiner, Carl: 241
Strangle. *See* Operations
Strategic
    air campaign: 11
    Air Command (SAC): 96, 99, 103–4, 107–8, 117, 184, 221, 239, 248, 286, 291
    Arms Limitation Talks (SALT): 255, 280–81
    Arms Reduction Talks (START): 214, 220, 278, 282–87, 291–92, 315, 322
    basing: 124
    bombing campaigns: 4, 11–12, 100–101
    Defense Initiative (SDI): 219, 332–33
    force: 213
    nuclear capabilities, Soviet: 17, 45
    planning: 14, 318–19, 321
    program budget: 323
Strategy
    bombardment: 22, 28
    containment: 58–59, 149–50, 173, 272
    counterair: 46
    defense: 10, 177, 233, 245
    defense policy, changes in: 4, 17

    deterrence as: 15, 39, 41–42, 45–50, 52, 55, 167
    enemy: 24, 26, 326
    forward defense: 17, 115, 122, 127
    global: 4, 18, 194, 197, 201, 209
    national security: 11, 57, 60, 145, 169, 175, 240, 257–62, 275, 318
    purposes of: 29
    technology and: 43, 201
    theater missile defense: 46
Suppression of enemy air defenses (SEAD): 24–25, 27, 31–32, 35, 133, 136, 207, 222, 320
Surgical strike assets: 199–200
Surprise, element of: 185, 187, 201
Surveillance, air: 32, 53, 125, 156, 222, 247–48, 327
Syria: 152, 173, 202

Tactical
    Air Command (TAC): 99, 104, 106, 108–9, 184, 248
    air control center: 222
    air-to-surface missile. *See* Missiles: TASM
    fighter wing equivalents (TFWE): 266
    Information Broadcast System (TIBS): 208
    Missile Defense Initiative (TMDI): 333
    program budget: 323
Taiwan: 174
Target selection: 24, 26–27, 29, 36, 46–47, 49, 97, 258
Task organization: 84
Technology: 46–47, 50, 53–55, 57, 61, 67, 81, 92, 95, 101, 116, 119, 126, 152, 203, 236, 238, 280, 306, 313–14, 317, 323–24, 326, 329–44
Terrorist activity: 49, 150–51, 183
Textron Defense Systems: 318–21
Thailand: 174
Theater commander: 159–60
Third-world conflicts: 152
33d Air Rescue Squadron: 242
Tigris River: 73, 201
Tonkin Gulf: 301
Tornado aircraft: 28, 173, 203
Total Force policy: 226–28, 232–33
Total obligation authority (TOA): 263, 267, 269, 271
Training: 119, 229–30, 232–33
Transportation: 72–73, 219
Trenchard, Hugh Montague: 22, 108
Trident submarine: 283
Truman Doctrine: 141

Tucson, Arizona: 230
Turkey: 46, 147, 204

Udorn Royal Thai AFB: 108
Unguided bombs: 28, 34. *See also* Aerial ordnance
United Arab Emirates: 258
United Nations (UN): 9, 44, 100, 129, 200, 209, 231, 306, 315
United Nations Security Council: 12, 43
United States Space Command: 237
Unity of command: 107
Urgent Fury. *See* Operations
US Southern Command: 231
US-Soviet Interim Agreement on Strategic Offensive Arms: 280
USS *Stark*: 174

Vandenberg, Hoyt S.: 100, 102
Van Tien Dung: 143
Viccellio, Henry P.: 221
Vienna: 156
Vienna document on CSBMs: 288–90
Vietnam War: 4, 11, 25, 40, 44, 66, 76, 78–79, 91, 96, 98–99, 104–5, 107–9, 119, 140, 143, 148, 159, 161, 187, 209, 226–27, 236, 256, 269, 303, 330
Votkinsk, USSR: 282

Walesa, Lech: 3, 9
Wall Street Journal: 298
Warden, John: 18, 28
Warsaw Pact: 10, 96, 118, 122–23, 127, 139, 149, 217, 228, 287, 290, 292, 315
Washington, D.C.: 82, 159, 277–78, 305
Washington, George: 257
Washington Post: 122, 126
Watergate: 301
Weapons
    conventional: 151, 155, 167
    midintensity: 94, 143–44, 152
    multipurpose: 312
    national security and: 175
    NBC: 26, 40, 46–47, 70, 72, 152, 167, 188, 206, 232, 245–46, 277
    new: 325
    nuclear: 97, 100, 104, 182, 205, 277, 281, 283, 285, 292
    requirements: 318
    sea: 84
    smart: 137, 167, 174, 203
    systems, importance of: 323

Weinberger, Caspar: 141, 149, 153
Welch, Larry D.: 238
West Asia: 18, 30
Western Europe: 10, 17, 46, 98, 127, 193, 228, 292
Western Europe Union: 200
Weyland, Otto P.: 102, 104
White House Office of Science and Technology Policy (OSTP): 335, 337–38
White, Thomas D.: 247
Will, George: 9
William the Conqueror: 68
Wilson, Woodrow: 303
Wolfowitz, Paul: 213, 220
World War I: 59, 80, 105, 172, 226, 303
World War II: 4, 14, 19–21, 25, 28, 36, 39–40, 59, 63, 79, 91–92, 96–97, 99–100, 102–3, 115, 117, 122, 127, 141–42, 148, 172, 177, 225–26, 233, 239, 257, 261, 271–72, 304, 307

Yalu River: 101–2
Yugoslavia: 239

Zone of conflict: 18, 30, 52

*U.S. GPO: 2002-736-826